The CIM Marketi.., _ _____ ,

The Marketing Series is one of the most comprehensive collections of books in marketing and sales available from the UK today.

Published by Butterworth-Heinemann on behalf of The Chartered Institute of Marketing, the series is divided into three distinct groups: *Student* (fulfilling the needs of those taking the Institute's certificate and diploma qualifications); *Professional Development* (for those on formal or self-study training programmes); and *Practitioner* (presented in a more informal, motivating and highly practical manner for personal use).

Formed in 1911, The Chartered Institute of Marketing is now the largest professional marketing management body in Europe with over 24,000 members and 28,000 students located worldwide. Its primary objectives are focused on the development of awareness and understanding of marketing throughout UK industry and commerce and on the raising of standards of professionalism in the education, training and practice of this key business discipline.

Books in the series

The Marketing Book
Michael J. Baker

Practice of Public Relations
Sam Black

Market Focus
Rick Brown

Creating Powerful Brands
Leslie Chernatony and Malcolm H. B. McDonald

Strategy of Distribution Management
Martin Christopher

Relationship Marketing
Martin Christopher, Adrian Payne and David Ballantyne

Profitable Product Management
Richard Collier

Managing Your Marketing Career
Andrew Croft

Marketing Research for Managers
Sunny Crouch and Matthew Housden

CIM Marketing Dictionary
Norman A. Hart

Practice of Advertising
Norman A. Hart

Marketing Plans
Malcolm H. B. McDonald

Marketing Planning for Services
Malcolm H. B. McDonald and Adrian Payne

Retail Marketing Plans
Malcolm H. B. McDonald and Christopher Tideman

Market-led Strategic Change
Nigel Piercy

Trade Marketing Strategies
Geoffrey Randall

Finance for Marketers
Keith Ward

Below-the-line Promotion
John Wilmshurst

The CIM Marketing Dictionary

Fifth edition

Norman A. Hart,
MSc., FCIM, FIPR, FCAM

Published on behalf of The Chartered Institute of Marketing and The CAM Foundation

Butterworth-Heinemann
Linacre House, Jordan Hill, Oxford OX2 8DP
A division of Reed Educational and Professional Publishing Ltd

 A member of the Reed Elsevier plc group

OXFORD   BOSTON   JOHANNESBURG
MELBOURNE   NEW DELHI   SINGAPORE

First published as *Glossary of Marketing Terms* 1977
Reprinted 1979
Second edition 1981
Reprinted 1983, 1985
Third edition 1987
Reprinted 1988
Fourth edition 1992
Fifth edition 1996

British Library Cataloguing in Publication Data
Hart, Norman A., 1930–
   The CIM marketing dictionary – 5th ed. – (The marketing series)
   1 Marketing – Dictionaries
   I Title   II Chartered Institute of Marketing   III Marketing dictionary
   658.8'003

ISBN 0 7506 2346 2

Printed and bound in Great Britain by
Biddles Ltd, Guildford and King's Lynn

Preface

In commissioning this book, The Chartered Institute of Marketing and The Communication, Advertising and Marketing Education (CAM) Foundation were well aware of the need for authenticity in what would be a pioneer work. Clearly, their sponsorship provides an implied seal of approval. Whilst the author is in fact wholly responsible for the definitions, the views have been sought of all the leading trade and professional associations, and due regard has been paid to their frequently helpful comments.

The breadth of marketing and its related subjects has led to the inclusion of terms which cover a wide span of activities – research, management, export, packaging, advertising, raw materials, selling, public relations, law and so on. As a result, the terms when put into alphabetical order present an apparently confusing disarray. Nevertheless, the intention is to provide a comprehensive range, conveniently located to meet the needs of practising marketing men and women.

This completely revised edition, amounting to over three thousand terms includes for the first time a range of key IT words which might have a relationship to marketing. In all, some five hundred terms have been added.

The author will certainly welcome any advice he may receive regarding content and coverage which could help to improve future editions.

Norman Hart

Acknowledgements

The value of this dictionary has been enhanced considerably by the inclusion for the first time of a large number of IT terms. These have been the responsibility of Andrew Barber, a leading independent information systems consultant and managing director of Axemead Computers Limited. Many thanks for his considerable effort.

Also, grateful acknowledgement is due to marketing consultant, Ian Ruskin Brown (a course director at The Chartered Institute of Marketing College of Marketing) for his thorough vetting and helpful suggestions on definitions.

Finally, thanks are given to Nick Bailey, Manufacturing Sector Director, Sema Group Outsourcing plc, for a number of additional IT terms.

A

À la carte   The practice of choosing a range of creative and marketing services from ad hoc suppliers for a fee rather than having just one central source, e.g. an advertising agency.

AA   *See* Advertising Association.

AB   *See* Socio-economic groups.

Abandonment   To give up producing and/or marketing a product, usually towards the end of its life cycle and/or when it is becoming unprofitable. Also, the outcome of a rationalization of the product portfolio.

ABC   Audit Bureau of Circulation Ltd. An independent body supported by advertisers, advertising agencies, and media owners, which issues audited circulation figures for subscribing publications. Circulation figures lacking an ABC certificate may not be accurate.

Above-the-line advertising   Any form of advertising for which a commission or fee is payable to a recognized advertising agency operating on behalf of its client(s). Usually press, television, radio, cinema, and posters, sometimes referred to as Theme Advertising. *See* Recognition. *See also* Below-the-line advertising.

Absorption   Assignment of all costs, both fixed and variable, to goods and/or services provided.

Absorption pricing   'Total cost' costing; all costs are recovered in the price set for a product.

Accelerated motion   The apparently increased speed of movement obtained by projecting at normal speed a film that has been taken at less than normal speed when shooting.

Accelerator   Relatively small change in demand for consumer goods resulting in a comparatively substantial change in demand for capital plant supplying these goods.

Access provider   A company or organization that provides connection, or a gateway, to the Internet.

Access rights   The freedom to use a program or get information. As a marketer you need access to *all* the company's information base for strategic purposes.

Access time   The key to a marketer's productivity in analysing data. Most information should be available to you in less than three minutes, and working data in three seconds.

Accommodation bill   Bill of Exchange signed by one person to accommodate another. By signing, the person concerned becomes a *guarantor* but receives no payment. He/she becomes liable if the acceptor fails to pay by the due date.

Accordion fold   Small, usually inexpensive, leaflet having alternate folds – accordian like – so that it will pull out into one broadsheet. Often used as give-away or hand-out for sales promotion purposes Also called Concertina fold.

Account   (1) In sales, an invoice. (2) In advertising, a client of an advertising or other agency, that is to say, an organization providing a service in consideration of which an income is derived; hence, the term account.

Account conflict   Situation in which an advertising agency or other outside service house is offered a business opportunity which is similar to that of an existing client or account. An advertising agency handling an automobile account could not thus take on another competing and therefore conflicting client in the same field. The problem can be overcome only partially by having a number of separate account groups. A more satisfactory solution is for there to be a separate company with no more than a financial connection.

Account executive   An executive in an advertising agency, or other such organization, responsible for the overall managing of a client's requirements. Sometimes known as Account Supervisor, Account Manager, or Account Director, the different titles indicating degrees of responsibility.

Account group   Sub-unit of an advertising agency, handling a group of clients or accounts. May be fully or partly self-contained.

Account planning   The production of an advertising plan by an agency for its client. Usually headed up by an agency researcher.

Accredited   Relating to an agent; appointed by a company to act on its behalf.

Acetate   Thin plastic transparent sheet, originally cellulose acetate, used in graphics as an overlay on layouts or artwork.

Acid test ratio   Synonym for liquidity ratio.

Acknowledgement   Written notification by a supplier to a customer that an order has been received and is being processed.

ACORN   An acronym of A Classification of Residential Neighbourhoods. Is classified in such a way as to identify areas in socioeconomic terms, thus facilitating direct mail to narrowly defined target audiences.

Acquisition   Purchase of other companies, or manufacturing rights, as a way of expanding a company's activities or increasing its share of a market. Also may be a means of diversification without the risks accompanying the development of a new product; or countering competition with greater certainty than by mounting a direct campaign. *See* Diversification.

Acronym   A word formed from the initial letters of a group of words, e.g. AIDA from Attention, Interest, Desire, Action.

Across-the-network Schedule for a particular advertiser or programme series that specifies transmission simultaneously from all the transmitters constituting the network.

Action close Proposal by a sales person, the acceptance of which concludes the sales transaction.

Action device *See* Response mechanism.

Active file The memo, letter and data you can see on the screen at the time of using it.

Active message sources *See* Message sources.

Activity sampling An observational technique, using discontinuous tests to estimate the incidence of any defined activity.

AD (Administrative domain) A collection of networks managed by a single administrative authority.

Ad hoc As and when required. Often refers to occasional market surveys.

Ad valorem A tax, duty or levy based upon the value of goods rather than by weight or quantity.

Adaptation Use of a basic idea, as in an advertisement, for other media, e.g. posters, point of sale, literature. Also to adapt an advertisement to another shape or size.

Added value Increase in value acquired by materials, components, or other commodities (including labour for example) as a result of any input, whether processing, assembling, handling, distributing, or any other marketing activity.

Address line Part of advertisement or promotional material which contains the address of the advertiser, or the address to which any inquiries should be sent. *See* Base line.

Adequate distribution   Ensuring that an adequate number of the appropriate type of retail outlets have sufficient stocks of goods to meet demand arising from any promotional programmes.

Administered prices   Price levels established by an industry or group of companies within an industry, forming either a monopoly or a cartel. The practice of Resale Price Maintenance was stopped in the UK during 1963, rendering the 'administration of prices' illegal.

Administrative domain   *See* AD.

Adnorm   A term used in Starch ratings (primarily in the USA) as a measure of the percentage of readers 'noting' an advertisement. Can also apply to editorial matter. *See* Page traffic.

Adoption of innovation   The acceptance by consumers of a new product or service. The first grouping of such people is known as innovators, and this is followed by 'early adopters', 'early majority', 'late majority', and 'laggards'. *See* Hierarchy of effects.

Adshel   Form of poster site incorporated into a bus shelter.

Advance freight   Freight dues paid in advance. Enables an importer to take immediate delivery of shipment following endorsement of a bill of lading.

Advanced interactive executive   *See* AIX.

Advertisement   Often used loosely to refer to any persuasive message or slogan forming part of an organization's publicity or promotion. Strictly the message should be incorporated into a paid-for space or time slot in a periodical or on television or radio. *See* Advertising.

Advertisement analysis   An assessment of the levels of advertising in above-the-line media in respect of the competition. Such data is provided by MEAL (Media Expenditure Analysis Limited).

Advertisement department Part of a publishing or other organization in the communications business concerned with selling advertising space or time, either to an agency or direct to a client.

Advertisement manager Executive responsible for selling advertising on behalf of a publisher, television, radio station or display contractor. Also responsible for managing the advertisement department. Not to be confused with an Advertis*ing* manager.

Advertiser Organization or person on whose behalf an advertisement appears, and who ultimately pays the bill.

Advertising Use of paid-for space in a publication, for instance, or time on television, radio or cinema, usually as a means of persuading people to take a particular course of action, or to reach a point of view. May also be taken to include posters and other outdoor advertising. *See* Above-the-line or Below-the-line advertising. *See also* Publicity.

Advertising agency Business organization set up to provide a service to clients ranging across booking advertising space, designing advertisements and producing them, devising media schedules, commissioning research, providing consultancy, and any associated marketing service. Origin was as agent of a publisher by whom a commission was payable. This system of remuneration still survives in the case of most advertising agencies.

Advertising allowance An arrangement whereby a manufacturer gives financial assistance to a distributor/retailer to support advertising or promotion on its behalf.

Advertising appropriation *See* Appropriation.

Advertising Association National body bringing together the interests of advertisers, agencies and media, and representing them at national and international levels. Also the source of authentic statistics on advertising expenditure, and of other published data.

Advertising budget   Sum of money set aside for spending on an advertising campaign. Sometimes represents total sum available to cover all advertising expenditure including overheads. Alternatively referred to as 'Advertising appropriation'. *See also* Budget and Task method.

Advertising campaign   *See* Campaign.

Advertising commission   *See* Media commission. *See also* Agency commission.

Advertising effectiveness   A measure of the extent to which members of a target audience can recall an advertising message. *See* Post test.

Advertising funded   Media which is funded completely or partly by revenue obtained from the sale of advertising, as against media which is dependent on subscriptions.

Advertising manager   Executive responsible for planning and implementing his/her company's advertising, also for managing the advertising department. Alternatively, may be known as Marketing communications manager, Publicity manager, Sales promotion manager, Marketing services manager. Not to be confused with Advertise*ment* manager.

Advertising medium   Vehicle of communication which provides for some form of advertising, e.g. the press, television, radio and transport services. Alternatively, a communication channel designed specifically for the purpose of advertising, e.g. direct mail, exhibitions, poster sites, and some printed publications, e.g. catalogues.

Advertising novelty   Cheap, possibly gimmicky, gift carrying advertising message, brand name or symbol. Typical examples are key rings, ball pens, scribble pads, stick or pin-on badges.

Advertising objectives   Specifically, what is to be achieved by an advertising campaign in quantified terms, and over a given period of time. *See also* Marketing communications objectives.

Advertising 'packages' Communications mix for publicity purposes.

Advertising rates Basic charges made by advertising media for use of their services or facilities. *See* Rate card.

Advertising reach *See* Cumulative audience.

Advertising regulations Conditions imposed upon advertising by media owners, trade associations, or government. *See* Voluntary controls.

Advertising research Evaluation of the efficiency of an advertisement or of an advertising campaign in terms of the task or objective it is set to achieve. Pre-testing and copy testing examine the likely results whereas post-testing deals with actual achievements. *See also* Media research.

Advertising reserve Financial allocation in a budget set aside for unforeseen expenditure. Also referred to as a contingency.

Advertising response Reaction by consumers to an advertising campaign, often measured according to a percentage scale.

Advertising schedule Programme of planned advertisement insertions, showing detailed costs, timing, nature of media and the bookings to be reserved. *See* Media schedule.

Advertising scheme *See* Scheme advertising.

Advertising slogans Catchwords or phrases used in association with brand publicity.

Advertising space That part of a publication or periodical which is set aside for advertising as opposed to editorial matter.

Advertising speciality Give-aways carrying a company or product brand name or slogan, such as pens, key rings, paper knives, etc.

Advertising Standards Authority *See* ASA.

Advertising Standards Board of Finance *See* ASBOF.

Advertising style Classification of advertising approaches. May be Informational, Strategic, Customer benefits, Transference, or Positioning.

Advertising testing A means by which the efficacy of an advertisement or a campaign is measured.

Advertising theme *See* Theme advertising.

Advertising threshold Point at which a consumer is likely to make an initial response to an advertising message. *See also* Maximal awareness.

Advertising to sales ratio An expression of the percentage of advertising expenditure in relation to sales or turnover. Sometimes used as the basis of budgeting.

Advertising wearout Point at which a consumer becomes indifferent to an advertising message.

Advertorial An advertisement which is designed to have the appearance of an editorial.

Advice note Document stating that a transaction has been completed. *See* Delivery note.

Advocacy advertising Corporate advertising to put across a company's position in relation to a major national or international issue.

Advocate A customer who, without any prompting, recommends a particular product. *See* Ladder of loyalty.

AE *See* Account executive.

Aerial advertising Persuasive message in the air, e.g. streamer trailed behind aircraft, slogan on a hot-air balloon, symbol on a helicopter.

Aerosol Pressurized canister containing a liquid (or cream) which is ejected, usually in the form of a vapour, on the operation of a valve connected to a press button.

Affinity card A credit card whereby a small contribution is made to a specific charity or other organization for every transaction.

Affinity lists A mailing list which has been built up by research specifically to serve a perceived need, as opposed to a list produced as a result of, say, a direct mail or advertising campaign.

Affinity marketing A campaign jointly sponsored by a number of disparate companies who are non-competitive but have a particular interest or event in common, e.g. the Olympics.

'Affordable' method One of a variety of ways of arriving at an advertising budget, on the basis of what a company can afford, rather than what task has to be achieved. *See* Task method.

Affreightment, Contracts of Contracts for the carriage of goods by sea. Standard contracts are shown in bills of lading.

After date Date of payment after that shown on a bill of lading.

After-sales service Service of carrying out repairs, maintenance and the supply of advice or spares after a sale has been transacted; also with a view to further sales. The provision of the service is usually essential to the sale of the product.

After sight A bill of exchange drawn after sight, becomes payable after acceptance, fixing a date of acceptance from acceptor.

Against all risks Term used in marine insurance meaning insured against all generally accepted risks.

10

Age cycle The changing of consumer demand patterns in line with those consumers' age/life style.

Agency audit A system whereby a client company makes a periodical, formal and structured assessment of an advertising agency's performance. Can also be applied to other marketing service organizations such as PR consultancies.

Agency bills Bills of exchange drawn on and accepted by the UK branches of foreign banks, usually in London.

Agency commission *See* Media commission.

Agency network A group of similar, but non-competing, agencies who collaborate to provide services covering the potential markets of a client. Usually international. Can also apply to public relations consultancies.

Agent (1) Person or organization with express or implied authority to act for another (the principal) in order to establish a contractual relationship between the principal and any third party. Also can act as legal representative. Advertising agencies are an important exception to this role, acting as principals for the services they purchase on behalf of their clients. (2) Term may be used in a general sense indicating the person or organization representing another.

Agent's lien Where the agent legally possesses goods still owned by its principal, it is said to have a lien for monies due from the principal.

Agent's torts Principal is jointly and severally liable for his/her agent's torts where the agent has been acting for him/her in the normal course of its agency or upon the instructions of the principal. An advertising agency is an exception.

Aggregate demand Expression of total demand for goods and services within a national economy, usually divided into consumer, industrial, public purchases and exports.

Aggregating Adding together data from a market research survey so as to give a quantitative output. Such data comes usually from pre-coded questions.

AIDA A mnemonic for Attention, Interest, Desire, Action, denoting the progressive steps of customer reaction in the process of making a sale. Dates from the late nineteenth century.

Aided recall Prompting respondents by inducing association of ideas to help recall, particularly of television or cinema viewing. *See* Recall.

Aim *See* Goal.

AIR Average issue readership.

Air brush Device which sprays atomized dye or paint in a controlled manner. Used for retouching photographs and for producing artwork.

Air date Normally refers to date of first transmission of a commercial or campaign via a broadcasting service.

Air time Amount of time devoted or allocated to an advertisement on radio or television. May also refer to actual time of transmission.

Airway bill May also be known as Air consignment note. Is used as a contract of carriage by air.

Aisle Passageway in a supermarket either side of which are display units.

AIX (Advanced interactive executive) IBM's version of the UNIX operating system.

Algorithm Rule for the solution of a problem in a finite number of steps, e.g. a full statement of an arithmetical procedure for evaluating Sin X to a stated precision (BS 3527).

Align   In which irregular lines of type in the body copy of a proof are marked so as to line them up, e.g. to justify them.

Allonge   Attachment to a bill of lading allowing for the inclusion of extra endorsement.

Alpha/Beta testing   Two systems for checking the likely success of a new product. Alpha relates to internal testing, and Beta to tests carried out in the market place.

Alternative closes   When seeking an order, giving buyer options to purchase but each choice involves a 'yes', so avoiding a 'no' to any alternatives offered.

Amongst matter   Position of an advertisement, where it is situated amongst editorial material.

Amortization   Accounting procedure for extinguishing initial investment in new product launch over a period of years. Also relates to depreciation of plant and equipment.

Ampersand   Symbol for 'and', i.e. &.

Analogue computer   A machine or electronic circuit designed around numerical data represented by variable physical or electronic quantities (e.g. rotation or voltage), in contrast with digital values of either 0 or 1.

Analysis   Resolution into simple elements, e.g. summary of data into tabulated form. May take the form of a chart of diagram.

Analysis of variance   Statistical term relating to an examination of variations of data about a mean.

Anchor store   In a shopping mall, a large and well known store which acts as an attraction to shoppers, thus benefiting other smaller retail outlets.

Aniline printing   Method of printing using aniline dyes. *See* Flexography.

Animation Movement added to static objects, especially in relation to cartoons.

Annual report Document published by a company and sent to its shareholders giving them the statutory financial information together with other information about the organization's performance and its future prospects. Increasingly used to inform other groups of stakeholders such as employees.

Annuals Periodicals which are published once a year, usually in the form of reference books.

Anonymous product testing Tests in which different basic products are all presented in a common anonymous form, e.g. a plain pack. This complements the Pseudo product test in evaluating a consumer's ability to perceive intrinsic product differences.

Answer print The first print of an edited colour film.

Anti-competitive practices Actions likely to restrict, distort, or prevent competition in the production, supply, or acquisition of goods or services in Britain. Contained within the Competition Act 1980.

Anti-dumping Action to prevent dumping by investigation following evidence of injury (not necessary in USA) to the domestic home market.

Anti-virus program A vital piece of software that is mandatory to use if you value your data and programs. It vaccinates your software against undesired viruses.

Appeal Basis of a selling proposition or advertising message designed to match a 'customers' want', i.e. the appeal identifies what customers desire and what the product or service concerned can supply.

Application A complete and self-contained program performing a specific function (e.g. word processing) as opposed to other software such as an operating system.

Appreciation   (1) Increase in value of asset, e.g. following excess of demand over supply. (2) Summing up or appraisal of a situation or problem.

Appropriation   Used in advertising to refer to the total sum of money set aside for all parts of the advertising mix. Equally, there can be appropriations for other parts of marketing or general business activity. Sometimes referred to as Advertising budget.

'Arbitrary' method   Method of arriving at an advertising budget unrelated to calculation and without reference to the task to be achieved. (*See* Task method.) Arbitrary method (*as also* Affordable method) is still a commonplace means of determining how much should be spent on advertising.

Architecture   The design of a computer, or any complex system (e.g. 'network architecture').

Archive   To physically store files on a disk or tape and physically lock them away. Also known as 'backup'.

Area sampling   A form of geographical segmentation in which research is conducted on a trial or sample basis which might then be seen as representative of the whole universe.

Arena advertising   Posters placed around a sports stadium or other such public place in order to gain publicity from the spectators, but more importantly from any television coverage.

Arithmetic mean   *See* Average.

Armchair shopping   Making purchases from home without visiting a retail outlet. Classically, this applies to mail order but is moving into the use of videos.

Arousal method   *See* Galvanometric response.

Array   Organized display of a set of observations in a statistical analysis.

Arrears   In which copies of a periodical are sent free of charge to lapsed subscribers in order to maintain circulation figures, and perhaps to gain a subscription renewal.

Art buyer   Person responsible for purchasing artwork or photography, usually in advertising agency.

Art director   Individual charged with the task of overseeing the transforming of a creative idea into visual form.

Art paper   High quality paper coated with china clay to give good reproduction. Varying surfaces are available from smooth to very high gloss.

Article   *See* Feature.

Artificial obsolescence   Annual model changes to bring dissatisfaction among consumers for their existing machine or appliance.

Artists' medium   Material used by artist for his/her particular visual expression, e.g. pencil, ink, paint, photography.

Arts sponsorship   Use of sponsorship to support an artistic event as against the perhaps more popular 'sport'. *See* Sponsor.

Artwork   Pictorial, illustrative or text part of an advertisement, or publication, in its finished form ready for platemaking or production, e.g. a retouched and masked photograph.

AS/400   An IBM minicomputer.

ASA   Advertising Standards Authority. An independent body set up and paid for by the advertising industry to ensure that its system of self-regulation works in the public interest. The Authority has an independent chairman. Its members are appointed by him to serve as individuals and not as representatives of any section or interest. Half of its members must be from outside advertising. The Authority maintains close contact with central and local government departments, consumer organizations, and trade associations and deals with complaints received through them or direct from the public.

Ascender   Stroke, in typography, rising above the x height of a lower case letter, e.g. h, b, k. *See* Descender.

Aspiration levels   Levels which consumers expect or desire to reach in class of product or service; in their aim or ambition to own a particular prestigious (according to their perception) product or brand.

Assertiveness   A personal skill, usually in a face-to-face situation, to achieve a goal without being unduly passive (submissive) or aggressive (belligerent), i.e. standing up for one's own rights while recognizing and not infringing the rights of others.

Assumptions   Factors on which any plan or campaign is based; are essential to the success of any activity.

ATM (Asynchronous transfer mode)   A new network transport technology which will allow voice and data (text, images or video) to be transmitted at higher speeds than have so far been possible over a single channel.

Atmosphere   Qualitative or subjective value of a medium or publication for advertising purposes.

Atomistic evaluation   Evaluation of specific elements or steps in advertising, particularly using indices of advertising effectiveness. *See* Holistic evaluation.

Attention value   Extent to which an advertisement can secure the initial attention of a reader, sometimes expressed in quantitative form in Starch or other page-traffic studies. *See* Starch ratings.

Attitude   State of mind reflecting a negative or positive personal view about an object or concept; a state of indifference indicates a mid-point between these opposites. *See* Behaviour.

Attitude change   Extent to which an attitude varies, usually as a result of external stimuli. A principal goal of public relations.

Attitude research   An investigation, often by personal interview or group discussion, into the attitude of people towards an organization or its products.

Attitude testing   Research into the likely reaction of consumers to proposed promotional strategies or tactics.

Attributes   The features of a product which are thought to appeal to customers. A more relevant term to 'product attributes' is 'customer benefits' which may not be the same, i.e., the product is looked at from the consumer's point of view rather than the seller's. An even more relevant term is 'perceived benefits' since this is the real factor which motivates purchase.

Attrition   Gradual wearing away of an individual's loyalty to a product or organization, attributable largely to competitive claims and promotions. May occur with advancing age but can often lead to a change of purchasing behaviour for no very apparent reason.

Auction sales   Public sale where items offered are sold to the highest bidder.

Audience   Group of people exposed to any of the media, but more usually associated with television, radio, or cinema. Audience is a passive word and does not necessarily imply 'attention' to an advertisement. *See* Reach.

Audience composition   Classification of audiences by particular characteristics, usually demographic.

Audience data   Information relating to size and/or nature of an audience.

Audience duplication   *See* Duplication.

Audience flow   Gain or loss of audience during a programme.

Audience loyalty   The acquisition by a television or radio series of a regular following, a targeted group of people whose characteristics might coincide with a market segment for a particular product.

Audience profile Information on the nature and characteristics of readers, viewers, or listeners of advertising media.

Audience research *See* Media research.

Audimeter Continuous measuring device for monitoring the use of television sets and hence, by careful sampling, television audience.

Audio news release An increasingly popular type of press release for radio stations, but in the form of an audio cassette ready for radio transmission.

Audiovisual Any form or combination of visual (ciné film, transparency or video) and sound (record, tape, cassette, optical or magnetic sound track).

Audiovisual sales aids Equipment incorporating facilities for communicating by sight and sound, used by salespeople to simulate an actual demonstration.

Audit Formal examination of accounts or management resources. *See* Agency audit.

Audit Bureau of Circulation Industry body formed to monitor and authenticate circulation of publications.

Audited circulation Circulation which has been verified by an independent body such as the Audit Bureau of Circulation.

Authorized dealer Retail or wholesale outlet which has exclusive rights over the distribution/sale of a product or service in a given geographical region.

Autocue Moving written message/script giving a prompt to a speaker usually in front of a camera. Placed in such a position that the audience is unaware of such an aid.

Automatic selling Form of distribution outlet in which goods are retailed through some automatic device such as a vending machine. Also in use by banks for dispensing money and garages for petrol.

Auxiliary sales/merchandising team Mobile force, available to undertake work that is out of the ordinary and cannot be coped with by the permanent staff. *See* Commando selling.

Average Usual or normal; most often refers to 'mean' or arithmetic average, the formula for which is:

$$m = \frac{x_1 + x_2 + x_3 \dots x_n}{n}$$

where 'm' is the mean. The mean is unfortunately not always representative of each item in a series and, in such cases, other forms of average, such as the mode or median may be used.

Average cost pricing Pricing policy where an average price is established over a product range based on average cost.

Average frequency Average opportunities to see a commercial announcement among those who are reached at all, i.e. gross reach divided by net reach.

Average issue readership The number of people who read or look at an average issue of a publication.

Average propensity to consume That part of national income devoted, on average, by the nation's individuals to consumption of goods and services.

Average revenue Total revenue divided by number of units sold.

Awareness Movement of object or idea into the conscious mind. Often a desired objective of an advertising campaign. A principal goal of public relations.

B

Back bench Senior editorial executives in a newspaper.

Back-checks System of following up interviewers in research to ascertain the extent to which instructions have been followed.

Back cover In advertising, the back cover of a magazine usually available at premium rates for advertising. Special rates apply to both inside and outside back covers. *See* Front cover.

Back-door selling Direct sales approach to the real decision-maker, by-passing the purchasing department which might otherwise act as a barrier.

Back freight Additional charges payable due to freight not being collected within a reasonable time at the port of discharge. Often includes master handling goods at owner's expense and may include transferring goods to another port. May refer to charges for goods to consignor.

Back-to-back Where two commercials for the same advertiser are run consecutively in the same television slot. Usually for the same product or for complementary ones.

Back-to-back credit Credit provided to a buyer by finance house acting as contact between foreign buyers and sellers, particularly where the seller does not disclose identity. The terms embodied in the credit reflect the terms of the original sale.

Backed note An authority, endorsed by broker, to master of ship arranging the loading of goods for shipment.

Background (1) Secondary information relating to a marketing campaign. (2) Remoter part of an illustration or advertisement layout. (3) Sound effect or musical strain in a broadcast or film.

Backhander An underhand financial payment as an incentive or a reward for help in securing a business deal. A bribe.

Backward integration   Increasing turnover, business and profit by acquiring suppliers: thus vertical integration.

Bad debts   Accounts going out of business and still owing money to suppliers. Also an item in financial accounts referring to actual amount of monies so lost, or written off.

Bag   Open ended container for wrapping goods usually at the point of sale. Made from paper or plastic, and sometimes including paperboard for added protection. Often bearing distinctive printing indicating origin, and advertising goods or services.

Balance of payments   Details of credit and debit transactions of one country against all foreign countries and international institutions. Government control over balance of payments usually affects international marketing policies.

Balance of trade   Nation's balance of payments for visibles on current account. *See* Invisible exports.

Balloon copy   As in cartoons in which the words spoken by a character are displayed within a circle from which a line is drawn to the person's mouth.

Banded pack   Special offer combining two related or unrelated products in one integral unit.

Bandwidth   A quantitative term used to measure the amount of data that can be sent through a communications circuit per second (or more specifically, the difference in Hertz (Hz) between the highest and lowest frequencies).

Bank papers   Medium papers used for stationery and other such documentation.

Banner   Relating to an advertisement headline stretching across open space. Also large board or piece of fabric held or towed aloft bearing some slogan or symbol.

Bar chart   Illustration of data using bars or columns. Also known as a histogram.

22

Bar code   A pattern of vertical bars of variable width containing encoded information (according to the spacing, width and number of bars) which can be read and decoded with a special scanner and associated software.

BARB   *See* Broadcasters Audience Research Board.

Bargain   (1) To negotiate for terms. (2) An offer providing unusual value, e.g. a reduction in price. The benefits may be largely illusory but are found to have a motivating influence.

Barter   Transaction in which goods are exchanged without the use of money. Originally on a person-to-person basis, but now occurs more frequently in international trading.

Base line   Part of an advertisement or promotional material, usually containing address, company name, logotype and maybe a slogan, situated at foot of page; often conforms to common house style. *See* Address line.

Basic human needs (desires)   Compound of human characteristics submerged in the subconscious, conditioning behaviour patterns and personality traits.

Basing-point pricing system   Pricing system which ensures that final selling prices in an industry are identical irrespective of the location or freight charges involved. In calculations each plant is given a 'base' price and a variable charge per mile.

Basket   Container made from various materials including cane, wood or paperboard, and having a carrying handle, used in horticulture mainly for tomatoes and soft fruit but also, in wire, used in self-service stores for collection of merchandise by customers.

Batch   (1) Group of similar documents used as input for one computer run. (2) Small production run, often the result of Economic Batch Production Techniques. (3) General term used to refer to a collection of items with a common identity or relationship.

Batch processing Data can be processed instantaneously for immediate results (in 'real time') or it can be 'batched' first, i.e. collected and collated, then submitted to the computer, and finally unbatched and redistributed.

Battered letter Typeface which has been damaged or is in some way faulty; shows up in printing as an indistinct letter.

Bayes Theorem (Bayesian Theorem) Recently acquired sample information combined with prior personal probabilities, so producing revised probabilities in order to embark on new courses of action which may then, repeatedly, be subjected to further inputs of information and revised. It is close to the process of elimination with the use of probability theory.

Bayesian decision theory Statistical technique for assisting decision-making under conditions of uncertainty. Used primarily for deciding when to implement a decision and what to do when made; it provides a framework for alternative courses of action particularly in new product development.

Behaviour Actions by people as against a mental inclination towards taking such action (behavioural intent) which may or may not be preceded by a change in attitude.

Behavioural intent A mental state arising out of awareness (of a product), perception (a positive feeling towards a product), and then an intention to buy a product. It is a well known fact that this does not necessarily lead to a change in behaviour, i.e. to actually purchase a product. *See* Behaviour.

Behavioural research Research into human behaviour, singly or in groups, particularly in connection with consuming or buying habits but also concerned with wider aspects of social and organizational conduct.

Beliefs The properties and benefits attributed by a customer to a product or service, whether they are true or not. *See also* Brand image *and* Perception.

Believability   The extent to which an advertising message is accepted as being credible. Also referred to as 'credibility of the message source'.

Below-the-line advertising   Advertising activities which do not normally make provision for a commission to be payable to an advertising agency. These include direct mail, exhibitions, demonstrations, point-of-sale material, sometimes referred to as scheme advertising. *See* Sales promotion with which it is often confused. *See also* Above-the-line advertising.

Benchmark   (1) A pre-determined standard against which future activity is measured, particularly in market research in order to carry out tracking. (2) A system of investigating 'best practice' for a particular function, and in a particular industry. This is then taken up and leads to increased efficiency which impacts upon marketing, giving the company a competitive edge.

Benchmark test   If you plan to buy a software program, get the various bidding companies to 'benchmark' their software on your *existing* computer installation, and compare ease of use and speed.

Benefit segmentation   The grouping together of prospective customers according to the particular benefits they seek.

Benefits   *See* Attributes.

Best before date   *See* Date coding.

Best practice   Superior performance of a system, process, or other activity which puts the company concerned at an advantage compared with its competitors. Also referred to as 'best-in-class', or 'best-of-breed'.

Bias   Statistical term referring to errors in sample survey results which may be due to the use of an unrepresentative sample but also to undue influence upon response by the agency conducting the survey or a combination of such causes.

Bid The price a person is willing to pay for a product or service.

Bidding theory Quantification of purchasing determinants and the application of probability theory to arrive at a pricing policy; the numerical expression of relevant factors and their measured likelihood of acceptance at different price levels

Bill (1) Invoice. (2) Short for billboard – a placard or poster in outdoor advertising. (3) Announcement listing persons in a broadcast programme.

Bill of entry Document showing final clearance of imported goods by Customs officers.

Bill of exchange Unconditional order in writing, addressed by one person to another, signed by the person giving it, requiring the person to whom it is addressed to pay on demand, or at a fixed or determinable future time, a certain sum in money to, or to the order of, a specified person, or to bearer.

Bill of lading Shipping document used as consignment note, indicating contractual terms and the parties to the contract. There are normally three copies (1) retained by seller; (2) held by master of ship; and (3) sent to buyer of goods. It is often presented with a bill of exchange and may give good title to goods.

Bill of sale Document indicating transfer of title, although possession usually remains with the transferer. Used to raise money on loan. Similar to Building Society mortgage.

Bill of sale (absolute) Document indicating transfer of title and possession, and witnessed by a solicitor.

Bill of sale (conditional) Document indicating transfer of title but where transferer reserves the right to retake title upon fulfilment of specific conditions.

Bill of sight Used by an importer for declaration on goods where full details of a particular consignment may be uncertain. After inspection by Customs the entry details are 'perfected'.

Bill of sufferance An authority to coastal vessels to carry dutiable goods between ports with bonded warehouses.

Billboard Outdoor poster site. In the UK it refers to a particular size (double crown) whereas in other countries, especially the USA, it has a more generic use.

Billing Total value of business handled by an advertising agency in a given period. Gross turnover.

Bin Container for bulk display of merchandise at the retail outlet. Often used in supermarkets to dispose of goods on special offer.

Binary (1) Of, or appertaining to, two (BS 3527). (2) Variable which can have one of two values only (0 or 1). It replaces the normal counting system of 1, 2, 3, 4, 5 ... n, by the values of 0 and 1 only. The basis for rapid computing in electronic data processing systems.

Bind-in A piece of promotional material bound into a magazine. Often printed on a heavier stock in order to increase its visibility. *See also* Inserts.

Binding Process of joining together pages of a book or other publication by means of stitches, staples, canvas, plastic, glue, rings, or other such devices.

Bingo card Enquiry card bound into a magazine and containing matrix of numbers or letters which correlate with similar keys in advertisements or editorial items. Facilitates reader enquiries and is usually prepaid for return to publisher. May also be referred to as readers' enquiry card.

Bit (Binary digIT) A unit of binary, either 0 or 1, representing the result of a yes-or-no question and forming the basic element of computer memory.

Black economy Informal economic system in the UK, involving the evasion of tax, including casual employment for cash, fringe benefits, and even immoral, and criminal activities.

Blanket coverage Advertising without prior selection of specific target audience.

Bleach-out A photograph from which all the middle tones have been removed, thus creating a dramatic and eye-catching visual.

Bleed Advertisement or printed page which utilizes the entire page area, i.e. print extends beyond the margin to the edge of the page.

Blind (1) Term in printing indicating the impression of letter or symbols without the use of ink, but by raising the surface, i.e. embossing. (2) Also used in product testing, where the commercial identity of the product(s) tested is unknown to respondents.

Blind advertisement An advertisement which is anonymous, i.e. it omits the name of the sponsor as in 'situations vacant' where the company does not wish to disclose its identity and uses a box number or similar device instead.

Blind embossing An impression made in a sheet of paper, say a letterhead, in which a symbol or logo protrudes, but without an ink coating. *See also* Blind.

Blind product test Evaluation of a product in such a way that the respondent is unaware of the brand.

Blink-meter Used in advertising research to measure the frequency of a person's blinking, so giving indications of interest or arousal.

Blister pack Sheet of transparent plastic, moulded into the form of a 'blister' and laminated onto a backing sheet. This enclosure might then contain a quantity of small units, like screws or drawing pins, or just one item, e.g. an electric switch.

Blitzkrieg advertising *See* Fastmarketing.

Block Plate of metal, rubber or plastic engraved, moulded, or cast for printing purposes (other than body type), e.g. of photographs or drawings.

Block pull Carefully printed proof from a block to enable the accuracy and quality of reproduction to be checked before printing order is executed.

Blocking out Re-touching a photograph or illustration in order to remove any unwanted parts before moving to artwork stage.

Blow-up Considerable enlargement of photograph or other illustration.

Blunderbuss *See* Shotgun approach.

Blurb Brief, written, description usually having the connotation of bias. Originally associated with details of a book printed on the cover.

Board Frequently used in reference to the Board of Management of a firm or other organization. *See* Paperboard and Fibreboard.

Body copy Main copy in advertisement, as opposed to headlines or illustration.

Body language (1) Non-verbal form of communication. (2) Sign language and non-verbal communication used where parties to a meeting may not have a common language. *See* Chronemics, Olfaction, Proxemics.

Body matter (or type) Small type which forms the bulk of the text in an advertisement, or indeed any piece of printed material.

BOGOFF A mnemonic for Buy One Get One Free, i.e., a promotional practice whereby on the purchase of one product, another one is given free.

Bold face Typeface in printing which is particularly heavy so that it stands out from the other printed matter. Used especially for titles or headings requiring prominent display.

Bona fide In good faith. Most often used in the law of contract. Sometimes used to indicate genuine travellers, e.g. in Scotland, where licensing laws are more tolerant to the needs of the traveller.

Bond papers Quality papers used for stationery and other such documentation.

Bonded goods Imported goods on which duty has not been paid. They are held in a bonded warehouse, e.g. supervised by a Customs and Excise official, awaiting payment of duty or for re-export or for use in goods due to be re-exported. Sold only to those going abroad at duty-free shops.

Bonding of salespeople Buying indemnity against possible loss arising from negligence or dishonesty through employment of salespeople.

Bonus/extra sized packs Larger pack, or pack with an additional smaller package of the same product but sold at the price usual for a standard pack.

Bonus payment An incentive payment to salespeople for above-the-norm achievement, often *ex gratia* rather than contractual.

Book face Type which is commonly used for body copy (or books) because of its particular legibility. Mostly these are serif faces, which *see*.

Book token Card containing a voucher which can be used in exchange for a book of the same value.

Bookends Two commercials, usually at the extreme ends of an advertising slot, for the same product.

Booklet Small book containing up to fifty or so pages. *See* Brochure.

Boolean operation An operation depending on the application of the rules of Boolean algebra. By extension, any operation in which the operands and results take either one or two values or states, i.e. any logical operation on single binary digits (BS 3527).

Boomerang effect Where advertising of product 'A' alienates the consumer as being too 'hard sell' and who, as a result, deliberately buys product 'B'.

Booth Exhibition stand. *See* Shell scheme.

Born salespeople Sales or other personnel attributed with natural qualities that result in superior selling achievement.

Boston box *See* Product portfolio.

Bottle Narrow necked container, usually of glass, stoneware or plastics (BS 3130). The latter may be rigid, e.g. containing carbonated drinks, or pliable, e.g. for washing-up liquids, where hand pressure assists dispensing of contents.

Bottom-up planning In which the various divisions/departments/subsidiaries develop their own plans which are then put together into one integrated corporate plan. Thus managers and executives feel that they have made a contribution to the future development of the organization and are, therefore, more strongly motivated. Has particular relevance in the compilation of marketing and communications budgets. Opposite of the more common Top-down planning.

Boutique agency (1) A specialized agency which sets out to concentrate on one specific element of advertising services, but to do it very well, e.g. creativity, design, writing, media planning and buying, as opposed to a Full service agency. (2) Also applied to shop carrying a range of trendy feminine wear.

Box   Rigid container, completely formed at the point of manufacture, constructed of cardboard (strawboard or chipboard) and often covered with decorative paper, e.g. gift boxes, quality chocolate boxes. Also may be made from rigid plastics.

Box number   Code put into an advertisement by the publisher, and to which replies can be sent without the identity of the advertiser being known. Frequently used in recruitment advertising.

Boycotts   Refusal to deal with or to trade with another person, organization, or country.

BRAD   British Rate and Data.

Brainstorming   An intensive group discussion to stimulate creative ideas and to solve business problems ranging from new product concepts to improved sales performance, brand names to co-operative strategies, advertising slogans to PR events. The essence of a brainstorming session is that no idea, no matter how apparently irrelevant, should be discarded without adequate consideration and debate, the intention being to repel normal inhibitions and stimulate every kind of suggestion.

Brand   Established product name, wholly of a proprietary nature, and usually listed with the Register of Patents.

Brand awareness   Extent to which a brand or brand name is recognized by potential buyers, and correctly associated with the particular product in question.

Brand conditioning   Marketing action to develop a favourable impression for a brand.

Brand differentiation   *See* Differentiation.

Brand extension   To add a new product to a current range all under the same brand name in order to benefit from the existing level of awareness and positive perception. *See also* Halo effect.

Brand image   Perceived impressions of a brand by market segments. Frequently related to abstract associations. May be the result of contrived marketing action or an accident of market perception. *See* Brand Personality, Image, and Product image.

Brand leader   Product which holds the greatest single share of a market.

Brand loyalty   Active support by consumers in continuing consumption of a particular brand in the face of competition by other branded substitutes. Such loyalty is often subjective or subconscious.

Brand manager   Executive responsible for the overall marketing, and particularly promotion, of a specific brand. Job function ranges from a co-ordination role to one in which profit objectives are built in. Sometimes titled product manager, especially in USA.

Brand personality   Collection of attributes giving a brand a recognizable unique quality. May be the result of contrived marketing action or an accident of market perception. *See* Brand image.

Brand positioning   Development of a perception of a brand such that it occupies a distinctive niche in relation to competitors. Thus it might be seen to have a high rating in terms of quality, reliability and status.

Brand preference   A primary advertising/promotional objective, to establish a situation in which a particular brand is regarded as more desirable than its competitors. A brand preference is a prerequisite of a first sale whereas brand loyalty is necessary for repeat purchases.

Brand properties   Actual attributes that collectively provide a brand personality.

Brand rationalization   Reducing the number of brands on offer; often involves making one brand available but providing different labels and packaging and different brand names.

Brand recognition   Advertising or promotional objective, to reach a level of awareness among consumers or prospects.

Brand reinforcement   Reassuring consumers' current beliefs or attitudes to a brand. Common advertising objective.

Brand share   Percentage sales by (or consumption of) a given product related to its total market. Can be expressed in monetary or unit terms and, since these provide different values, should always be defined in terms of the method used to calculate it.

Brand value   An estimated worth of a brand (either a product or a company) which is represented as an asset when being sold off. Debatable as to whether it can appear in the balance sheet, but certainly appears as 'goodwill' in any company valuation.

Branded goods   Goods identified with a proprietary name, normally prepacked by the manufacturer, for promotional, security or trading purposes. Branded goods offer some protection to the retailer or the distributor under the 1893 Sale of Goods Act, the Trade Descriptions Acts, 1968 and 1972, and the Supply of Goods (Implied Terms) Act, 1973.

Breadboard   Early form of prototype in which the performance of a product is reproduced but without the associated appearance or other characteristics. Derives from electrical or engineering products in which components are laid out on a board, thus facilitating changes in order to obtain optimum performance.

Break   Time period in television or radio when commercials are to be transmitted. Often referred to as commercial break.

Breakdown Detailed assembly of data within defined categories. An advertising breakdown, for instance, would show the nature, medium and cost of each item within the campaign.

Breakeven Point at which any commercial venture becomes financially viable, i.e. when total expenditure is exactly matched by income, and therefore the point after which a profit begins to be made. This is of particular importance in the launching of a new product where a certain risk investment is necessary; therefore forecasts must be projected before proceeding, as to the circumstances and time within which the breakeven point will be reached. This provides both the information required for policy decisions but also a yardstick against which performance can be measured progressively. Hence the expression 'payback period' to denote time to elapse before all investment costs are recovered and profit will subsequently be generated.

Breakeven analysis Examination of relationships between sales revenue, fixed costs, and variable costs to determine the most profitable level of output or the most profitable product mix.

Breakeven point Point at which sales revenue covers all expenditure and no profit or loss is being made. The *time* required to achieve this is often characterized as the pay-out period.

Breaking bulk Function of wholesaler who buys in bulk and then distributes in small quantities to local retailers.

BRG (Boston Research Group) *See* Product portfolio.

Brief Summary of facts, objectives and instructions relating to the requirements for the creation of a campaign, an advertisement, or any other element of a marketing operation.

British Code of Sales Promotion Practice Similar in concept and structure to the code relating to advertising, but dealing specifically with the regulation of sales promotional activities. Administered also by the ASA.

British Market Research Bureau (BMRB) Subsidiary of the British constituent of the worldwide J. Walter Thompson advertising agency and source of many notable marketing research studies and techniques, e.g. TGI.

British Rate and Data A detailed guide to media buyers.

British Standards Institution Operating under a Royal charter, the Institution is government assisted. It is an independent body promoting the co-operation of both users and producers in the improvement, standardization and simplification of designs, products, and industrial materials in order to eliminate production of an excessive variety of patterns and designs intended to serve one purpose. Furthermore, BSI sets standards of quality and dimensions by specification and registers and licenses standards of all descriptions. It also operates THE (Technical Help for Exporters), a body used to provide technical advice, guidance and information on foreign standards and competitive performances.

Broadcast Transmitted message by electro-magnetic radiation (over the air), e.g. radio and television.

Broadcasters Audience Research Board (BARB) An industry body charged with the task of commissioning and publishing audience research data in relation to all television channels. It is concerned with both audience measurement and audience reaction.

Broadsheet (1) Printed promotional material usually with one or two folds, but opening up into a relatively large sheet. (2) Term referring to newspapers other than tabloids.

Brochure Stitched booklet, usually having eight or more pages, often with a prestige connotation. *See* Booklet.

Broken lot Goods offered for sale in smaller than normal quantity. Includes damaged packaged goods where some contents have been lost or removed.

Broker Agent who does not physically handle the goods with which he/she deals, nor having control over the terms involved in a contract. He/she may represent either a buyer or a seller.

Brown goods Goods (usually electrical) which were originally coloured brown, e.g. radios and televisions.

BSI   British Standards Institute.

Bubble pack   *See* Blister pack.

Bucket shop   Retail outlet selling cut-price wares. Mostly refers to travel agents selling cheap air fares. Perceived by some to be unreliable.

Budget   Estimate of future sources of income and expenditure including statements of intentions within a given period of time. Can relate to individual parts of the marketing mix, when it may include expenses only, or to the total marketing operation. *See* Advertising budget.

Budgetary control   Methodical monitoring of planned income and expenditure by issuing sales targets, placing orders and authorizing payments within the context of a previously approved and detailed budget. Provision is made for continuous feedback which relates to all financial commitments and projected surpluses or over-expenditures.

Build strategy   Deliberate actions to increase market share, usually by investing more into advertising, marketing communications and, indeed, marketing.

Built-in obsolescence   Technique used to increase the need for replacement for products in an effort to maintain continuous high volume of output and sales. *See* Obsolescence.

Built-in stabilizers   Automatic buffers against violent fluctuations in the economy, reacting without related government intervention at any one time. Sometimes manipulated by Government to achieve desired effects on national economy.

Bulk cargo   Cargo of one commodity on board ship, sometimes as loose storage in hold.

Bulk discount   Reduction on standard price in consideration of purchasing a large quantity of goods or services, or, in the case of advertising, space or time.

Bulk goods   Products or materials distributed in loose form and often in large quantities such as coal, grain and sand.

Bulk mail   Supplying mail to the postal service in specified groups, e.g. postal codes, in order to qualify for a discount.

Bulkhead   An advertising position for posters in buses which appear above the windows.

Bullet   A mark in a visual which is placed adjacent to a selling proposition in order to draw attention to it. Usually in the form of a large dot, square or triangle. Often referred to as bullet points.

Bulletin   (1) Brief, periodically issued, mailing or announcement. (2) Painted outdoor sign or display.

Bulletin board   (1) Poster, illuminated outdoor sign, or transparency, size forty-eight sheet or even larger. Often found in city centres or on trunk roads. (2) Notice board.

Burst   Concentration of television commercials into a short space of time.

Bus side   Space on the side of a bus, available for advertising. Usually 17 ft 6 ins long by 1 ft 9½ ins deep.

Business cycle   *See* Trade cycle.

Business gift   *See* Advertising novelty.

Business objective   Long-term purpose of an organization. Usually expressed in terms of markets to be covered, products or services to be developed, and financial targets to be achieved, i.e., profit.

Business partner   Where two companies work together for some common aim, e.g. a principal and an agent both for overseas markets and/or a principal and a distributor. *See* Partnership pricing.

Business plan   A document which sets down the overall objectives of an organization, and the means by which it intends to achieve them. It takes in all the other functional plans as sub-sets, e.g. the marketing plan. In a commercial business, the ultimate and sole objective is profit. All other objectives, however laudable and logical, are set with that ultimate objective in view. *See also* Corporate planning.

Business portfolio   *See* Product portfolio.

Business presentation graphics   Graphically oriented software programs which allow all types of non-text data, e.g. bar charts to be displayed. Excellent for presentations.

Business press   Periodicals dealing exclusively with business subjects. Can be horizontal (*Management Today*) or vertical (*Campaign*). *See* Technical press.

Business reply service   Service offered by the Post Office in which the respondent (say to a direct mail shot) is not required to pay the postage, which is then paid by the originator or licence holder.

Business strategy   The means by which a business aims to achieve its objectives. This is enlarged upon in the business plan. Similarly, each function (e.g. marketing, financial, human resources, R&D, etc.) has a set of objectives, strategies and plans.

Business-to-business advertising   *See* Industrial advertising.

Business-to-business marketing   The marketing of goods or services in which the potential market comprises businesses or organizations rather than the general public. Thus a lemon is a 'business' product when viewed in relation to hotels or airlines (and actually retail outlets) but a 'consumer' product when the appeal is to the general public. Industrial marketing and technical selling fall within the business-to-business sector. *See* Industrial selling.

Buy classes In which organizational purchasing decisions vary in complexity according to which of three patterns they fit. The simplest is the 'repeat purchase' – buying the same product from the same supplier. This is followed by the 'modified rebuy' where the same type of product is purchased from an alternative supplier. Finally, the 'new buy' situation, i.e. a first time purchase in which a larger number of people are likely to be involved and in which the evaluation is likely to be more complex. *See* Decision-making unit.

Buy grids Competing products objectively compared for their attributes and then matched against specified requirements. Used by industrial buyers.

Buyer (1) Person responsible for making a final purchasing decision. (2) Executive in a company heading up the overall purchasing function. (3) Department head in a department store.

Buyers' market Market situation in which excess manufacturing capacity and over-supply of a commodity puts buyers in strong negotiating position as the result of an imbalance between supply and demand. Particularly affects movement of prices for seasonal goods.

Buying centre *See* Decision making unit.

Buying committee In retailing, a group of people who decide on the range of goods their outlets will sell, and hence what has to be bought.

Buying criteria The various factors which go into the purchase of a product or service. Usually a combination of objective criteria such as price, delivery, performance and service, coupled with a whole range of perceptions such as brand and corporate images, ego, fear, and personal feeling towards the selling contact.

Buying incentive A sales promotional aid to persuade a customer to make the decision to buy, e.g. a discount or an incentive such as 'buy one get one free'.

Buying intent   The penultimate stage in making a purchase. Starts with awareness followed by a positive perception, then behavioural intent, and finally behaviour. 'Intention' by no means always leads to a sale.

Buying motives   All those factors within a person or organization which combine to create a desire to purchase. Such factors are usually complex and comprise logical criteria like price, quality, delivery; but also highly subjective considerations, often difficult to locate, let alone measure, such as prestige, brand image, colour, shape and packaging.

Buying signals   Indirect indications of a prospect's growing interest in the product being presented.

Buying syndicates   Collective negotiating and buying group. *See* Co-operative.

By-line   Reporter's name printed above his/her story.

By-product   Product, commodity, or service which becomes available as a result of production of some primary product.

Byte   (Literally 'by eight'.) Arithmetically speaking, a group of eight binary digits, or bits, corresponding to a single character of information and representing the smallest addressable unit of computer memory. It is not unknown, particularly on older architectures, for a byte to consist of 6, 7 or 9 bits although such usages are nowadays quite rare.

C

C1/C2   *See* Socio-economic groups.

Cable television   System whereby incoming signals to domestic television sets is by cable connection to a central receiving source rather than each set having its own aerial. Of growing interest as more channels become available with increasingly complex aerial systems, and with the opportunity of specialized programmes being received by particular audience categories thus facilitating narrow-casting.

CAD (Computer aided design)   An element of computer aided engineering concerned with the drawing or physical layout of steps of engineering design.

Call analysis   Study of salesperson's customer calling patterns.

Call frequency   Frequency with which salespeople visit or contact customers. Distinguished from conventional journey cycle by customer categorizing into groups of varying priority.

Call frequency schedule   Salesperson's journey plan.

Call planning   A procedure whereby information is obtained, usually by telephone, which enables a call to be planned in advance as regards selling strategy and the timing of the call.

Call rate   Number of personal contacts made with customers or prospects within a given period of time. *See* Journey planning.

Call report   Summary, usually in writing, of visit by salesperson to a customer, account executive to client, or similar business meeting.

Call to action   The element of an advertisement which indicates to the reader, viewer, or listener what action to take next. Of growing importance in direct marketing and in relationship marketing. *See also* Response mechanisms.

Callback   In market research, a call which is not answered, or to which there is no response, is further contacted in order to maintain strict sampling accuracy.

Callendered   A paper whose surface is smoothed on the paper-making machine by passing it through rollers to achieve such an effect.

Calligraphy Handwriting, or lettering, as an art form.

Calling cycle Average period between calls on a given customer.

Camera-ready copy Finished artwork ready to be photographed for subsequent platemaking.

Campaign Organized course of action, planned carefully to achieve predefined objectives. Can relate to marketing, advertising, sales, public relations, or any part of the promotional mix.

Campaign plan Formal documentation of a campaign, beginning with campaign objectives and finishing with campaign monitoring and evaluation proposals.

Can Diminutive of canister. A metal container, usually of tin-coated mild steel or aluminium, for containing, preserving or dispensing liquids or solids, especially foodstuffs. Hence, colloquial form is 'tin'. Opened except in the case of aerosols by a metal-cutting tool or by means of a 'ring pull'.

Canned presentation Any sales or advertising presentation committed to memory and used consistently for all prospects. Often used by inexperienced or new personnel not yet able to deliver their own spontaneous presentation. May figure prominently in sales training sessions.

Cannibalism Brand sales being achieved at the expense of another brand within the same company.

Canvass (1) To interview a selected group either for research purposes or within a selling procedure. (2) Used in research to indicate coverage of an entire population rather than just a sample. Synonymous in this sense to polling or conducting a census. (3) In form of 'cold' canvass, reference is made to salesperson calls on prospects not previously contacted.

Canvasser Sales representative or selling agent calling direct on users or consumers. Cold canvassing is the term used to describe a salesperson's uninvited (often the first) call on a prospect.

Capital   Monetary measure of assets employed in a business, hence return on capital (ROC). *See* Yield.

Capital goods   Goods, usually for industry or commerce, which are likely to remain permanent fixtures or to be used continuously for a long period of time, e.g. plant and machinery. Contrary term is consumer goods, those entirely consumed shortly after purchase, e.g. soap, foodstuffs, oil.

Capital intensive   Firms or organizations using a high proportion of machinery relative to labour. As labour costs rise, there is a tendency to move towards automation, particularly in situations where machines prove cheaper or more efficient than manpower.

Captain's entry   Details provided by the master of a ship when requesting permission to unload.

Caption   Short description relating to an illustration or diagram.

Captive audience   Audience which, by virtue of its particular situation, is likely to be exposed to an advertising message *in toto*, e.g. a cinema or conference audience.

Captive market   Group of purchasers who are obliged to buy a particular product due to some special circumstances, either where there is no other source of supply or where the supplier is the owner of the buyer's company.

Car card   Small poster displayed mostly above the windows of an underground train. Sometimes called 'tube car panel'.

Card rates   *See* Rate card.

Cardboard   Popular term for paperboard.

Career salesperson   Sales personnel choosing selling as a career rather than as a step in the promotional ladder.

Caret   The symbol ʌ used as a mark of omission in typescript or proof, showing where added matter is to be inserted in a line.

Carnet   International Customs document allowing temporary duty-free import of certain goods into specified countries; normally used for the import of sales promotional samples of no commercial value or for works of art or capital equipment, etc. for temporary use, e.g. for exhibition purposes.

Carrier   Organization or person undertaking to transport people or goods.

Carrier bag   Plastic (or paper) bag for shopping. Often branded with a store or product name, and is reusable.

Carry-through rate   Charging the higher time segment rate when a broadcast programme spans two segments.

Cartel (Kartel)   Organization of a number of firms operating in one market intending to minimize competition. May take the form of 'bulk agreements' as used between the suppliers of post office exchange equipment; outstanding orders are shared out between the participating companies. Under progressive attack from EU Common Market institutions.

Carton   Strictly a folding carton constructed from paperboard, 'set-up' or closed by an adhesive and/or by interlocking of end or side flaps. Most commonly made out of a white-lined board which is printed. Can contain one or a number of units, or dry goods such as powder. Sometimes wrongly used to describe a fibreboard case.

Cartridge paper   Strong compressed paper with a natural uncoated surface.

CASE (Computer aided software engineering)   A computerized technique for designing, producing and maintaining software in a structured environment.

Case   *See* Fibreboard case. *See also* Packing case.

Case study   Case history produced in such a way as to facilitate study/learning, e.g. final solution is omitted to allow student to formulate his/her own.

Cash and carry wholesalers Wholesale supermarket frequented by small retailers or caterers.

Cash cow A product, usually well established, which is more than capable of generating revenue in excess of costs, whilst maintaining its market share. Thus it can be 'milked'. *See also* Star and Dog.

Cash discount Reduction in cash price as incentive to purchase by cash as opposed to some form of credit.

Cash flow Change in the supply of available cash in a given period in a business as a result of income and expenditure transactions.

Cash on delivery System of payment in which goods are paid for on delivery. Safeguards seller in that merchandise is not handed over without payment; similarly, safeguards buyer who takes delivery without any prior financial commitment.

Cash premium coupon Element of an advertisement or part of a pack which, if presented at a retail outlet, will result in a reduced price. Also referred to as a 'voucher'.

Cash refund offer A sales promotional tool in which the purchaser is offered a rebate.

Casting The choice of an actor or actress to be part of the cast of a commercial.

Casting off Estimating space in printing required to accommodate a given number of words of a certain typeface and size.

Catalogue Publication containing descriptions or details of a number or range of products.

Catalogue buying The process of selecting and purchasing goods from a catalogue, ordering by post or telephone, and taking delivery by post or other carrier. *See* Mail order and Direct response marketing.

Catch phrase A product slogan in advertising which is so popular that it becomes part of everyday language, at least for a period of time.

Causal norms Object of research to discover why people behave as they do.

Caveat emptor Legal expression meaning 'let the buyer beware'. Has almost ceased to apply following the Trade Descriptions Acts, 1968 and 1972 and the Supply of Goods (Implied Terms) Act, 1973. The original assumption implied that a person was legally obliged to exercise his/her own commonsense in buying and would not obtain sympathy from the law if he/she failed to protect himself/herself against deception.

CCTV Closed-circuit television (*See* Closed circuit).

CD-i (Compact disc interactive) An application of CD-ROM technology which allows users limited interaction with CD-based material, such as games or educational applications, via a specialized controller.

CD-ROM (Compact disc – read-only memory) Optical-based data storage medium, similar to an audio CD. Commonly used for reference material or computer games where high storage capacity and fast access times are important.

Ceefax BBC variant of computerized television information service being developed by collaboration between ITC, BBC and the Post Office. *See also* Oracle, Viewdata.

Celebrity endorsement Someone chosen to be featured in an advertisement as a well known and respected person who uses a particular product. The celebrity needs to be chosen with care so as to be meaningful to the target group.

Cell The intersection between a row and a column in a spreadsheet. Marketers use spreadsheets for forecasting sales and market trends.

Census Study of an entire population – a government census of population is usually carried out in the UK every ten years. Other censuses, e.g. of production and distribution, are also periodically taken in UK.

Census sample Apparently contradictory term but meaning a sample drawn from compiled census data.

Central Office of Information Production centre of the UK Government world-wide publicity network, available to the British exporter.

Central processing unit *See* CPU.

Centre A typographical instruction to place a particular element of a layout or visual in the middle, with equal space on either side.

Centrespread Double page spread at the centre of a periodical. Usually regarded as desirable position since it occupies one continuous sheet of paper, enjoying the advantages both of extra size and a solus position.

CEO *See* Chief Executive Officer.

Certificate of origin Used to identify source of goods or materials. Useful for economic trading or political reasons, particularly where some privilege is granted in respect of certain producers or where restriction upon movement of goods has been imposed.

Chain stores Group of outlets, under single ownership, each offering a wide variety of merchandise according to local demand.

Champion A person charged with a specific responsibility such as to 'own' a campaign. *See* Product champion.

Channel (1) *See* Channel of distribution. (2) *See* Channel of communication. (3) Often used as synonym for television or radio station, distinguishing one contractor from another by geographical area, based on terminology associated with frequency bands.

Channel of communication Any particular link between a communicator, e.g. an advertiser, and a receiver, e.g. potential customer. *See* Medium.

Channel of distribution Specific means of channelling goods from their point of origin to their point of sale or consumption, e.g. wholesale to retail distribution or manufacturer to customer.

Channel selection Means by which suppliers serve their ultimate consumers either direct or indirect through wholesaler and different categories of retail outlet.

Character In printing, a single letter or symbol.

Character count In a type mark-up the number of letters and spaces are added together to arrive at an accurate visual representation of the finished job.

Character merchandising A form of merchandising based upon popular characters, e.g. Mickey Mouse.

Charge accounts Credit facilities offered by stores to established customers making periodic payments.

Chart Clearest and most effective method of interpreting and presenting a subject visually. A chart can be used to clarify complex problems, reveal hidden facts, or to detect mistakes in statistical work.

Charter Statement of prime responsibility for a department or organizational unit.

Cheap Low price relative to other prices for similar goods. Usually avoided in business, because it tends to be associated in the minds of consumers with inferior goods; alternatives used may be inexpensive, competitive, or covered by the use of the expression 'Sale price', or 'bargain'.

Check list   Comprehensive categorization of actions to be taken in order to achieve a given effect with maximum efficiency.

Checked copy   Typed or printed matter that has been proof read for accuracy, authenticity, or merit.

Checking copy   Examining a periodical to ensure that a particular advertisement appeared on time, in the right position, and in good quality. *See also* Voucher.

Checkout   Cash till at exit(s) of self-service stores and supermarkets where payment is made for goods.

Cherry-picking   In which a shopper selects goods which are on special offer in a store.

Cheshire   Make of labelling machine which cuts computer-printed continuous address labels to size and affixes them to envelopes.

Chi-squared   Statistical test to check whether and in what ways distributions of data differ from each other.

Chief Executive Officer   The senior most important operational executive in an organization. Can be a managing director, a general manager, or even a chairperson.

Chimeric customer wants   Numerous ever-changing needs or demands among customers.

Chip   *See* IC.

Chipboard   Cheap quality of cardboard made from wastepaper. Most common form is white lined chip, in which a higher quality lining of white wood pulp is applied during manufacture. This provides a good printing surface and is used widely in packaging, e.g. of cereals, toothpaste, games and hardware. *See also* Paperboard.

Chronemics   Timing or pauses between verbal exchanges, due either to custom or to give emphasis.

CIF *See* Cost insurance and freight.

Cinema Theatre where motion pictures are shown; usually provides also an outlet for advertising films. In some cinemas, there is more than one theatre with different films showing in each theatre.

Circular Piece of printed matter distributed, or circularized, to a defined group of people.

Circulation Total number of distributed (subscribed or free) copies of a periodical or publication. *See* Readership.

CKD Completely knock down. *See* Knock down.

Class magazine Periodical intended for readership by people having a particular common or specialized interest. In practice, usually applies to consumer, rather than business and professional magazines.

Classified advertising Grouping together into categories or classifications of advertising usually comprising small type-set or semi-display advertisements, e.g. situations vacant, properties required or for sale.

Classified directory Publication listing products, organizations, or people, classified into specialized groups, and listed in alphabetical order.

Classified display advertising Compromise between display and classified advertising whereby a classified advertisement is presented in a display size and format.

Clean In direct mailing practice refers to improving a mailing list by removing duplicates, correcting addresses, etc.

Clean bill of lading Bill of lading without superimposed clauses or endorsement expressly declaring some defective condition of the goods on consignment.

Clearance sale   Good offered at reduced price to clear surpluses or end of season stock. Loss of profit in such sales is balanced by an increase in liquidity, which provides resources for new investment.

Client   In the 'ladder of customer loyalty' a customer who makes a repeat purchase is referred to as a client.

Client-Server   A computing model in which two programs work in co-operation with each other. The program that initiates the work is the client which makes requests on the second, the server. An example could be a desktop workstation making enquiries over a network of a database resident on a central file server.

Clip   (1) Shot or sequence of shots cut or clipped from a complete film. (2) Fastener for retaining connected documentation on movements or transactions.

Clipping   *See* Press cutting.

Clipping service   An agency which will extract relevant news items or advertisements concerning a product or company in return for a monetary consideration.

Close up   Instruction on a proof to move characters together, i.e. to have less space between them.

Closed circuit   Transmitting pictures to a television receiver by wire instead of radio waves. Alternatively, using a TV camera to record events on videotape which can then be used to reproduce the record on suitable TV receivers.

Closed-ended question   A survey technique in which a respondent is asked to choose from a number of specific questions, thus facilitating precise quantification, e.g. 'please state marital status: single, married, divorced'.

Closing date   *See* Copy date.

Closing prices   Price of a commodity or a company's shares in the market at the end of a day's trading.

Closing techniques Variations of method in soliciting buyer action.

Closing the sale Salesperson technique in requesting an order from a buyer (and securing it).

Closure Means by which a pack is closed up, e.g. the top to a bottle, the cap to a can.

Cluster analysis Grouping attitudes by tendency to agree. Used in research to associate slightly different attitudes that, in general, have a tendency to agree.

Cluster groups A number of people or families in a relatively small geographical area.

Cluster sampling Sample units devised in local groups, often chosen geographically to reduce interview travelling costs.

Coarse screen Printing plate having larger than usual screen to facilitate its use on lower quality paper, e.g. newsprint.

Cobweb theorem Analysis of supply and demand situation where supply is a reflection of demand at an earlier time and has, therefore, little relevance to current demand levels. Applies where short-term production capacity is fixed or dependent on seasonal patterns.

COD *See* Cash on delivery.

Codes of practice Laid down conditions under which business should be conducted in a particular area of activity. In marketing, best known perhaps is Code of Advertising Practice (CAP) but Market Research Society and the Chartered Institute of Marketing also publish codes. Similar codes govern practice in sales promotion (issued by International Chambers of Commerce).

Coding (1) Keying of an advertisement to enable the origin of an enquiry to be traced. (2) Use of numbers or letters in a questionnaire against specific questions in order to facilitate analysis.

Coefficient of correlation Measure of the interdependence between two variables. Perfect positive correlation may be indicated by a measure of +1, whereas perfect negative correlation may be indicated by a measure of −1. No correlation at all may be inferred by a measure of zero or close to zero.

Coefficient of variation Standard deviation of a distribution of values divided by its arithmetic mean. It is used to compare frequency distributions and their variabilities.

Cognition Process which uses all human senses to observe the outside world and to form perceptions, attitudes, comprehension and memory. Loosely used as synonym for Perception, which also *see*.

Cognitive dissonance State of mental conflict caused by taking an action which is in direct opposition to a particular belief or attitude. In marketing, an example would be pre or postpurchase anxiety as to the advisability of having made a particular choice, usually for more expensive goods.

COI *See* Central Office of Information.

Cold calling Uninvited call by a salesperson with the intention of securing an interview leading to the placing of an order.

Cold canvassing Calling on prospects without warning and assessing their needs without any prearrangement.

Cold mailing Using a rented or compiled list to mail for new business.

Collage Mounting objects onto a surface in order to make up a pictorial illustration, often in abstract form.

Collate Put together individual pages in a pre-determined order.

Collateral Term used to refer to promotional elements of a campaign other than advertising, e.g. direct mail, exhibitions, literature.

Colour separation   Photographic process whereby the colours in an illustration are filtered to produce a set of three or four negatives from which printing plates are made. *See* Four-colour set for the application involved here.

Colour supplement   A colour magazine supplied free of charge with a newspaper.

Column centimetres   *See* Column inches.

Column inches   Measurement of area derived from the width of a column of type in publication, multiplied by its depth. Column centimetres now applies under metrication and is replacing column inches in practice.

Comb binding   *See* Mechanical binding.

Combination   Printing block which combines both line and screen (half-tone) etching.

Combination rate   This applies when an advertiser books space in more than one publication by the same publisher. A form of quantity discount which may have to be negotiated.

Commando or pioneer selling   Intensive selling into new markets, often with an entirely new product and sometimes by a specially employed sales force instead of or augmenting existing personnel.

Commercial   Advertisement in television (or radio) either in colour or monochrome.

Commercial break   Break in a television or radio programme in order to transmit an advertising message or 'commercial'. *See* Break and Time segment.

Commercial counterfeiting   Trademark and tradename piracy; may include designs, models, and copyrights. *See* Pirated products.

Commission (1) Agreed financial share of a transaction accruing to a salesperson or selling agent responsible for initiating or introducing business. (2) To hire or brief another concern to undertake a defined assignment. (3) Term used to describe discount allowed to an advertising agency by media owners in consideration of its space/time purchases on behalf of clients: usually 15%; trade and technical publications pay 10%.

Commitment (in advertising) Action whereby advertising space or time becomes chargeable at the full fee, whether cancelled or fulfilled. This occurs automatically to all bookings at a given time prior to scheduled appearance.

Common carrier Carrier prepared to transport goods of any description for anyone willing to hire its services. While it may normally specify the type or size of goods, or even the area in which it is prepared to work, providing it implies it will work for anyone it is considered to be a common carrier, whereupon it is legally obliged to carry goods when requested to do so, subject to any limitations previously publicized.

Communication mix Combination of different media in a specific promotional campaign to reach a pre-determined target audience.

Communication objective The level of awareness and the attitude of particular target audiences which it is desired to achieve in a given period of time.

Communications audit As for a Marketing audit, which *see*.

Communications media Vehicles used to carry messages, informative, educational, or entertaining, to large groups of people; e.g. television, cinema, or radio. *See also* Channel of communication.

Communications spectrum (1) *See* Marketing communications mix. (2) Stages of awareness, *viz* unawareness, aware, comprehension, conviction, action. *See* Hierarchy of effects.

Compact disc interactive   *See* CD-i.

Compact disc – read-only memory   *See* CD-ROM.

Company profile   Description of an organization in terms sufficient to make direct comparison with other organizations, such as, number of employees, product range, sales turnover, market penetration, or promotional expenditure.

Comparative advertising   Drawing attention to one's own product's performance against those of particular competitors, in a recognizable form of measurement such as miles per gallon or usable space. Allowed since 1975 in UK, began in USA in 1964, but became universal in 1974. Known as 'Knocking copy'. Freedom to make direct comparisons with competitive brands.

Comparative analysis   Comparison of quantitative factors relevant to different advertising media or vehicles, based usually on cost factors taking into account the demographic penetration of different publications.

Comparison shopper   Researcher, often employed by a retailer, who investigates merchandising activities in (competitive) retail outlets.

Comparison shopping   Studying competitive brands and selecting according to assessment of value. Most often attributed to those who look for the cheapest brand available at the time. Brand loyalty is not relevant.

Comparison test   Detailed comparison of competing products or services available in the market, usually by an independent third party financed by subscribing members.

Compatibility   Describes the ability of a component such as a PC or network of software to interact in an error free way with another component. Vital to get right and normally needs expert advice in a company with more than one PC!

Compensation (in advertising)   Money negotiated as a refund by the agency, media or production departments for advertising which has appeared incorrectly, the fault lying, at least in part, with the publisher or contractor.

Compensation (as applied to remuneration)   Amalgam of different forms of remuneration for sales executives.

Competition   Existence of rival products or services within the same market (direct competition).

Competitions   Promotional device, whereby prospects are invited to compete for prizes by submitting solutions to problems along with a required number of 'evidences of purchase'. Nearly always involve tie-breakers in the form of apt descriptions or advertising slogans in order to limit number of applicants for prizes, though some competitions offer a multitude of small prizes. Strictly controlled by gaming legislation.

Competitive advantage   Some benefit or value provided by a product or company, often unique to the organization concerned, that gives it superiority in the market place. *See also* Competitive edge.

Competitive bidding . Estimating the probability of being awarded a contract based on different price levels and submitting the price that best suits the company according to its current needs.

Competitive claims   Particular benefits or values promoted by manufacturers or advertisers.

Competitive edge   *See* Competitive advantage and Differential advantage.

Competitive parity   A method of budgeting for marketing communications in which parity with the competition is the basis.

Competitive price   Reduced price compared with those currently prevailing or similar price together with additional incentive. Sometimes offered to selected customers because of their value at any point in time.

Competitive strategy   Determination of business objectives and policies through marketing intelligence, including pricing strategy.

Competitor   Business rival, usually offering similar products or services.

Complementary demand   Demand for one product bringing joint demand for an associated product.

Complementary products   Products sold separately but dependent on each other for sales performance.

Complete refund offer   Offer by manufacturer to refund entire cost of purchase after a complaint by a customer. Frequently includes reimbursement of postal expenses in addition.

Compliment slip   Small sheet of paper (e.g., ⅓A4) to accompany a leaflet, sample or product where a letter is not necessary, and which identifies the name and address of the sender.

Composite demand   Total demand for a material usable for a number of different purposes.

Composite pages   The gathering together of a number of advertisements on a particular topic thus perhaps gaining extra reader attention, e.g. holidays.

CompuServe Information Service   A service run by Compu-Serve Corporation providing access to a variety of information and services including electronic bulletin boards, on-line databases, electronic mail, news services and the Internet.

Comprehension   An understanding of the facts and benefits of a product. An important part of the mental process which a prospect goes through before making a purchase. *See* Hierarchy of effects.

Computer   Nowadays an electronic device for the high-speed processing of information according to given instructions.

Computer aided design *See* CAD.

Computer aided software engineering *See* CASE.

Computer bureau An outside service providing data-processing facilities.

Concept Abstract idea associated with the promotion of a product or service, or with full understanding of a particular business principle or technique.

Concept testing Means by which a new product idea is tested for its acceptability in the market before a prototype is made. Used as a first stage in screening a new product concept. The potential benefits are put to prospective buyers and users to test their reactions to an idea. May also be used for pretesting advertisements.

Concertina fold *See* Accordion fold.

Concession closes When seeking an order, giving buyer small concessions to the proposed deal so tempting an immediate favourable response.

Concessionaire One who operates a business or trade within premises supplied by another.

Condensed Type-face which is especially narrow thus enabling a larger number of letters per inch to be used.

Conditional sale agreement Agreement for the sale of goods, wherein the purchase price may be payable in parts and where the property in the goods remains in the hands of the seller until the terms of the agreement are fulfilled.

Conditioned reflexes Reaction of consumers following a reminder stimulus to earlier brand conditioning.

Confidence level *See* Normal distribution.

Confidence limits   The limits within which a research finding is likely to be accurate.

Confirmation note   An acknowledgement to an order. Often sent as a blank form with an order for the recipient to return, thus providing evidence of the order having been received.

Conglomerate   Holding company, generally consisting of a group of subsidiary companies engaged in dissimilar business activities, but centrally controlled.

Congruent marketing   In which all the separate promotional components are brought together into one unified campaign with similar, identical or complementary messages, thus providing a synergistic output. *See* Integrated marketing.

Congruent production diversification   Widening of product range in line with technological or manufacturing capability or expertise as opposed to the needs and wants of the market, i.e. basis of 'production orientation' as opposed to 'marketing orientation'.

Conjoint analysis   A statistical term used in market research to evaluate and compare product or service attributes, and to discover those most likely to affect buying decisions.

Conquest strategy   A marketing operation in which the main purpose is to attract new customers. Often has many disadvantages which has led to the growth of relationship marketing. *See* Retention strategy.

Consideration   In a contract, the promise of one party must be supported by the agreement of the other party to do, or not to do, some act or to pay some money. The agreement by the other party is known as the consideration. If consideration does not pass, then no contract is enforceable. However, consideration, to be effective, must have some value, i.e. it must be subject to some definition in monetary terms.

Consignee   Person to whom goods are to be delivered.

Consignment note   Shipping term for a document accompanying a consignment of goods often used as an alternative to a bill of lading.

Consignment selling   Goods sent to distributors who take possession but title remains with manufacturer until consignment is paid for. *See* Sale or return.

Consonance   Harmonious blending of basic needs; agreeable reaction to proposition.

Conspicuous consumption   Consumption for approbation instead of utility; tends to be inherent in all purchases, irrespective of the actual utility of the product. Attributed to the American economist, Thorstein Veblen.

Constraint   Any limiting factor involved with the development of an idea or venture.

Consular invoice   Importing countries often insist that goods destined for their country are accompanied by a supporting invoice checked and stamped by their own consul in the exporting country. This enables the importing governments to exercise some control over the flow of imported goods.

Consumer   Strictly, the ultimate consumer of a product, the ultimate user of a product or service; the person who derives the satisfaction or the benefit offered. The 'consumer' is not necessarily the customer, since there are often 'customers' in the buying distribution chain; moreover, the consumer is frequently not the person who makes the buying decision; for instance, in the case of many household products, where the housewife may make the purchase but consumption or use is by the whole family. 'Consumer' is not normally applied to the purchase of industrial goods and services where the customer is usually a corporate body. Nevertheless, consumable goods are sold to industry for corporate purposes and the consumers of these goods can be identified for marketing practice.

Consumer advertising   Loosely relating to all advertising of goods or services to the mass markets of individuals or families. Used in contrast to industrial or capital goods advertising.

Consumer behaviour Buying habits or patterns of behaviour of consuming public either in general or in specific groups.

Consumer benefit A product or service attribute expressed in terms of its value to the user rather than the product itself. Thus consumers buy the 'sizzle' rather than the 'sausage', and engineers buy 'holes' rather than 'drills'. *See* Competitive advantage.

Consumer benefits advertising Style of advertising identifying either a functional or an abstract advantage or benefit to the consumer.

Consumer buying power Available discretionary income; surplus after commitments have been met, but including those amounts currently committed via discretionary agreements such as hire-purchase, credit sale, or bank loan repayments which will eventually become available for future expenditure. Excludes taxation, rates and any other obligatory call upon income the consumer has no power to evade.

Consumer credit Loans to customers to enable them to buy the seller's output. Often the seller is helped to provide credit by the resources of a finance house or other intermediary, such as Barclaycard or Access.

Consumer diary In which consumers make a record of some continuing event such as purchases of a particular product group, watching television, and other activities which are aggregated to give a measure of consumer behaviour.

Consumer durables Goods which are intended for mass markets, but are not in fact consumed immediately, but have a lasting life, e.g. washing machines, cars, furniture. *See* White goods.

Consumer goods Products or merchandise intended for use or consumption by individuals, as opposed to organizations, companies or businesses.

Consumer magazines Periodic publications promoted and sold to members of the population as individuals, as opposed to trades, professions, or industries or to people having a common involvement in such working areas.

63

Consumer need Reference to any desire or requirement a person (consumer) might have, whether existing and perceptible, or latent and unrecognized. The determination and evaluation of consumer needs could be said to be at the root of the marketing concept from which all subsequent activities develop. Not to be confused with consumer want, which *see*.

Consumer panels Groups of consumers selected as representative of the population reporting on their purchases and purchasing behaviour. *See* Continuous research.

Consumer patronage Established customer groups purchasing regularly with little thought to alternatives.

Consumer preferences Collective scales devised to indicate relative levels of preference for available goods and services.

Consumer price Accepted retail selling price for a particular type of product or service.

Consumer profile Household, domestic, cultural and demographic characteristics and details of consumers, including their hopes, aspirations, and expectations for the future.

Consumer promotion *See* Sales promotion.

Consumer protection Movement to raise trading standards by legislation; Consumer Protection Agencies, and voluntary codes of practice.

Consumer reaction Behaviour of the consuming public on exposure to any particular stimulus. Often associated with interpretation of product promotion or advertising concept.

Consumer research Study of consumer attitudes, motives, habits and behaviour in relation to their buying products and services.

Consumer satisfaction Satisfaction of a consumer want is an essential part of the marketing operation. Fundamentally, a person buys (acquires) a product or service for the satisfaction it will provide. This may be tangible or intangible (as indeed will be the 'want') but providing a product gives consumer satisfaction, a main aim of the marketing concept has been fulfilled.

Consumer sovereignty   Recognition of power of consumers to determine the success or otherwise of any goods or services offered for sale or hire.

Consumer surplus   Difference between the actual price of a product and its maximum worth to the consumer.

Consumer want   Human physiological and psychological requirements which may or may not be at a personal level of awareness. These are capable of generating psychic impulses which the 'consumer' recognizes as needs. To 'want' a product is to form a conscious desire to acquire it and is clearly different to that condition of simply experiencing a 'need' for it. The transition from 'need' to 'want' can be part of changing social behaviour as, for example, the wider use of bathrooms or it can be aided by some form of persuasion, as has been the case with deodorants. Marketing action is highly significant in this process. *See* Consumer need.

Consumerism   Movement by individuals and pressure groups designed to ensure that 'consumers' interests are safeguarded. In a society where marketing orientation is universal, consumerism would be said to be obsolescent since, by definition, the consumers' interests would be fully catered for by the competing firms. In fact, consumerism has aims which may be identified with those of marketing.

Consumers Association   Independent non-profit-making organization established in 1950 to help shoppers by testing goods and services on sale to the public. The Association buys goods, simulating the consumer buying process anonymously and then tests them. Its findings are published in a monthly magazine, 'Which'.

Consumers' choice Expression of preferences by consumers for different goods where some sacrifice is involved, or where some alternative has been foregone.

Consumption Rate at which a product or commodity is consumed or used.

Consumption patterns Indexes of consumption by customers within classifiable product groups.

Contact print Reproduction on photo-sensitive paper of the image from a negative by direct contact exposure which produces a print of the same size.

Contact report Written summary of a meeting or conversation between client and agency giving the specific actions agreed.

Container A generic term used to describe any form of pack or receptacle containing goods, liquid or solid. More often applied to large units.

Contest A competition in which an individual is required to show that he/she is in some respect superior, whether in knowledge, memory, expertise or guesswork, and for which prizes will be awarded for the best performance(s).

Contingency plan Part of a marketing plan which attempts to anticipate eventualities, both negative and positive and to make provision for them. *See also* Crisis management.

Continuity Repeated use of a theme, medium, script, or idea over a period of time.

Continuous billing Preparation of invoicing procedure throughout a business period rather than at a single time each month.

Continuous research Research studies undertaken on a regular ongoing basis. Used by many sponsoring companies as a performance monitoring method.

Contra-deal Agreement between two organizations to supply goods or services from the one in exchange for goods or services of the other. Thus a magazine might supply free advertising space to an airline in exchange for free seats on an aircraft.

Contract Legally binding document or situation in which a seller undertakes to supply goods or services to a buyer in 'consideration' of some financial or other return.

Contract publishing An outside service which provides publishing for periodicals, such as house magazines.

Contribution analysis Estimating the difference between product selling prices and their variable costs per unit, so calculating the extent to which each unit contributes to fixed costs and profits.

Contribution pricing Pricing technique which ensures some contribution to profit, even where normal profit margins are not being maintained.

Control group Identical sample to one which is exposed to experimental stimuli but to which no such stimuli is given. Thus, its reactions, or lack of them, can be compared with those of the experimental group giving a base point from which to make measurements.

Control question Used in a questionnaire as a hidden means of checking the validity of answers to other questions.

Controlled circulation In which the method of circulation of a publication is controlled by some specific criterion relating to the status of the reader, and for which no separate charge is made.

Convenience foods Ready-prepared dishes bought usually from a supermarket and capable of serving with little effort and in little time.

Convenience goods (1) Goods which are very widely distributed and which are bought more according to convenience of acquisition than by 'brand' or particular value, e.g. petrol, cigarettes. (2) Goods having an element of processing, historically carried out by customer or user, that gives an added value to the product and for which a premium price may be obtained.

Convenience store A local shop selling food and convenience goods, open for long hours, and usually on Sundays.

Conversion rate Measure of conversion of inquiries or replies to an advertisement or mailing shot into sales. *See* Response rate.

Conversion value Cost of converting or assembling product plus profit. Sometimes known as 'added value'.

Cooperative Voluntary organization set up by producers and/or consumers to service their own needs by democratic control, distributing profit according to purchases, sales or fixed return on capital. *See* Retailers' cooperatives.

Cooperative advertising (1) Promotion by group of concerns in the same industry. (2) Local advertising by a retail outlet in conjunction with the suppliers of a nationally advertised product.

Cooperative marketing Campaign in which a number of marketing companies cooperate to create demand for a common product or service, e.g. the now defunct Tomato and Cucumber Marketing Board.

Copy Text or written matter for reproduction.

Copy brief Detailed statement of aim(s) in relation to preparation of an advertisement, or series of advertisements, with the purpose of ensuring that copywriters are aware of their purpose and that their submissions may be evaluated by continuous reference to it.

Copy claim Benefit, or value, attributed to a product or service by an organization in its promotional activities. Usually refers to the claim(s) made for a product in advertising literature.

Copy clearance Refers to the process whereby claims, or themes, adopted in advertising are given acceptance by specialist representatives of media concerned in order to avoid misleading or offensive statements or ideas.

Copy date Date by which advertising or editorial matter should reach a publisher for inclusion in a particular issue. *See* Press date.

Copy plan Statement of theme(s) and other material for the development of a copy platform.

Copy platform Main copy theme of an advertisement.

Copy-rotation Using a systematic rota of different advertisements in order to enhance attention and impact.

Copy test Test of advertising copy, either before or after publication, aiming to discover readers' comprehension, interest, brand preference, company image, etc. *See* Advertising research.

Copyright Sole legal right to produce, or to reproduce, a work or any substantial part thereof, in any material form whatsoever.

Copywriter Person who writes copy for advertisements or other promotional material. Usually employed by an advertising agency, but, in technical areas, will more frequently be employed by the firm manufacturing and/or distributing the products concerned.

Core strategy Dominant elements in marketing mix, referring usually to the promotion of the differential advantage.

Cornering the market Person or organization contriving to take advantage of a monopoly situation, during which prices and terms can be unilaterally controlled.

Corporate advertising Any form of advertising which has as its objective the building up of a company's reputation. Has a closer affinity to public relations activity than to marketing. *See* Institutional advertising.

Corporate affairs   *See* Public affairs.

Corporate brand   A synonym for 'corporate image'. A popular term but misleading since 'brand' is also associated with 'product', e.g. in 'brand image'.

Corporate communications   Strictly this term is synonymous with public relations. It takes in all communications activities which contribute to the reputation or corporate image of an organization. This, in turn, is not an end in itself, but must be an integral contributor to the business or corporate objectives. The target audiences or publics might be said to be all those groups of people who have a stakeholding in the business. Often linked, incorrectly, with media or press relations, or editorials and publicity. *See* Public relations.

Corporate culture   The way the people in an organization behave, or are expected to behave, and which may colour its perception by the outside world. Increasingly, businesses are setting down the culture they would like to apply, and then producing a programme designed to achieve a culture change.

Corporate identity   The 'message sources' by which an organization develops and enhances the way it is perceived by its various publics. Commonly thought to refer only to the corporate logo, and its use on letter headings, brochures, uniforms, etc., but equally important are corporate culture, customer care, third party endorsement and so on.

Corporate image   The image which is conjured up by mention of a company's name. This can be positive or negative, weak or strong, and it is argued by some that it is the sole purpose of any public relations campaign. Its value is in increasing the propensity to buy, to join a company, to acquire shares and, in general, to facilitate the profitable operation of a business. It also has a tangible value in the form of 'goodwill' when a business is sold.

Corporate mission   *See* Mission statement.

Corporate objective   *See* Business objective.

Corporate planning Setting down of long-term plan of development in a methodical manner, based upon all the available facts, in relation to the ultimate goals of a company and the ways it intends to achieve them. Time scales vary from three to ten years (even more in certain industries). Fundamental to the preparation of a corporate plan is the need to define exactly the area of business in which to be operative. A second requirement is that any such plan be flexible, subject to regular updating as events move to change the criteria upon which it is based.

Corporate positioning The place occupied by an organization in the minds of its various groups of stakeholders as to its relationship to other businesses. The criteria for such positioning can be various, such as quality, value for money, innovation, good employer, customer care, and so on. *See also* Brand positioning.

Corporate purchasing Buying by an organization rather than a private individual. Implication here that the buying decision is a 'corporate' one, i.e. made by a number of people, and that arguably it may be made upon more objective grounds than many consumer purchases. *See* Organizational purchasing and Decision-making unit.

Corporate strategy The means by which the corporate objectives are to be achieved. It will take in and integrate all the various functional strategies, e.g. marketing, human resources, finance, R&D, and so on. In short, it is a summary of the corporate plan.

Correlation Measure of the degree of relationship found to exist between two distinct sets of data, e.g. telephone ownership with age.

Corridor traffic A measure at exhibitions of the value of a particular stand location based upon the flow of visitors past the site.

Corrugated board Fibreboard comprising corrugated inner fluting pasted to two flat outer paper surfaces known as inner and outer liners. Commonly constructed from kraft paper resulting in a light, inexpensive and tough material much used in packaging, particularly for outer cases. *See* Fibreboard.

Cosmetic   Refers to the appearance of a medium, particularly publications: hence the use of such expressions as, 'giving it a facelift'.

Cost analysis   Study and interpretation of all cost figures; of particular use in considering future likely costs in the launch or development of a product or service.

Cost and freight (C and F)   Terms used in foreign trade contracts, where the exporter agrees to pay the freight charges in addition to the consignment costs of getting the goods 'free on board'.

Cost benefit analysis   Investigation into the social costs and social benefits of community investment projects.

Cost centre   Application of responsibility accounting; a unit or centre of activity to which costs are assigned or allocated. *See* Profit centre.

Cost comparison   Studying the relative costs of two or more alternatives.

Cost effectiveness   Measure of most economic activity in achievement of given objective.

Cost insurance and freight (CIF)   Term used in foreign trade contracts, indicating a price which includes the freight and insurance charges in addition to the charges incurred to transport the goods 'free on board'.

Cost insurance freight and interest   Term used in foreign trade contracts, where the exporter agrees to pay the freight, insurance, and interest (interest charges on the value of the goods) in addition to the charges incurred prior to 'free on board' status.

Cost of living index   Index number representing the trend of a series of prices paid by consumers for a representative sample of items, so revealing the changes in the cost to households of typical purchase needs. Known officially as the Retail Price Index.

Cost per inquiry Cost of producing a single inquiry in an advertising campaign. Most usually expressed in the form of an average, i.e. not any particular or selected inquiry but a resultant reflecting the average cost of all inquiries received.

Cost per order A term frequently associated, but not necessarily so, with mail order where the profitability of a particular promotion is measured by dividing the advertising spend by the number of orders received. *See also* Cost per enquiry.

Cost per thousand Means of providing some form of standardized costing of advertising to facilitate inter or intra-media comparisons. Basis of calculation is to express the rating of a publication or programme in terms of the cost of reaching one thousand recipients, subscribers, readers, viewers, or other common base.

Cost plus Pricing method whereby actual production cost, or an estimate thereof, is added to a profit figure to arrive at a selling price. Originally used for war contracts, the system is still used in development work where eventual costs cannot be realistically estimated. The principle is used widely in industry but as a pricing policy where historical costs, together with agreed profit margin, give the selling price.

Cost profile Identification of production costs, and cost distribution for order processing, packaging, storage, inventory, transportation, materials handling, and each element in the marketing mix.

Costing Allocation of expenditure where reliable costs may be determined and presented in order to provide for control of a business.

Counterpack *See* Display pack.

Coupon (1) Redeemable voucher supplied to consumer as purchasing incentive, usually by allowing a price concession. (2) Part of an advertisement enabling enquirer to complete required details in order to obtain further information or place an order. *See also* Direct response marketing.

Coupon price reductions Making a price concession by providing coupons, of fixed value, sometimes printed upon the pack to encourage the initial and subsequent purchases. The coupon may, however, appear in a printed advertisement or be distributed direct to householders and may, or may not, require a previous purchase.

Cover Outer faces of a magazine usually available for advertising purposes, i.e. front, back, inside front and inside back cover.

Cover date The date which is printed on the cover of a magazine or other publication.

Cover page Either front or back page of a publication, usually available for advertising purposes at premium prices as they constitute preferred positions.

Cover price Normal retail selling price of newspaper or magazine, usually shown on front cover page.

Coverage (in advertising) Proportion (expressed in percentage terms) of a market exposed to advertising.

Cow Expression used to describe products whose performance is past their best but which remain profitable. They are 'milked', i.e. provide a source of funds for new product development. *See* Cash cow.

CPT Cost per thousand.

CPU (Central processing unit) The static memory area, or 'brain', of a computer where all data processes are handled, but more commonly used to refer to the whole computer itself (as opposed to peripherals such as terminals, printers, etc.).

Crash System failure from which a computer cannot normally recover without some form of manual intervention. The term originally described the action of the read/write heads of a hard disk crashing onto and damaging the surface of the magnetic platters, causing sudden and drastic system failure.

Crate Type of container, constructed of wood, often built around the product. Specially in relation to bulky heavy goods. *See* Case.

Creaming Selling product range at a higher than average price in order to improve quality, known as upmarketing a product, whereby it becomes the accepted purchase of the more affluent members of society. Upmarket products tend to ride the storms of economic depression better than cut-price products.

Creative Relating in advertising to the conceptual input upon which a campaign or an advertisement is based and incorporating the copy and visual content – the creative expression.

Creative department Part of an advertising agency concerned with creating ideas and expressing them in copy and design.

Creative director The head of the creative department in an advertising agency. Responsible for the overall creativity of all the contributing personnel such as copywriters and visualisers.

Creative group Collection of individuals specializing in the development of creative ideas, particularly for the origination of advertising campaigns.

Creative hot shops Specialist firms offering only a high standard of creative advertising or publicity.

Creative salespeople Users of original material or ideas and their presentation in developing a sales territory.

Creative strategy Statement of advertising goals, the target audiences, the intended creative propositions and the means of expressing them in a particular advertisement or series of advertisements.

Credentials presentation Demonstration by an advertising agency or PR consultancy to a potential client of some of its past work. *See* Pitch and Presentation.

Credibility Extent to which claims made for a product or firm are believed by its markets. Exaggerated claims may often destroy a product's, or even a company's, credibility.

Credibility (of the message source) The extent to which a customer or prospect accepts the validity of an advertising proposition is influenced by the perception of the medium. Thus an advertisement in the 'Economist' may be more highly regarded than one in a periodical which is less well regarded.

Credibility gap Difference between commonly accepted levels of performance and the expectations aroused by extravagant claims on behalf of a person, organization, product or service.

Credit (1) Supplying goods in advance of full payment. (2) Bank credit: loans and overdrafts to bank clients. *See* Consumer credit.

Credit account (1) Purchase made on credit and account settled, monthly or otherwise by agreement. (2) Regular monthly payments made by bankers' order to retail establishment against which persons may make purchases up to an agreed multiple of the monthly instalment. (The amount is subject to Government fiscal controls over the circulation and velocity of cash within the economy and will therefore vary according to the level of economic activity.)

Credit cards Identification Cards, possession of which enables the consumer to make a range of purchases from member retailers and then settle the full amount monthly, or, alternatively over a longer period together with interest charges. Mainly but not exclusively issued by the banks in UK. Agency cards are issued chiefly for regular industrial purchases, e.g. petroleum.

Credit note Document conveying credit of a stated amount, often against returns or allowances but most frequently adjusting errors or omissions related to previous charges.

Credit rating Systematic rating of customers for credit worthiness.

Credit sale   Sale made on credit over a short term, where the ownership of the goods passes with possession. In the case of hire-purchase extending over a longer period, the creditor retains ownership, until a statutorily fixed portion of the debt has been paid. After this point the goods cannot legally be repossessed, although the buyer remains legally liable for the outstanding portion within the statutory period.

Credit squeeze   Government intervention over credit facilities in order to limit the rate of consumption for fiscal purposes.

Creditor   Party to a credit transaction who is owed money by another party involved in it.

Crisis management   A growing practice in PR in which detailed plans are produced in advance to cater for any likely crisis which might conceivably occur, e.g. strike, explosion, fire, sub-standard product. *See* Issues management.

Critical path   Technique derived from network analysis that assists planning by scheduling all necessary happenings to bring about a complex outcome at the right time and in the correct sequence. *See* Critical path analysis.

Critical path analysis   Planning technique applied usually to a complex project, in which a large number of variables inter-relate and where the failure of any one will set back the entire scheme. Any sub-set whose timing is critical to the whole project is shown thus in advance, usually in diagrammatic form, and the whole series forms a linear sequence (or critical path) from which the minimum project time can be calculated. *See also* Network analysis.

Crop   To cut down in size a photograph or illustration, either to focus interest upon particular features or to make most effective use of limited space available.

Cross couponing   A coupon on or off pack which is making an offer for some quite different product.

Cross-elasticity of demand   Response of demand for one commodity to a change in the price of another, e.g. a transfer occurring as when the price of electricity increases, demand for less expensive alternatives, possibly gas or oil, increases.

Cross fade   To reduce volume of one form of sound whilst simultaneously increasing volume of another. Commonly used in radio, for instance, to introduce a scene or subject change and also in audiovisual media, like TV and cinema, where the usage of the term extends also to the gradual replacement of one scene by another. *See* Dissolve.

Cross-headings   Smaller than a headline, these are inserted throughout the body-copy to break it up. *See* Sub-head.

Cross tracks   Poster site on other side of railway track and facing travellers.

CSI   *See* Customer satisfaction index.

CTN   Abbreviation of Confectioners, Tobacconists, and News-agents.

Cues   Symbols or sources of marketing messages which together add up to a total corporate or product identity. Cues can be broken down into the four Ps. Product cues relate to the various messages transmitted (and/or received) by the product other than the intrinsic product performance. Such messages could be product presentation, packaging, weight, smell, etc. Price cues are particularly important when there are few other criteria upon which to base a judgement on quality, i.e., quality is perceived as being higher as the price is increased. Place cues relate to the impression created by the appearance or reputation of a retail outlet for instance. *See* Message sources.

Culture   Relating to an organization or a country, this is an important element in developing a marketing strategy. It is based upon the habits, behaviour, beliefs, values and customers of a particular society. *See* Corporate culture.

Cumulative audience   Aggregate of persons or homes reached by successive issues or broadcasts; synonym for Cumulative reach. *See* Reach.

Cumulative reach   Number of people in a target audience reached without duplication by a given promotional schedule over a particular period of time.

Currency of a bill   Period of time between the drawing of a bill of exchange and the final date when it becomes payable.

Current awareness   Up-to-date data and information on operational results made available to functional managers. May be distributed in printed sheets or available on-stream by disk to computer terminal.

Current demand   Present willingness in the market to pay the ruling price for goods.

Cursive script   A typeface which tries to look like handwriting.

Cursor   The screen position at which input is required, or where output will be displayed (usually signified by a blinking underline character or block).

Custom-built   Made to specific individual customer specification.

Customer   Person or organization actually making the purchasing decision not necessarily the 'consumer' or 'user'. Legally, a party to a contract for the sale of goods.

Customer care   A new marketing concept in which everyone in the whole organization is encouraged to think and act with the customer in mind. Has special significance in service organizations.

Customer database   *See* Database.

Customer delight   Term used in a customer care programme in which one does not aim for satisfaction but rather sets out to achieve customers who are very pleased, or delighted, with the product, service or company. In other words, it exceeds expectations.

Customer driven   *See* Customer led.

Customer facing   All people in an organization who, at some time, are likely to come in contact with customers face-to-face, e.g. sales people, service engineers, technical consultants, etc. Some authorities include telephone contact and correspondence.

Customer focused   In which all the operations of a company are carried out with the customer in mind. Not just marketing activities but production, R&D, and finance, for instance.

Customer group   Classification in some form, e.g. demographic, of members of the population likely to be customers.

Customer led   In which all functional plans, particularly marketing, are led by customer requirements, (as opposed to customer 'needs' and 'wants' which are quite different).

Customer loop   Logistics process necessary to monitor traffic, and complete orders through company administration procedure.

Customer magazine   *See* House magazine.

Customer need   *See* Consumer need.

Customer orientation   Preoccupation with customer needs within an organization. Basis for marketing theory and practice which dictates that competitive survival, growth and returns on investment are proper rewards for the achievement of consumer satisfaction. *See* Marketing concept.

Customer profile (1) Description of a group of customers in terms sufficient to make direct comparison with other groups, such as washing machine owners, owner-occupiers, professional classes, demographic and/or socio-economic classifications. (2) Total list or estimate of all customers divided into pertinent categories, e.g. age-groups, with each group expressed in percentages of the total.

Customer records Tabulation of inquiries and orders received, deliveries, and any other pertinent information concerning a customer and his/her satisfaction.

Customer relations The deliberate and planned building of good relations with customers. Strictly a sub-set of public relations, but also the basis of Relationship marketing, which *see*. The measurement of customer relations is the customer satisfaction index.

Customer responsive The culture of an organization in which it is second nature to react to a customer's requirements with positive action.

Customer satisfaction An increasingly important factor in marketing in which the purchasing decision, particularly repeat purchase is determined by the extent to which a customer feels satisfied with both the product and the company behind it. An important contributor to providing an additional competitive edge, especially as products become more and more undifferentiated. As a qualitative measure, this can be expressed as the customer satisfaction index (CSI).

Customer satisfaction index A quantitative measurement of the extent to which a customer feels happy with a product and the service behind it. A range of criteria are set and weightings put against each. These are then evaluated by sampling a number of customers and getting their reactions.

Customer service No longer a matter of putting things right which have gone wrong, this can be broken down into pre-sales service, sales service and post-sales service. A contributor to customer satisfaction, it is also coming to the fore as a critical element of Relationship marketing.

Customer service department   Set-up in an organization which sees to it that customers are satisfied with the performance or their product. Deals particularly with complaints, faults and problems.

Customized marketing   In which products are designed specifically to match a customer's requirements as opposed to mass produced. Obviously an important factor in the field of industrial products.

Customs bills of entry   Lists published daily by the Customs and Excise authorities of ships from British ports, showing details of cargo and destinations.

Customs tariff   List of dutiable goods published by Her Majesty's Stationery Office for showing the levels of duty payable.

Cut-price merchandise   Goods subjected to cut prices. May or may not refer to goods of inferior quality.

Cut prices   (1) Used by suppliers hoping to compensate for reduced profit margins by selling a larger volume of goods. (2) Reducing prices temporarily to stimulate trade for particular, especially new products or using particular products as loss leaders to induce a higher turnover of other lines. (*See* Loss leader.)

Cut-throat competition   Prices in the market reduced to the point where no supplier is likely to make a profit. Usually means all suppliers selling at prices below cost in order to minimize possible losses, particularly of perishable or depreciating goods. Normally a result of supplies temporarily exceeding demand.

Cuttings   (1) Clippings from newspapers or magazines of items relevant to company operations. (2) Surplus film pieces edited out of a commercial or programme shooting. *See* Press cuttings.

Cybernetics   Study of communications systems whether of human or mechanical form. Also refers to means of controlling activities in order to keep them directed at a particular objective.

Cyberspace A 'virtual' or conceptual meeting place of on-line networks, databases, E-Mail, Internet and any other electronic forums.

Cycles of trade Repetitive periodic movements in trade, especially in relation to upturns and recessions. Cyclical analysis of industries, for example, has been found useful in sales forecasting.

D

DAGMAR Originally title of a book advocating evaluation of advertising effectiveness by communications goals rather than sales. Acronym for Defining Advertising Goals for Measured Advertising Response.

Daily report of calls List of interviews obtained and visits made by salespeople, sometimes submitted daily but may be given in form of weekly summary to regional or head office.

Dandy roll A special fitment to a papermaking machine to cause a watermark to appear. Invented by John Marshall.

Data (1) Facts or information, often numerical. (2) The numbers and letters that are typed into a computer. When converted into a document or chart it becomes information.

Data analysis Careful study of tabulated figures to establish trends or exceptions. May involve study for current or future problems or opportunities.

Data capture Information taken on to a computer.

Data collection Accumulation of facts and information with a view to inputting it into a database.

Data processing Arrangements of data into a systematic form and its further analysis, most frequently by mechanical or automatic means.

Data sheet Leaflet containing factual information and data about a product and its performance.

Database A centrally-held collection of data or information allowing access and manipulation by one or many users.

Database Management System A program that provides control for a database including utilities such as security and access rights.

Database marketing A growing form of marketing in which messages are sent to narrow target groups as a result of detailed information about their characteristics. Direct mail is thus sent to a company's narrowly defined Database, which *see*.

Date coding Practice of showing manufacturing date or, more commonly, date by which product should be sold to reach consumer in an acceptably fresh condition.

Date in charge Date from which the rental for a poster site is charged.

Day after recall A measure of advertisement impact by checking the extent to which a target audience can remember its appearance on the following day.

Days of grace Additional time allowed by customs for payment of a bill of exchange after the due date. Normally maximum of three days is allowed in this way.

DC Double column in an advertisement which spans two columns. Also stands for Double crown which *see*.

DE *See* Socio-economic groups.

Dead freight   Payable where the charterer is unable entirely to fill a ship with cargo and is therefore charged against empty space.

Dead matter   Typescripts, roughs of diagrams, proofs, etc., which have been superseded by the next stage.

Deadline   Time by which a particular stage of a job must be completed, particularly in journalism where the story becomes dead if not completed in time. Also with advertising and broadcasting and indeed has been generally adopted as a term in planning procedure.

Deal   Agreement reached between two or more parties to a contract.

Dealer   Intermediary in distribution chain, buying goods in order to sell them, usually but not always to the general public: generally synonymous with 'retailer' but often applied to the larger distributor. Term can apply more broadly to anyone 'dealing' in the transfer of ownership of goods, whether industrial, commercial, or consumer. *See* Distributor.

Dealer aid   Any material supplied to dealers (retailers) in order to assist them in their task of selling merchandise, e.g. point-of-sale display items, leaflets, samples and dispensers.

Dealer audit   *See* Retail audit.

Dealer brand   *See* Own label.

Dealer incentives   Special promotional offers to retailers to encourage buying, promoting, and active selling of branded goods.

Dealer leaders   Promotional device providing incentives to retailers to stock a product, or range of products, at predetermined quantities.

Dealer loader Providing an incentive to dealers to over-stock and promote a manufacturer's range of products, e.g. discounts, special offers and competitions. *See* Dealer incentives.

Dear money Applies when interest rates (the price of money) are high and loans have generally become more difficult to obtain.

Debit card Plastic card issued to an individual which enables a retailer to debit directly a customer's account in consideration of a purchase of goods or services.

Debug Logically to trace and eliminate errors from a program (BS3527).

Decentralization Assignment of accountability from central unit of control to individual units within an organization, involving transfer of decision-making authority and responsibility.

Decision-making unit Group of people who together contribute to a decision on whether or not, and what to purchase (DMU). Used more in industrial marketing but can apply for example, to a consumer situation, e.g. the multiple household. Usually comprises specifier, influencer, authoriser, gatekeeper, purchaser and user.

Decision theory Quantitative techniques for reducing complex problems to a limited number of easier problems.

Decision tree Display of events, past, present and future, leading to and effecting the outcome of a business decision.

Deck Subsidiary section of a headline.

Deck cargo Cargo stowed on deck rather than in the ship's hold. Deck cargo may often be of a hazardous nature and must, therefore, be easier to jettison in a situation of jeopardy.

Decreasing returns Occur when economies of scale cease to operate, because of the counter-acting effect of increasing average costs and resulting in a decrease in profitability. *See* Diseconomies of scale.

Dedupe   Identifying and removing duplicates from a mailing list.

Deep-rooted demand   Continuing loyalty to a product or brand, even where its original competitive advantage or value may no longer be significant. May sometimes be the result of cultural or traditional beliefs.

Defensive marketing   *See* Retention strategy.

Deferred rebate   Rebate or discount on goods accumulated for an agreed period; used as an incentive to customers to remain loyal to supplier or to buy all needs from one supplier. A form of contract where the discount allowed is conditional upon both the total and period of the purchases.

Definition   In communications, this refers to the clarity or fidelity with which an illustration or image is reproduced.

Deflation   Reduction in the amount of available money causing incomes to fall and unemployment to grow.

Del credere agent   Agent who accepts responsibility for the payment of money due to the principal, and who earns an increased commission for taking the additional risks involved.

Delayed response   Reaction to marketing initiative at a later time but often within the expected period of time. *See* Gestation period.

Deliverables   Any promotional items which can be handed out or 'delivered'. *See also* Collateral.

Delivered price   Ex-works selling price plus all costs involved in freighting or transportation.

Delivery note   Document accompanying goods on delivery to buyer. Used as a means of checking delivery, dealing with claims for shortage, damage and empties and subsequently clearing the invoice for the goods.

Demand   Derived from economics, its usual reference in marketing is to the aggregate of effective purchasing intentions in a community regarding a particular product or service.

Demand analysis   Study of demand for product or service in order to establish reasons for its success or failure or in order to discover how sales performance may be improved.

Demand curve   Statistical distribution of demand expressed in the form of a graph.

Demand forecasting   Undertaking a series of value forecasts at different selling prices to establish the optimum profit opportunity. It is based on the principle of elasticity, whereby demand increases at lower prices and decreases at higher prices.

Demand function   Relationship between demand and the determinants of demand such as price, substitute products, income, or credit facilities.

Demand management   Exercising control over the amount and levels of demand for company products in terms of quantity, quality, price, and timing.

Demand pull   Resultant of demand stimulants applied in marketing: works in conjunction, for example, with sales push.

Demand theory   Branch of economic theory devoted to the analysis of demand determinants and consumers/users scales of preferences.

Demarketing   Deflating demand when in short supply; effective rationing of supplies by marketing methods.

Demographic segmentation   The breakdown of markets into specific groups having the same characteristics such as age, sex, occupation and region.

Demography   Science of social statistics, particularly population statistics, essential to market research and effective campaign planning. *See* Socio-economic groups.

Demonstration   Showing the product or service in action. Sometimes used to refer to an artificial situation where audiovisual equipment is used instead of the actual product/service itself.

Density sales   Product achieving the highest level of sales within a company or an industry relative to others within that product field.

Department store   Large store selling a wide range of commodities, particularly clothing, where merchandise is segregated into different departments, each having a specialist manager, usually wholly responsible for own buying and selling but subject to central control. Frequently offers credit and delivery facilities to customers and usually will be located only in urban marketing centres.

Dependent variable   Statistical term describing a factor which changes as a result of some other directly linked factor – another variable – which is independent, e.g. sales, which may increase as a result of advertising. Advertising is then the independent variable and sales the dependent variable.

Depreciation   Diminution in value of an asset due to use and/or lapse of time. Normally, such reductions in value are charged against the profit and loss account with an accounting formula, which spreads the value of the asset over its expected life, in order to show a more realistic cost of operations to the business. In most cases, the amount written off is put into reserve in order to provide for a future replacement.

Depression   Period during which a nation's productive resources are persistently underemployed; often manifests itself through a long period of high unemployment among a community's labour force.

Depth interview   Informal conversation between interviewer and respondent but with underlying cross-examination following clearcut objectives. Intended to discover facts which might not emerge from direct questioning. *See* Group discussion.

Derived demand Indirect demand for capital goods, materials or other factors of production which are used to provide goods for which there is direct demand.

Descender Lower case letter in which the stroke drops below the base line, e.g. g, p, q, y. *See* Ascender.

Design In marketing, used as a generic term embracing all types of visual work, e.g. roughs, typography, graphics, finished art, for all kinds of application – advertising, exhibitions, print work, house styling.

Design factor Measurement of relative efficiency of sample design against a reading of 1–0 for a completely random sample.

Designer products Ostensibly up-market products, created designs by notable people giving an image of prestige or superiority.

Desire Expression of human appetite for given object of attention.

Desktop PC A personal computer of a size suitable for use on a desk or other solid work surface. Desktop PCs are usually mains powered and are not designed to be used while 'on the move' (unlike portable computers).

Desktop publishing Nowadays, a frequently in-house function in which computer technology is used to place and position upon a screen all the elements of a proposed publication. Its popularity comes from the ease with which changes can be made, and thus economies. The finished copy can be put straight into artwork form.

Desk research Obtaining facts and information from sources which are already published (e.g., directories), or which are readily accessible (e.g., sales records). As opposed to field research. *See* Secondary data.

Determinant Factor determining, limiting, or defining, a decision.

Devaluation   Reduction in the value or price of one currency or commodity relative to other currencies or commodities.

Development tools   Programs used by software developers to create, modify and extend other software programs quickly and easily and in a structured and disciplined environment.

Deviation, standard   Statistical term used to describe, by formula, movement of the spread of data around an average.

Diadic   Paired comparison test involving informants reporting on two products or advertisements, one against the other.

Diary method   Research technique in which respondents keep a regular written record of events such as reading a publication, viewing television or purchasing certain goods.

Dichotomous question   In market research, a question to which there can be only two possible answers, either 'yes' or 'no'.

Die stamping   Raised impression on a sheet of paper of a design or symbol, produced by compressing the sheet between two dies. Also known as Embossing. *See* Blind.

Differential advantage   Perceived benefit of a product, whether real or imaginary, compared with a competitive product. With undifferentiated products particularly, there is a need to build in a differential advantage in order to produce a motivation for purchase. *See also* Unique selling proposition.

Differential pricing   Different prices charged to different customer groups, but for the same product.

Differential sampling   Weighted samples adjusted to allow for known bias in penetration or spending power.

Differentiation   Providing a product with a benefit, making it able to be promoted as a unique brand, to a segment of the market which is seen as valuable and for which people will pay, as they believe it is not available elsewhere.

Diffusion of innovation The process by which new ideas are communicated to members of a particular target audience. Not to be confused with adoption of innovation which *see*.

Digital Data represented as numbers or characters, usually in binary notation (contrasted with analogue).

Dimension Measurable quantity, used in marketing research to compare responses at different levels or in regard to platforms.

Diminishing returns, law of States that where one 'factor of production' is increased while others remain constant, output will change by steadily decreasing amounts.

Direct costing Method of producing a statement of costs which are directly attributable to a particular product, brand, or function. Especially significant at extreme ends of the product life cycle, e.g. during the growth and decline stages.

Direct expenses All costs directly attributable to a product, a project, or an accounting centre.

Direct mail Mailing of a piece of informative literature, or of any other promotional material, to selected prospects. Not to be confused with direct marketing or direct response marketing.

Direct mail shot One single batch or mailing in a direct mail campaign. One mailing shot might therefore comprise a large number of items and a campaign might consist of several mailing shots.

Direct marketing Producer supplying direct to consumer without the use of any retail outlet. Includes mail order companies and direct response firms selling through the media or by post.

Direct response advertising Increasingly, advertisements and commercials are offering to supply information and promotional material 'direct'. This applies obviously, but not exclusively so, to direct mail and telemarketing.

Direct response marketing   A rather loosely interpreted term, often referred to as simply direct marketing. Strictly, it refers to marketing in which purchasing is made directly between the manufacturer or supplier and the customer, without going through the intermediary of a retail outlet. The offer of goods is not just by means of direct mail and/or telephoning, but also by press, television and radio advertising. Direct response marketing does not refer to offering and supplying promotional material: this is the subject of Direct response advertising which *see*.

Direct selling   Where the sales and distribution are direct to the end customer. *See* Direct response/consumer marketing.

Direct taxation   Taxes on individuals or organizations levied directly by income or wealth.

Directory   Published source of reference, usually on annual basis but possibly more frequent, setting out comprehensive coverage of companies and services in a particular area of business and/or their range of products, e.g. *Advertisers' Annual* and *BRAD*.

Directory advertising   The placement of advertisements in directories, annuals, and such publications for long-term benefit, e.g. Yellow Pages.

Dirty proof   Proof with many corrections.

Discontinuous products   New product idea in different market group.

Discount   Reduction on the quoted or list price of a product, usually in the form of a percentage. Examples include discounts for prompt payment, large quantities, bulk deliveries, special sizes and deliveries at off-peak times.

Discount house   Large store or branch of chain, offering mainly durable consumables at heavily discounted prices but providing little or no handling, delivery or credit services to customers.

Discount rate Rate at which bills of exchange are discounted. Linked with the now discontinued Bank Rate – since termed Minimum Lending Rate.

Discount store Retail outlet offering goods at reduced price by limiting or eliminating the range of customer services at the point of sale. Compare with Discount house, an alternative term.

Discrete data Research information used in stochastic process, where data or numbers are discontinuous. Refers to evidence bearing on changes in brand preferences by users.

Discretionary buying power That part of an income which remains after essential purchases have been made, and which thus can be retained as savings or disposed of in the purchase of non-essential goods, i.e. at the discretion of the buyer.

Discretionary income Amount of income left over after fixed regular outgoings have been paid. It constitutes the amount of money not yet committed and therefore its expenditure is subject to persuasion techniques. *See* Discretionary buying power.

Discrimination test Investigation aimed at discovering the incidence of customer differentiation for a product or package.

Discussion group *See* Group discussion.

Diseconomies of scale Point at which the economies of scale have ceased to operate and average costs of production and/or marketing begin to increase. *See* Decreasing returns.

Disk drive A hardware unit of a computer – where it is usually found built into the main central processing unit chassis (or it can be external as with floppy disk drives on some portable computers) – or of a workstation, which stores information to, and reads information from, floppy or hard disks. The drive contains an electric motor to rotate the disk platter(s) and one or more read/write heads which facilitate the transfer of information to and from the disk surface.

Disk operating system   *See* DOS.

Diskette   *See* Floppy disk.

Disinflation   Fiscal control in which excess purchasing power is being syphoned off by the government in taxation.

Disparaging copy   *See* Knocking copy.

Disparate responses   Numerous needs in the chosen market requiring custom-built products, yet may be consolidated into acceptance of a 'designer' product.

Dispersion   Degree of scatter shown by observations in statistical analysis, usually measured against a central tendency or average, using a mean or standard deviation.

Display   Commonly used in retailing to refer to an exhibition of merchandise, whether in store or in window. Also describes panels – display boards. *See* Window dressing. May also refer to arrangement of control dials, meters and switches for industrial products.

Display advertising   Advertising other than simple typeset lineage advertisements of the classified kind. Also implies an element of design, e.g. use of display type faces as opposed to uniform body matter.

Display classified   *See* Classified display advertising.

Display outer   Outer container for protecting goods in transit, which converts into a display unit at the point of sale. Usually a carton containing a convenient small quantity for counter show and dispensing.

Display pack   Pack which, in addition to performing a 'packaging' function, also serves as a means of displaying the product at the point of sale. Usually applies to single items as opposed to the display outer.

Disposable income Residue of personal income after statutory deductions at source.

Dissolve In which a projected image fades and is simultaneously replaced by another, usually by use of two linked projectors. Also referred to as Cross fade.

Dissonance *See* Cognitive dissonance.

Distribution, theory of Economic theory explaining the determinants of the prices of 'factors of production' and their income, together with all processes and media for the distribution of goods and services available for consumption.

Distribution channel *See* Channel of distribution.

Distribution check Survey taken at retail outlets to measure levels of distribution being achieved.

Distribution logistics Organization and costing of effective distribution of goods and services to required destinations or outlets.

Distribution missions Set of goals to be achieved by the system within a specific product/market context.

Distribution network (1) Type and extent of coverage of the consuming market through appropriate outlets. (2) Logistics of physical distribution.

Distributive trades Collective term for wholesalers and retail firms, especially those directly involved in selling to the public. Often abbreviated colloquially to 'The Trade'.

Distributor Firm which buys and sells on its own account but which deals in the goods of certain specified manufacturers. Common in trades where special representation, stocking and service facilities are required, e.g. motor transport.

Distributors' brand (1) Brand name used by a retail outlet. Generally referred to as 'Own Label' or private label goods that are usually competitively priced and are intended to promote outlet loyalty, rather than brand loyalty. (2) Sometimes used to include brands marketed by a collection of retailers such as MACE, or VG.

Divergent marketing Setting up separate organizations for each of a company's products or product groups; thus each has its own individual marketing goals and is in itself a profit centre.

Diversification Introduction of new products into existing markets or of existing products into new markets to extend life cycles and offset decline. Rarely involves introducing new products into new markets. Also to hedge against a company's future being tied too closely to a small number of products/outlets. Achieved either by new investment or acquisition. *See* Acquisition.

DIY Do It Yourself. Used as indicative sign for shops specializing in the supply of construction, repair, decorative or assembly goods or materials mostly used by skilled artisans but made available in convenient quantities for people wishing to do the work themselves.

DMU *See* Decision-making unit.

Dock dues Toll on all vessels entering or leaving a dock.

Document management system A combination of software programs which when integrated provide authoring, configuration and version control of complex documents such as manuals ready for production onto CD-ROM.

Documentary Cinema or television film, or radio programme, dealing with actual facts of a situation as opposed to fiction. Often used as part of a public relations plan. Sometimes referred to as sponsored promotion, i.e. where its purpose is primarily or wholly commercial.

Dog Expression used to describe products retained in production for sentimental reasons but whose retention is not justified by any contribution to profitability. *See* Cash cow.

Domination (1) Refers to situation of market leader, with significant share of total market. (2) Concentration of promotional effort in one area or medium so as to dominate that area or medium.

Door drops Unaddressed leaflets, samples, or other promotional material delivered by hand.

Door-to-door Practice of selling by calls upon householders, may also be used to distribute promotional material. *See* Canvass.

Dormant accounts Accounts once active as customers but not now buying, for whatever reason.

DOS (Disk operating system) A family of computer programs (e.g. Digital Research's DR-DOS, Microsoft's MS-DOS) which control the operation of the computer hardware and its interface with other resident software programs, for example applications such as word processing software, spreadsheets, etc.

Dot matrix printer A member of the family of 'impact' printers which uses a combination – or matrix – of pins striking an inked ribbon to form an image on paper. The pins themselves are contained within a print head and are activated in particular combinations and sequences depending on which characters are to be printed. The quality and definition of the resulting composite character image largely depends on the number of pins comprising the print head (more pins will lead to better resolution).

Double column *See* DC.

Double crown Basic unit of size in posters, a sheet, size 20 in wide by 30 in deep.

Double-decker Two outdoor advertising panels sited one above the other.

Double front Twin poster sites arranged to utilize both sides of the front of a bus or other commercial vehicle. Usually each a 'single sheet' or smaller.

Double page spread Two facing pages in a magazine or newspaper, used in advertising as if they were one single sheet, i.e. the design carries right across the gutter in the centre.

Down market Market segment where the lowest prices dominate the buying behaviour.

Down time Period during which a machine is not operative due to mechanical failure, machine adjustment, nonavailability of materials, labour or maintenance work. Average down-time is built into product prices to ensure that such hidden costs are covered by sales revenue.

DPS *See* Double page spread.

Drawback Rebate on duty paid for imported goods when used in the manufacture of products for export.

Drawing accounts Credit made available to salespeople in anticipation of future earnings most usually operative where a substantial part of remuneration derives from a commission on sales. Particularly related to industrial goods, for example, where the number of sales over time is low but the value of each is comparatively high.

Drip Advertising campaign covering a long period of time – usually over twelve months.

Drip mat A type of coaster on which glasses are placed, and which is made of an absorbent material to take in any spilt or overflowing liquid. Usually has printed upon it a brand name or slogan relating to alcoholic or soft drinks. Commonly used in pubs and clubs.

Drive time In radio broadcasting, the time during which many listeners are driving to or from work.

DRM   Direct response marketing.

Drop shipment   Describes arrangement where goods are not shipped by person or organization receiving the initial order; commonly a despatch by wholesaler, retailer or agent on advice from manufacturing or marketing company.

Drum   Large cylindrical metal container mainly used for bulk packaging of liquids. Term can also apply to a small fibreboard cylinder often with metal end closures and containing powders in convenient quantities for household use, e.g. salt, custard powder and abrasive cleaning products.

Dry goods   Products in a retail outlet other than perishable grocery items.

Dry-run   Pretransmission television rehearsal where action, lines, cues, etc. are perfected.

Dry transfer lettering   Letters printed on to a plastic sheet in such a way that by rubbing the reverse side they can be transferred on to another surface, e.g. for use in creating artwork.

DSVD (Digital simultaneous voice and data)   A transmission method which allows the mixing together of voice telephone calls with data channels over a single communications line.

DTP   *See* Desktop publishing.

Dubbing   Superimposing sound upon an already completed film, as opposed to simultaneous recording.

Dumb terminal   A type of terminal consisting simply of a screen and keyboard and used to enter and receive data. It has no computing power of its own, unlike a workstation, and cannot therefore work independently of a host computer.

Dummy   Simplified representation of a proposed publication, package, or other promotional item. *See* Mock-up.

Dump display   Unit of fibreboard or woven wire into which a quantity of products is exposed in random order for self-selection at a retail outlet. Particularly associated with supermarkets in connection with product launches or clearances and carrying special price or other offers.

Dumping   Distribution of goods overseas at a price much less than the equivalent in market of origin and which would not normally be expected to make a full contribution to the recovery of overheads.

Duplication (in advertising)   Extent to which the audience of one medium or vehicle overlaps that of another. *See* Reach.

Durable goods   Goods providing a service over a period of time rather than extinguished at the moment of consumption. Includes goods like TV, motor cars, refrigerators.

Dustbin check   Survey at consumer level to establish purchases over an agreed period according to brand and pack. Emptied containers are retained in a bin known as a dustbin. It is a form of household audit for which greater reliability is claimed because tangible evidence of consumption is provided.

Dutch auction   Bidding starting at a high price and reducing until a bid is made. Most often associated with charities but may be used as a method of sales promotion which gains an audience for a required exposure or demonstration.

Duty free shop   Retail establishment in which selling prices do not include Customs and Excise duties and may, therefore, be fixed at a lower level than those prevailing generally within a particular country. Most often located at air or seaports where operators can, as a result, take a higher margin of profit than other retailers.

DX   Usually, and very generally, signifies that a particular microprocessor (e.g. Intel 486) has not been 'cut down' in terms of speed or performance (as opposed to SX chips which have).

Dynamic obsolescence (style, creative, artificial) Deliberate restyling of goods or services, often including a technical advance, to out-date established models. *See also* Style obsolescence and Planned obsolescence.

Dynamically continuous Same basic product idea but innovation in technology takes product into new product field.

Dysfunctional Element in strategy or plan that fails and disrupts part or all of other elements.

E

E & OE Errors and Omissions Excepted. Used on quotations, invoices and other financial documents.

Ear Advertising space at top left or right of a newspaper's front page.

Early adopters *See* Adoption of innovation.

EAV *See* Equivalent advertising value.

Econometrics Application of mathematical/statistical techniques to the solution of economic problems, usually with the aid of electronic data processing devices.

Economic dynamics Analysis of economic systems, through time, and particularly in relation to behaviour of markets, firms and the national economy in general.

Economic growth Increase in productive capacity for entire economy with the result of increasing national income.

Economic life Period during which a machine or device works efficiently or profitably.

Economic order quantity (EOQ)   Minimum order value producing a profit for a supplier.

Economic price   Price which includes full consideration of elements of direct and indirect costs together with an allowance for the opportunity cost.

Economic rent   Earning differential between the most efficient and alternative uses of a factor of production.

Economic trend   Pattern of economic development for a country or industry.

Economies of scale   Reduction in unit cost attributable to overheads being divided over a larger volume, often due to introduction of mechanization or automation leading to greater output at lower overall cost.

Economy size   (1) Used to describe a larger than usual size package in order to encourage an increase in consumption. (2) Best value for money in available package choices.

Edit   To modify an original manuscript, text or film in such a way as to make the meaning clearer, improve the grammar, reduce the size, or in some other way prepare it for multiple reproduction and distribution.

Editing   (1) Preparing written copy or film for publication. (2) Critical analysis or censorship of material to be published.

Edition   Particular issue of a publication.

Editorial   Leading article in publication or broadcast, usually explicit statement of editor's views. Sometimes used to distinguish news or feature items from advertising content.

Editorial advertisement   Advertisement designed in the form of a piece of editorial matter. Such advertisements must, however, be clearly labelled 'advertisement'. *See* Advertorial.

103

Editorial calendar Advance notice given by a publisher to advertisers and likely editorial contributors regarding any special features which are planned.

Editorial columns That part of a publication devoted to non-advertising matter, i.e. containing editorial matter.

Editorial copy All the printed material in a publication other than advertisements. This may include feature articles, new stories, reviews, and, indeed, the 'editorial' itself. *See* Editorial.

Editorial matter News or entertainment section of publication or broadcast, i.e. excluding any advertising matter it may carry.

Editorial mention Reference to an individual, or a company, favourable or otherwise, in the editorial columns.

Editorial publicity Space in a journal or newspaper in which a product, service, or company is discussed or publicized at the discretion of the editor. Commonly referred to as 'publicity'. *See* Press relations.

Editorial write-up News story or feature about an individual, product, service or company.

Educational advertising (1) Advertisements referring to educational matters. (2) Advertising devoted to improving consumers' knowledge about a product or service in order to render them more favourably disposed towards it, particularly if it involves some change in beliefs or attitudes.

Effective cover Known otherwise as the '4 plus syndrome', whereby the members of a target market will have seen a commercial at least four times on average. Compares with simply 'Cover' which means the same coverage but limited at least once only.

Effective demand Willingness and resources to pay the price asked for a product.

Ego   Term borrowed from psychology, indicating an individual's conception of himself, often having an influence over his purchasing behaviour patterns.

Ego superego concept   Determination of how individuals seek satisfaction within the bounds of conscience based on moral and ethical conduct.

Elasticity   Measure of the degree of responsiveness of one variable (the dependent variable) to changes in another (the independent variable), where a causal relationship is observed to exist.

Elasticity of demand   Demand is considered elastic when a decrease in price results in an increase in total revenue. It is inelastic when the reduction results in a decrease in total revenue. Unit elasticity means volume increases sufficiently to compensate for loss of revenue. Zero elasticity is the term used to define a change in price where no change in demand results.

Electronic bulletin board   A computerized version of a conventional bulletin or notice board on which users can leave messages and files for other users. Typical operators of bulletin boards would be government, educational and research institutions as well as commercial organizations and private individuals.

Electronic mail   *See* E-mail.

Electronic media   (1) Advertisements making use of neon signs or lights, and capable of movement by electric impulses. (2) General term referring to television, radio and other electronic based media.

Electrotype   Duplicate of an original printing block; produced by electrochemical deposition onto a matrix. Commonly known as 'electro'.

Em   The square of any size of type, for instance, a 12 point em is 12 points wide. Ems are also used to measure the width of type on a page, irrespective of the size of the typeface being used.

E-mail (Electronic mail)   A computer-based mail or messaging facility for sending, receiving and storing text files (or any kind of computer file reduced to text format) via mailboxes. The concept is largely based on conventional postal systems where letters and packages are delivered to and collected from post office boxes.

Embargo   (1) Restriction on the import of certain specified goods into a country. The embargo may be imposed either by the importing country or the exporting country. (2) In relation to news releases, a time or date before which a particular item of news must not be published.

Embossing   *See* Die stamping.

Emotional appeal   Product advertising appealing to emotional desires rather than logic, economy or utility.

Emotions   Arguably defined as bodily changes, together with mental change, influencing one's decisions, sometimes out of the normal pattern for the individual, used particularly in reference to buying behaviour.

Empathy   Identifying oneself completely with the problems and aspirations of others; often used in connection with the necessity for a salesperson to see his/her task through the customers' eyes and to establish a reciprocity with them effective in concluding business agreements.

Empirical   Data based upon observation or experiment as opposed to theory.

Empirical research   Study by observation and accumulated experience. Does not normally involve theory or formal research procedures.

Employee communications   A system of personal and non-personal communications between an organization and its employees in order to inform and motivate them. Equally important is for there to be communications from employees to senior management. *See* Employee relations and Internal communications.

Employee relations The building up of good relationships with employees, future and, perhaps, past employees. Strictly, this is a personnel or human resources function rather than a public relations one. The latter activity is more properly contained within the term 'Employee communications'.

Empty nesters People whose children have left home, maybe thus adding to their affluence – a stage in the family life cycle/life style.

En The measure of one-half an em; the measure used in casting-off or estimating the length of a typescript.

Enclosure Object inserted into envelope or package, usually in addition to the main or principal content.

Encryption A security technique designed to disguise data by scrambling it.

End-aisle display A promotional device to put on show a particular offer in the form of a display at the end of an aisle in a supermarket.

End-user The person actually using a product as against the person buying it or authorizing its purchase. *See* DMU.

Endorsement Transfer of the property in a bill of exchange by the signature of the owner. Increasingly used to indicate some amendment to the original composition of a contract or legal document.

Enlargement Reproduction in size larger than the original, particularly with reference to a photographic print.

Enquiry In business terms, 'inquiry is preferred to enquiry' to distinguish between a general request for information (enquiry) and a firm request for details prior to placing an order (inquiry). *See* Inquiry.

Enterprise zones Geographical areas given financial support and development help from national government or from the EU or both.

Entrepot trade Business consisting of re-exporting of imported goods, with or without any additional processing.

Entrepreneur Individual with talent for creative business activity, exercising initiative and pulling together the various multifunctional activities into one co-ordinated and usually profitable enterprise.

Envelope stuffer *See* Stuffer.

Environment Refers to surrounding conditions of an activity, particularly in marketing, the social, physical and psychological conditions.

Environmental analysis Study of market conditions particularly culture, life-style, and purchasing patterns and behaviour.

Environmentalist Person, usually one of an organized group, devoted to the protection of the environment against such hazards as pollution, effluent, industrial development, etc.

EPOS Electronic point of sale.

Equilibrium price Price at which supply equals demand and there is no tendency to change, upwards or downwards.

Equivalent advertising value The amount of editorial coverage (publicity) gained from a press relations campaign, expressed in terms of the cost of such space if it had been purchased as advertising space.

Ergonomics Study concerned with the working environment and its effect on a person's efficiency with a view to applying anatomical, physiological and psychological knowledge to the solution of problems which may arise from this relationship.

Escalation clause Device to enable companies to pay rising rates of commission for higher levels of sales turnover by agents, salespeople, etc.

Escalator panel Specialized poster displayed on the walls of an escalator as in the London Underground.

Essential commodities Goods considered essential to maintain a minimum acceptable standard of living. Some essential goods in an advanced affluent society would be considered luxuries in poorer countries.

Established brand, image, market, product Widely acknowledged and accepted in the market place. Sometimes may be prematurely described as such in order to secure early credibility.

Estimating Strictly, producing an estimate of the cost/price of an activity particularly in one-off jobs and in contracting. Term sometimes applied to the calculation of a price upon which a firm quotation is based. Almost entirely confined to industrial goods and services but also used in the case of some consumer durables.

Ethical advertising Advertising of ethical pharmaceutical products addressed to the medical profession. Also applied generally to describe honest, informative advertising, as distinct from unscrupulous and misleading practice. *See* Codes of practice. *See also* Voluntary controls.

Ethnic media Broadcast or printed media aimed specifically at a particular national group, often in their own language.

Eurodollar American currency (dollars) held either by individuals or organizations outside the United States.

Events marketing A promotional activity in which an organization stages an event to which customers and prospects are invited, e.g. a private exhibition, a concert, a sports fixture, or a competition.

109

Ex ante Ex ante demand is the level of demand for commodities which are expected to be bought at a certain given price.

Ex gratia As a matter of favour. Usually refers to payments which are made where no legal obligation exists to make them.

Ex post Actual value attributable to a variable factor. Ex post demand, for example, is the actual quantity bought at the price realizable.

Ex works price Basic price of a product at the point of manufacture, i.e. excluding delivery and insurance, and sometimes packaging.

Excess capacity Existence of more productive capacity than is warranted by the demand existing at any given time.

Excess demand Existence of more demand than presently existing productive capacity is able to satisfy.

Excess supply In which supply exceeds demand at the prevailing price.

Exchange rate Fixed price at which one currency may be exchanged for another or for gold. A floating exchange rate exists when the rate is not fixed but is allowed to find its own level in trading negotiations.

Exchange value Translation of product qualities into people statements; exchanging a technical benefit into a human desire.

Excise duty Tax on the production of particular goods in high general demand such as alcoholic drinks, tobacco and petroleum goods.

Exclusive In press relations, relates to a story and/or illustratory photographic or other material which is supplied to one publication alone.

Exclusive agency agreement   Agreement binding two parties, one as principal, the other as agent, involving a product, a market, or a geographical area, being limited in availability to the agent for a period, and fully supported by the principal.

Executive gift   An item given to customers and prospects as a momento or reminder of a product or organization. Usually more expensive than simply an Advertising novelty, which *see*.

Exempt rating   Classification of a business which is not required to add VAT to its charges, neither is it able to reclaim VAT charged to it.

Exhibition   Putting on display a company's products or services for promotional purposes. Particularly the gathering of a number of such displays which are either on view to the public in general or merely to invited guests. May be commercially or privately sponsored.

Expanded type   A typeface which is broader or wider than normal.

Experience effect   Improvements in efficiency resulting from experience; leads to improvements in cost effectiveness.

Experimental advertising   In which a campaign concentrates upon getting the consumer to at least want to experience the product benefit. Heavy emphasis here might be on sending out or offering samples.

Exploded drawing   An illustration, usually a line drawing, which shows the inside of an object which would not be seen from a photograph.

Exponential smoothing   Statistical process applied to moving averages, to reflect most recent changes in a series of data.

Export agent   A person or organization in one country operating exclusively on behalf of a principal in another. Remuneration is by commission on the selling price. The goods or services are frequently supplied direct to the customer.

Export declaration   Details, to be submitted within six days, of the export of all goods from the country.

Export house   Organization specializing in selling into foreign markets. Originally called Forwarding agents, they now provide a large range of services to exporters big or small. Representative body is the Institute of Freight Forwarders.

Export licence   Document issued by the government giving authorization for a product to be exported.

Export marketing   Marketing goods or services in a country other than one's own. *See* International marketing.

Export sales manager   Person who manages the selling operation in countries other than the home market.

Exposition   Sometimes used as synonym of 'exhibition', but usually to imply a larger or more serious event, often accompanied by a conference or seminar.

Exposure   The extent to which readers, listeners, or viewers are in receipt of messages about a product or service, or indeed any other piece of information. *See* Cumulative reach.

Extended credit   *See* Credit sale.

Extended guarantee   Application of guarantee conditions past the expiry date of the original cover. *See* Guarantee.

Extended use tests   Similar to placement tests but used, especially in industrial marketing, where it is necessary for findings to be derived from use of the product in a work situation over a long term period.

Extensive selling   Selling products through every conceivable distribution channel, stocking in every possible retail outlet, and promoting sales to every likely market segment.

External house magazine   *See* House magazine.

External image audit   *See* Image audit *and* Internal image audit.

Extrapolation   *See* Projection.

Eye movement camera   Used in advertising research, this equipment tracks the movement of the eye over press advertisements, showing the path which the eye takes and indicating the sequence of interest that the features arouse.

Eye observation camera   Equipment used in advertising research to measure pupil dilation, so giving indications of arousal of informant.

Eye pupil dilation   Reaction to a communication with which levels of interest or involvement may be measured.

Eye-wash   Exaggerated claims.

Eyeblink test   A measurement of the reaction or emotion caused by a person observing a commercial or advertisement. Based upon the theory that blink rate changes with change of emotion. *See* Blink meter.

F

Face   In printing, a particular design or style of lettering upon which a typeface is based. Two broad categories, 'serif' and 'sans serif' distinguish between the more and less intricate characters.

Face-to-face interviewing   In which questions are put to a respondent directly on a personal and one-to-one basis, as opposed to postal or telephone interviewing.

Face-to-face selling   Personal selling usually on a one-to-one basis, i.e. a personal meeting between buyer and seller in which each can state a case and/or hear the other's point of view. Vulgarly referred to as 'belly-to-belly' selling.

Face value   Nominal value or price of a commodity.

Facia   In exhibitions, the headboard above a stand. Sometimes used for advertising purposes, e.g. featuring a brand-name, but usually carries the identity of the exhibitor.

Facility visit   Visit by journalists to a factory, installation, retail outlet or other place of interest where facilities are provided by the host for the preparation of an article or programme.

Facing matter   Positioning of an advertisement so that it appears opposite an editorial page.

Facings   The front (or faces) of a carton which can be seen when stacked upon a shelf in a shop or supermarket. A unit of shelf space, i.e. measurement.

Facsimile   Strictly an exact copy of writing or an illustration.

Fact sheet   Document which concentrates on presenting the facts about a product rather than performing any overt selling function. *See* Data sheet.

Factor analysis   Study of the component parts of an attitude research programme interview with the aim of discovering more meaningful conclusions than are apparent from the data taken as a whole.

Factoring   (1) Discounting of bills. (2) Intermediaries acting as go-between for sellers of commodities without a common interest. The factor arranges for the sale of products of both companies and then settles the accounts. Factors are often involved in processing as well as the usual wholesaling operations. Otherwise, they would be purely marketing agencies.

Fad   Usually a fashion adopted quickly by a number of people who subsequently lose interest as quickly as they originally gained it.

Fair copy   A clean proof without any printer's errors.

Fair trading   Regulation of monopolies and mergers, anti-competitive practices, and restrictive trading agreements.

False claim   Inaccurate claim or falsehood, whether deliberate or inadvertent.

Familiarity/favourability   A presentation in graphic form of the extent to which a company is known by a particular target audience compared with the way in which it is regarded. All the evidence suggests a correlation between the two, i.e., as a company name becomes more familiar, so it is perceived with greater favour. Useful for comparison with competitors.

Family   A particular style of typeface in which there are a number of variations such as 'bold', 'light', and 'italics', but all having a common resemblance

Family brands   A name or symbol used to identify and promote a number of different, related or branded products.

Family budget   Total family income devoted to expenditure for housekeeping purposes.

Family life-style Manner or style of living adopted by a family according to its background, income, or aspirations. Is becoming subject to closer scrutiny in the development of psychographics.

Fanfold *See* Accordion fold.

Fast food Meals or dishes which can be prepared very quickly.

Fast moving consumer goods (FMCG) Repeat selling, low unit value goods normally in universal demand.

Fastmarketing Use of a technique in which advertising is concentrated into a shorter time than usual in order to get a quick response. Sometimes referred to as Blitzkrieg advertising.

Fax mailing Direct mailing using a fax machine rather than the post.

Feasibility Expresses the degree of practicality, usually in financial or economic terms, of a product or business venture's success.

Feature (1) In press relations, an article or story which is written in some depth and at some length; usually exclusive. (2) A specific characteristic of a product (or service) which is only of value in that it yields a 'benefit' to the customer, e.g. 'a tyre is a radial ply' is a feature; 'yielding longevity' is the benefit. (3) A particular characteristic of a product which is thought to have special appeal to customers, maybe a USP.

Fee A single sum of money paid for the provision of a service, often based upon an hourly rate multiplied by the actual or estimated time taken.

Feed (1) To supply information to another, particularly on sales leads. (2) Relaying transmission of a broadcast from one station to another.

Feedback Response or reaction to a message, indicating to its communicator how the message is being interpreted.

116

Fibreboard Two or more sheets of paperboard pasted together to form a stronger, thicker material. Usually a combination of kraft and chipboard. Solid fibreboard is a straightforward laminate often used, for example, as a book cover. Corrugated fibreboard comprises two outer 'liners' in between which is sandwiched a corrugated 'fluting'. Both types of fibreboard are used extensively in the construction of 'cases', sometimes referred to as containers or cartons.

Fibreboard case Container constructed from either solid or corrugated fibreboard, intended for protection of goods during transit. A transit outer.

Field force Team of interviewers used for gathering information direct from respondents in or around the respondents' usual habitat. To be carefully distinguished from sales force.

Field organization Structure governing the operation of a field force, which may be for purposes of marketing research or act as a promotional device.

Field research That part of a market research survey involving contact with customers, potential customers, or a representative sample of the population.

Field sales manager Executive responsible for organization, direction, control, motivation and training of the field selling force in whole or in part.

Field selling The process of selling by personal visits of the sales force to potential customers at their own premises.

Fieldwork That part of a market research survey which involves face-to-face interviews with respondents by research investigators, as compared with other means of obtaining data, such as postal or telephone enquiries and the searching of relevant published material. *See* Desk research.

File A sequence of related information.

Filler Pre-prepared advertisement by publisher used to fill the gap left in a page after make-up.

Film rush First print of ciné film sequence; produced immediately after shooting in order to see whether a retake is necessary. *See* Rush.

Film strip Joined sequence of positive transparencies either black and white but more usually in colour. Each strip consists of a limited number of exposures, which together tell a story or put across a message. Often produced in conjunction with a sound script which can either be spoken during showing or coupled electronically for automatic reproduction.

Filter (1) Means of eliminating unnecessary information. (2) Receptionist or secretary protecting executive(s) from unexpected callers. (3) Question in research questionnaire intended to redirect interview.

Filter question Question used in a market research survey to identify required respondents. Interviews may be terminated if the respondents do not provide indicative answers.

Final Proof or pull of the corrected, locked-up printing forme or of a plate, showing the printed corrected work as it will eventually appear. It is thus distinguished from initial proofing which is for checking and correcting purposes only.

Financial advertising Advertising activity undertaken by companies, firms, or organizations involved in financial markets, such as Unit Trusts, Assurance, Building Societies, or Banks.

Financial relations Sub-set of public relations. *See* Investor relations.

Finder's fee Sum of money paid to an individual for bringing together two organizations to conduct business with one another, e.g. fee given to someone who introduces an author to a publisher. Can be in the form of a fee or a commission/royalty.

118

Fine grain Descriptive of a photographic emulsion or the developer used to process it; results in a negative which can be enlarged to a high degree without showing excessive graining.

Fine screen In printing, a halftone screen containing 100 or more lines to the inch.

Finish Quality of final work.

Finished art *See* Artwork.

Finished product A manufactured product which has been completed and is ready for sale.

Finished rough *See* Visual.

Firm quotation Quoted price and/or conditions which will remain unchanged, subject to previously defined criteria.

First in, first out (FIFO) Principle used in stock-holding policy.

First proof An initial proof of an advertisement or publication to be read for literals or printer's errors.

First revise A corrected proof following the revisions made on the first proof.

Fiscal policy Government policy in matters of taxation, particularly in controlling changing patterns of demand to meet other needs of the economy as a whole.

Fixed costs Accounting term referring to costs that are not expected to vary up to a given level of output.

Fixed spot Television spot for which a premium is paid (normally 15 per cent) to ensure that it is transmitted within a preselected break during a programme.

Flag In a mailing list, to apply an indicator against chosen addresses to identify them for some future action.

119

Flagship brand   The major product in a range of brands; the product by which the company of the brand is best known.

Flashpack   A specially produced package which carries a sales promotion message such as an extra quantity or a price reduction in the form of a 'flash', i.e. an apparent overprint with the main point of the offer, e.g. 10p off.

Flat rate   Uniform rate for advertising space or time, i.e. without allowing for discounts.

Flatbed scanner   An item of hardware which looks and works like a photocopier to import hardcopy documents into a computer file.

Flexible budget   Variable amount of funds for a given purpose subject only to accountability for achievement.

Flexography   Method of printing using rubber plates; cheaper but resulting in lower quality reproduction.

Flip chart   Large white paper fold-over pad used for conveying sales messages and making sales presentations. Used also in conferences, seminars and training courses.

Flong   Sheet of softened paperboard used in printing to produce a Matrix.

Floorwalker   Store security officer, usually mixing with customers and attempting to spot shoplifters.

Flop   An event or an activity which is a complete failure.

Floppy disk   A magnetic data storage medium, typically used to transfer information between computers or provide back-up copies of data and software programs resident on the computer hard disk. The disk itself is made of a flexible material (hence 'floppy'), which, taking the popular 3.5 inch format as an example, is then encased in its own rigid plastic cover for protection and ease of handling. A floppy disk will necessarily have a much lower storage capacity than a hard disk.

Flow chart (1) Graphical presentation of performance. (2) Stages in critical path procedure.

Fluff A mistake in speech, e.g. on television or radio, made in such a way as to be obvious to an audience.

Fly posting Illegal fixing of posters on another's property.

Flyer Inexpensive promotional piece, commonly comprising one sheet of paper, printed one or two sides, and used as a handout, a direct mailing piece, a stuffer, a handbill, or a circular, which *see*.

FMCG Fast moving consumer goods, which *see*.

FOB Free on board, which *see*.

Focus group discussion *See* Group discussion

Foil (1) Thin film of metal, usually aluminium, used in packaging. Often referred to as tin foil or silver paper. (2) Also term used by plate makers and printers when individual page films are attached to one large piece of clear film in the correct position ready for plate making.

Foil stamping Application of metal foil to paper or other substance by means of heat and pressure.

Fold-out Leaflet which opens out into a larger size. *See also* Accordion fold.

Folder Sheet of paper or board folded once or more, sometimes printed on and often to act as a container.

Folder technique Description of a means used to pre-test an advertisement in which a number of alternatives are presented to a panel who give reactions to each.

Folio Numbered sheet of copy.

Follow up   Sales contact, telephone call or letter sometimes but not always as a result of an expression of interest by a prospect and usually after his/her receipt of an initial promotional piece, e.g. a direct mail shot.

Following matter   *See* Following reading matter.

Following reading matter   Preferred position in advertising media for advertisers; an advertisement is placed immediately after a feature article or editorial and so attracts the attention of readers, whose eyes are said to migrate to the advertisement.

Font   *See* Fount.

Footage   Indicates the length of a piece of film. Each foot contains 16 frames; 35mm films run at $1\frac{1}{2}$ feet or 24 frames per second.

Forced consumption   An attempt to pressurize consumption patterns.

Forecasting   Predicting future events on the basis of historical data, opinions, trends and known future variables.

Foreigners   Private work undertaken by artisans for the customers of their employers with or without the employer's approval or knowledge.

Format   (1) Shape, size, or style of a publication. (2) Structure or organization of a business proposal or campaign.

Formatting   New or re-used hard and floppy disks need to be prepared by a software program, such as an operating system, before they can be used on a computer. This process is termed formatting and is carried out according to the specific platform on which the disk is to be loaded (for instance a MS-DOS formatted disk would not work on a UNIX computer using UNIX commands and software). An ordinary user will normally only be required to format floppy disks (although these can be obtained pre-formatted) as hard disks are prepared at build time. Re-formatting disks containing data will erase the contents thus preparing them for re-use.

Form letter *See* Standard letter.

Forme Frame with typematter and blocks assembled in it for letterpress printing.

Forty-eight sheet Very large poster. *See* Bulletin board. *See also* Double crown.

Forty-forty-twenty rule Postulates that the success of a direct mail campaign depends 40% on the mailing list, 40% on the advertising proposition, and 20% on the creative presentation.

Forward delivery (1) Deliveries booked in advance to meet fixed schedules. (2) Time lag between order and delivery.

Forward market Market in futures, where contracts are made to buy commodities or securities at prices then ruling but for delivery at a future date.

Forwarding agents Packaging and shipping specialists. *See* Export house.

Foul bill of lading Covers goods known to be defective; also known colloquially as a dirty bill.

Foul proof Corrected proof from which a revised set has been made.

Fount Complete set of type of same face and size.

Four-colour set Set of printing blocks or plates, one for each of the four major printing colours (red, yellow, blue, black) used to produce a full colour reproduction. Term sometimes refers to a set of colour proofs. *See* Colour separation. *See also* Progressives.

Four Ps Shorthand way of indicating the principal factors to be included in the marketing mix, i.e. product, price, place and promotion. *See* Marketing mix.

Four plus *See* Effective cover.

Four sheet Poster size of growing popularity, equal to four double crown posters.

Frame (1) One individual exposure upon a reel of film. (2) *See* Sampling frame.

Franchise Trading agreement, most often between a supplier and a retail outlet, where co-operation and support, often of promotional facilities, are provided to the retail outlet by the supplier as part of a contractual arrangement in return for a guarantee of sales income. A distribution device of growing importance particularly for service industries.

Franking Printing or cancellation of postage upon envelopes or labels which can be used to carry an advertising slogan.

Free alongside ship (FAS) All charges being met by the exporter up to the point of delivering to the ship.

Free continuous premium Coupons promotion whereby consumers secure some gift or price concession according to their number of purchases.

Free gifts Promotional gifts: (1) Mail-in: inviting prospective customers to send for a gift. (2) On-pack: gift attached to product at point of sale. (3) On-pack offer: inviting purchasers to send for gift, usually with evidence of a minimum purchase.

Free mail-in A sales promotion offer which is free but maybe requires some proof of purchase. Postage and packing might be charged.

Free market One in which forces of supply and demand are allowed to operate unhampered by government or other regulations.

Free on board (FOB) All charges being met by exporter to the point where goods are loaded on board the transit vessel.

Free samples Popular sales promotion technique, often at the introduction of a new product. Trial size samples are given away, distributed or mailed to potential customers to induce them to make a first purchase.

Free standing insert Leaflet, flyer, or other sales promotional piece inserted loose in a periodical. *See* Loose insert.

Free trade International trade operating without intervention of governmental restrictions or requirements.

Freeboard Distance between main deck and the waterline.

Freelance Journalist not on the staff of one newspaper, but usually contributing to several. Also refers to artists, writers and other self-employed suppliers of specialist services.

Freephone By quoting a freephone number a caller can be connected free of charge to the company or organization registering the number and paying for it.

Freesheets Local newspapers or magazines which are distributed without charge, depending for their revenue entirely on advertising support. Most of the space in these publications is sold for advertising, leaving little room for editorial content.

Freight forward Convention dictating that freight charges are payable at port of destination.

Freight liner Door-to-door container service provided by British Rail.

French fold Sheet of paper folded twice at right angles to one another. Usually printed on one side. Often used for greeting cards.

Frequency Number of times an advertising message is delivered within a set period of time.

Frequency curve Graphical expression of a continuous frequency distribution.

Fringe accounts Low profit customers making marginal contributions to a supplier's turnover and therefore liable to least service or even closure in times of financial stringency.

Fringe time Periods of time in television advertising which precede and follow Prime time, which *see*.

Front cover First page of magazine or journal, sometimes available for advertising. *See* Back cover.

Front end Software that provides an interface to another program 'behind' it, which may not be as user-friendly.

Front loader Administrative costs added to a financial arrangement; known also as handling fee.

Fudge (1) Mistake. (2) Part of newspaper printing machine carrying second colour for late news, or announcement on ears of front page.

Fulfilment Making provision to respond to a direct marketing campaign by sending out promotional material, answering enquiries, dealing with orders, and invoicing.

Fulfilment house An outside agency which provides a service in responding to a sales promotion or direct marketing campaign. Sometimes called a handling house.

Full-line forcing Selling a whole range of products as a result of maintaining a monopoly position for one or more of the constituent products which are essential.

Full-out Typesetting in which the opening line of each paragraph is not indented, but rather a space is used between the paragraphs.

Full plate Photographic print, approximate size 8 in by 6 in; sometimes known as Whole plate.

Full point Typographical term meaning 'full stop'.

Full service agency Advertising agency offering clients a wide range of activities and expertise over and above the normal creative and/or media facilities. Such services will include marketing research and planning, merchandising and below-the-line sales promotion, press and/or public relations, packaging, etc.

Function   Basic organization term referring to grouped activities of an enterprise, e.g. marketing, finance, production and R&D.

Functional benchmarking   A comparison of a particular function as between two or more organizations.

Functional budget   Method of budgeting where funds are allocated according to distinct functions within a business, e.g. marketing, production, finance, administration.

Functional product differentiation   Distinguishing a brand from competition by highlighting a functional feature that may or may not be unique to the brand concerned.

Futures   Refers to forward sales or forward purchases. A feature of markets used to guard against violent fluctuations in price.

Fuzzy logic   Logic which allows for 'shades of grey' between 'completely true' and 'completely false' statements (e.g. 'yes' or 'no' answers in binary). Computers designed to use fuzzy logic would therefore use decision making processes which would result in 'weighted' answers (e.g. 'more true than false').

G

G-spool   Copy of a video commercial as sent to a television station.

Gable-end   Description of a poster located on the end wall of a building.

Galley   First proofs of typesetting taken prior to the make-up of pages.

Galvanometric response   Change in skin conductivity due to change in moisture content (perspiration); measured by current flow as indicated on a galvanometer. Such change may have a correlation with psychological stimuli (e.g. fear or other emotion) and arguably may provide a measure of a respondent's reaction to an advertisement.

Game theory   Principles evolved from business games with players in conflicting situations where different outcomes result from alternative decisions. May be used prior to the commencement of a real business venture. Most often used, however, in training or selection establishments.

Gantt chart   Horizontal bar chart, frequently used as a means of showing the timetable in a marketing communications plan, such as Media schedule, which *see*.

Gap analysis   Methodical tabulation of all known 'consumer wants' of a particular product category, together with a cross-listing of the features of existing products which satisfy those wants. Such a chart shows up any gaps which exist and thus provides a pointer as to where new products might find an unfulfilled demand.

Gatefold   Four-page advertisement bound into a publication at one edge and folded at the other such that it opens out, as with a gate, to provide a double page spread.

Gateway   A physical access point to an external computer network.

GATT   General Agreement on Tariffs and Trade. International agreement signed in 1947 by numerous countries to liberalize trade by the reduction and removal of tariff barriers and quota restrictions. The agreement has no legal force but has had considerable influence in post-war developments.

GDP   Gross domestic product, which *see*.

Gearing Description of capital structure in limited companies referring to proportion of capital, whether debentures, preference, or ordinary shares making up total equity in the company. High gearing refers to a greater proportion of 'loan capital', i.e. debentures or preference shares, to risk capital, i.e. ordinary shares and vice versa with 'low gearing'.

General sales manager Senior manager with overall responsibility for sales activities, often encompassing both internal and external. May report directly to the CEO, and have control of the field force, maybe via regional sales managers. Also could be the national accounts manager. *See also* National account.

Generic products Goods sold, unbranded, for price-conscious consumers.

Generic term In marketing, applied to brand names which have come to be adopted as the general descriptive term for a product, often as the result of extensive promotion, e.g. Hoover, Biro, Linoleum.

Geodemographic targeting Identifying an audience by its location and demographic characteristics. *See also* ACORN.

Geodemographics Segmenting consumers by where they live.

Geographical concentration Limiting of a sales or promotional campaign to a particular geographical region.

Geometric mean Term used in advertising schedule building where three elements (cost effectiveness, market penetration, and advertising unit cost) are treated as being entitled to an equal share of the advertising appropriation. By using the technique, selected media are given shares of the appropriation according to the extent to which they provide combinations of the three elements.

Gestation period Length of time which elapses between an initial inquiry for a product and the placing of an order. More often applied to capital goods where it can amount to several years.

GHI Guaranteed Home Impressions. A guaranteed number of television or radio advertisements for a given sum of money.

Ghost writer Person who writes anonymously on behalf of another.

Ghosting (1) Providing an inner view of a package or product by cutting away part of the exterior. (2) Shadow on television film. (3) Shadow on printed paper caused by incorrect printing.

Giffen goods Goods for which demand moves in the same direction as price, instead of following the classical laws of supply and demand.

Gift voucher Special incentive to purchase, usually involving money-off against next purchase of qualifying brand or providing an opportunity for a special purchase.

Gigabyte A thousand million bytes.

Gimmick Idea or object which is novel or highly unusual within the context in which it is used. Lends news value to promotional activity; also helps to establish identity for a product image.

Give-away Inexpensive promotional piece, sometimes merely a leaflet, designed for wide distribution from offices or shops or direct to prospective customers. *See* Handbill.

Give-away magazines Magazines depending entirely on advertising for their revenues and distributed to readers free of charge. *See* Freesheets. *See also* Controlled circulation.

GLAMS Psychographic acronym for Greying, Leisured, Affluent, Middle-aged.

Global A name recognized throughout the world, referring to a company or product.

Glossy Applies to magazines, particularly those which are 'upmarket', maybe with a derogatory connotation.

Glut In which the supply of a good is greatly in excess of demand, leading in turn to a substantial fall in price.

GNP Gross national product.

Goal Synonym for business objective or aim to be achieved.

Gobbet In which a relatively small amount of copy in an advertisement is surrounded by a large amount of white space.

Going rate Current typical price for a product or service.

Gompertz curve Exponential curve using logarithms.

Gondola Shelving carrying displays of goods with aisles on either side in self-service shop or supermarket.

Goods on approval Goods, usually of a durable character, provided for a period of trial prior to a purchasing decision and returnable in the absence of such a decision.

Goods on consignment An arrangement whereby an agent takes possession of goods but no title to them. The agent will normally be working for a commission on their sale and the goods are returnable in the absence of a buyer being found for them.

Goodwill That part of the value of a business enterprise reflecting consideration of its established market connections, reputation and image. On sale, that part of the purchase price not accounted for by its total net assets. *See* Corporate image.

Government relations Branch of public relations dealing with the specific publics of local, national, and international relationships. Often dealt with under the heading of Corporate affairs, or Public affairs, which *see*.

Grammage Term for expressing a particular weight of paper expressed as g/m^2.

Graphic display A specialized visual display unit for handling graphical applications (as opposed to character-based).

Graphical user interface   *See* GUI.

Graphics   (1) Illustration or diagram in pictorial statistics. (2) Visual elements of communications, usually associated with artwork, dummies, photographs in media.

Gravure   *See* Photogravure.

Green marketing   In which special attention is given, particularly to environmental groups, to products and packaging which are biodegradable and/or recyclable. Also to products which have wholly or partially been produced from recycled materials, e.g. writing paper.

Gresham's law   States that bad money drives out good, i.e. where two coins with identical face value have a different bullion content, the more valuable coin will be taken out of circulation. A similar situation may often happen in marketing where inferior goods can create a poor market reception for sound goods.

Grey market   The older population segment (55+) which is growing in affluence and of increasing interest to many marketing operations. Also referred to as Grey panthers or Third age.

Grey panthers   *See* Grey market

Gripe session   Refers to a conference or other meeting at which sales people primarily offer complaints about company products, personnel policy or environment. Usually taken to be a symptom of poor motivation but may also reflect lack of positive planning by the management.

Grocery   Retail outlet offering wide range of consumable household goods such as foodstuffs, beverages, cleaning materials. Alternatively, especially in the plural usage, a term used to describe such merchandise itself.

Gross circulation   Total of credited circulations in groups of media, without discounting for any duplications or errors.

Gross cover (1) The product of adding the separate TVRs resulting from a number of commercials. (2) Similarly, the totalling of the separate readership figures achieved by individual advertisements. *See* TVR.

Gross domestic product (GDP) Total output of goods and services by the national economy in a full year.

Gross margin Difference between cost or purchase price and the selling price for a particular piece of merchandise.

Gross margin method Relates advertising expenditure to sales turnover minus the costs of production and distribution. Progressively being replaced by the 'Task method', which *see*.

Gross national product (GNP) Differs from gross domestic product by adding incomes from abroad to UK residents, e.g. salaries, dividends and interest, minus similar payments to residents of other countries.

Gross opportunities to see Number of advertisements or commercials appearing in a series multiplied by cumulative readership or audience. *See* OTS.

Gross profit Value of difference between cost of purchase of a product and its selling price, i.e. without allowance for overheads, promotion or other expenses. *See* Gross margin.

Gross reach Total number of opportunities for people to see the advertisements contained in a schedule; the sum total of the readership of each publication multiplied by the total number of insertions.

Gross sales Total sales volume before the application of any financial concessions such as quantity discount.

Grossing up A means of arriving at a gross figure given only the net figure, e.g. adding 17.65% to a bill from an advertising agency so as to conform to their usual practice of taking a commission of 15% on media bookings.

Group discussion Research technique in which a group of people is encouraged to express freely views and opinions on a selected subject. This might relate to the message contained in an advertisement, or any other component of a campaign upon which a viewpoint is sought. Group discussions are frequently used as a means of determining both overt and subconscious attitudes and motivation and discussion may range widely around the topic, a controlling psychologist ensuring that the topic is fully explored. The recorded proceedings are then subjected to further analysis. *See* Brainstorming.

Group interview Structured interview used for testing commercials or aimed at getting representative family views about a product.

Growth-share matrix *See* Product portfolio.

GSM Grammes per Square Metre – a measurement of substance or weight usually relating to paper and board.

Guarantee Undertaking by one party to answer for liability, or to perform a duty on the default of another, either in service or a product for which it is primarily responsible. The guarantee usually specifies the extent of the liability of the guarantee. Since the Supply of Goods (Implied Terms) Act, 1973 the extent of liability is governed by statute.

Guaranteed circulation In which the number of copies distributed by a periodical is authenticated by some independent body such as the ABC, which *see*.

Guaranteed home impacts, impressions, ratings *See* TVRs.

GUI (Graphical user interface) A pictorial or diagrammatical screen display enabling users to, for example, select menu options with a mouse using the 'pick and point' method instead of typing in commands from a keyboard.

Guiding question   In a focus group discussion, part of the 'topics list'. The particular area to be discussed as indicated by the convenor/moderator of a discussion group.

Guppies   Special interest groups and hobbyists.

Gut feeling   Hunch; opinion based upon intuitive grasp of a situation, arising from experience rather than logical deduction.

Gutter   Margin of a page adjacent to the fold in a publication; the vertical centre of a double page spread.

Gutter crossing   In which the headline of an advertisement runs across the Gutter, which *see*.

H

Habitual buying   The practice by a customer of always buying the same product, particularly where there is little or no difference between one brand and another in terms of price, product or availability. *See* Brand loyalty.

Hacker   A term with several meanings: (1) a malicious meddler who invades the privacy of computer systems or networks; (2) a person who is good at programming quickly; (3) an expert at a particular program.

Hackneyed   Words or expressions which are banal or over-used: perhaps the most familiar in marketing is 'new'.

Haggle   Process of discussional bargaining, prior to the negotiating of prices or terms of agreement.

Hairline   The finest of the lines used in printing or engraving. Hairline rules are often used in tabular material.

Halftone   Printing block or plate of a tonal illustration, the reproduction of which is facilitated by breaking up the continuous tones to leave a series of dots which pick up the ink.

Hall test   Research activity in which passers-by are invited into a hall, town hall, or other such place, in order to answer questions. Used to evaluate advertising, new products, brand images and so on.

Halo effect   (1) Describes the situation in which estimation may be coloured by the circumstances of the environment, e.g. in marketing, a company stance of frank sincerity will tend to add to a buyer's confidence in a product or service. (2) Statistical term of measurement applied to this area.

Hand held   Film shot made without the use of a tripod.

Handbill   Form of printed advertising delivered personally into the hands of likely prospects. *See* Give-away. *See also* Circular.

Handling house   *See* Fulfilment house.

Handout   Inexpensive leaflet for free distribution at exhibitions or for promotional purposes, especially at point-of-sale.

Hard-boiled, Hard-headed   Buyers, often with long experience, who habitually challenge or reject any new approach, organization, product or opportunity; such behaviour may be natural to the person or assumed in an effort to contain aggressive selling practices. Salespeople must be trained to anticipate and overcome sales resistance of this kind.

Hard copy   Paper-based output, as opposed to screen-based.

Hard disk   Also known as a fixed disk or hard drive and comprises a collection of magnetic disks, or 'platters', coated with metal oxide similar to the coating on magnetic audio tape. The platters, which form the permanent memory, or archive, of a computer, are mounted on a disk drive spinning at very high speeds, and are read from and written to by heads which move over their surfaces under the control of the computer.

136

Hard goods   *See* Durables.

Hard marketing   *See* Hard selling.

Hard news   Current topical news, mainly factual. *See also* Soft news.

Hard selling   Positive, sometimes aggressive, form of selling or marketing action.

Hardware   (1) Merchandise such as tools, building materials, garden equipment, do-it-yourself products – as distributed via hardware stores. (2) The physical apparatus and equipment comprising a computer system (as opposed to software).

Harmony   Essence of an advertisement or commercial reaching the desired theme or objective.

Harvesting strategy   A planned programme for withdrawing a product from the market at a maximum profit. All non-essential costs are eliminated, such as promotion, and the product is just allowed to decline.

Hawker   A door-to-door salesman or woman.

Hawthorne effect   A tendency for respondents in a piece of research to behave in a different way if they are aware of being observed. This might be to respond in the way they feel they are expected to respond, or, indeed, the very opposite. The use of a control group in this situation is particularly important. *See* Control group.

Head margin   White margin at the top of a printed page.

Head-on position   Advertising position which is sited such that it faces oncoming traffic.

Headhunter Recruitment agency which specializes in pinpointing very precisely just those few people known to be suitable for a certain vacancy, and then making personal contact to encourage their interest. A procedure which contrasts with the more commonplace method of placing recruitment advertisements which will probably attract more responses but may be missed by the most suitable people for the job.

Heading Title of report or published matter. *See also* Headline.

Headline Dominant line of type in printing or abbreviated statement in broadcasting; intended to particularize the essence of a longer, more complex message, to which attention is thus drawn.

Heavy users Consumers or customers whose purchases of a product are larger than average. A typical yardstick is one third of consumers purchasing two thirds of the total sales.

Heavy viewer Television viewer consistently watching for many hours each week.

Hedging Negotiation of contractual arrangements intended to protect a buyer or seller against changes in price, supply or other conditions which may be to his/her disadvantage.

Hedonomics Studies into the questions of choice and of people's capacity to enjoy the results of choice.

Her Majesty's Customs and Excise UK government department administering controls over imports and exports and the manufacture of dutiable goods together with the assessment and collection of customs duty on such goods; it is responsible internally for administering VAT (Value Added Tax) in UK.

Hertz A measure of the 'clock speed' of a computer processor. Usually expressed in megahertz (MHz). Generally speaking the higher the MHz, the faster the processor and the more it costs to buy.

Heterogeneous   Groups of people with diverse habits, attitudes, circumstances, tasks and requirements.

Heuristic   An adjective used to describe an exploratory method of tackling a problem, in which the solution is discovered by evaluations of the progress made towards the final result, e.g. guided trial and error (BS 3527).

Hidden decision   Any decisions taken automatically and without question; for example, renewing a contract when due without reviewing its continued usefulness.

Hidden persuaders   Popular term for abstract or subconscious appeals in advertising campaigns.

Hidden price increase   To decrease the value of a product as an alternative to an open price increase. Quantity or quality might be reduced.

Hidden value   Value not obvious at first sight. Marketing activity often constitutes such a hidden value but this should not be appreciated as such by customers unless the supplier chooses to exert effort to inform them.

Hierarchy of effects   The complete process through which a buyer progresses before making a purchase, e.g. unawareness, awareness, knowledge, liking, preference, conviction, and finally purchase. *See* Diffusion of innovation.

Hierarchy of needs   Ranking by individuals, according to their personal motivation, of particular needs usually conditioned by peer groups.

High involvement products   Products (or services) which are purchased only after very careful consideration. As against impulse purchasing. For example high capital value goods.

High key   An illustration in which the majority of tones in the subject or image lie at the light end of the grey scale.

High pressure selling   Aggressive selling activity to achieve sales revenue irrespective of a consumer's real need or resources.

Highlights The lightest parts of a photograph, sometimes painted in to give extra contrast.

Hire purchase An agreement for the bailment of goods under which the bailee may buy the goods or under which the property of the goods will or may pass to the bailee. Governed in UK by a series of Hire Purchase Acts, legislation which is frequently being reviewed and augmented in modern times.

Histogram *See* Bar chart.

Historical method Method of budgeting based upon what has been allocated in the past. *See also* Task method.

Historical trend Use of historical data to forecast future events, e.g. a sales forecast formulated after a study of past sales performance. *See* Forecasting and Sales forecasts.

Hit list Names of prospective customers, usually held by a sales person who then sets out to convert them into customers.

Hit rate The number of conversions from the hit list into customers, expressed as a proportion or percentage. *See* Conversion rate.

Hoarding (1) Withholding money or goods from circulation for later advantage. (2) Site for poster advertising.

Hoarding site Parcel of land or a building used for posters.

Hold-over audience Listeners or viewers who stay tuned to a station after having heard or seen a particular programme, thus facilitating accurate targeting.

Holiday junkies Psychographic term sometimes applied to people who take, or wish to take, more holidays than most.

Holistic evaluation Evaluation of an advertising or marketing campaign as a whole, quite separately from consideration of its constituent parts. *See* Atomistic evaluation.

Hologram   A special effect three-dimensional picture as used on credit cards for instance.

Home audit   Form of research in which a panel of homes keeps records of purchases of specified goods; usually FMCG. *See also* Dustbin check.

Home market   Geographical area or country in which an organization's headquarters are based, usually referred to as such by executives selling in the country where they are based.

Home sales   Sales in the home market.

Homogeneous goods   Competing products or brands with little or no real differences between them.

Honorific   A title used to precede a name, such as Mrs, Mr, Miss, Ms.

Horizontal integration   Grouping together, say, by acquisition, two or more firms having the same manufacturing operations for the same product range. *See* Vertical integration.

Horizontal market   One in which buyers from many different industries purchase a common product or service, e.g. a computer, typewriters. *See also* Vertical market.

Horizontal publication   Business publication aimed at readers in similar job categories over a variety of different industries, e.g. *Management Today. See* Vertical circulation.

Host   A term used when computers are connected to a common physical network to describe the computer resource which 'serves' the programmes for use by PC users.

Hot-line list   In database marketing, the names of customers and prospects most recently entered.

Hot shop   Creative studio which puts high value on novelty and topicality in the preparation of its advertising copy and designs.

House account Significant customer, usually serviced at management level; because of the volume of business transacted, prices are keen and leave little or no opportunity for the payment of commission on sales. In many cases, house accounts business makes the difference between profit and loss and the relationship therefore is usually close and strong. They many consist of a company's earliest customers who have grown along with it. *See also* National account.

House agency An advertising agency wholly owned and operated by a large business organization to which it provides services which are, however, not necessarily exclusive to that organization. Similarly such an organization may additionally or alternatively use the services of independent agencies.

House list A mailing list produced by the company itself and mostly comprising enquiries, sales leads, and customers. Sometimes rented out to other, non-competitive marketing companies. Response rate and level of accuracy usually better than a commercially available list.

House magazine Periodical published by a company or other organization for public relations and/or sales promotional purposes. Usually in one of two main forms, either purely external for influencing custom, or internal for employee motivation, although the former may be circulated internally and the latter known by those outside the firm's employ. Also known as House organ or House journal.

House mailing Mailing your own list.

House organ *See* House magazine.

House style Characteristic and standardized form which is applied throughout a company to such items as letter headings, publications, advertisements, vehicles and packaging. Usually includes a distinctive logotype design for instant recognition.

House-to-house   Calling direct on potential consumers and users at their own homes for purposes of distributing or collecting information, leaving samples or direct selling.

Household   Designation of the single family unit for research survey purposes.

Household names   Brand names with established reputations known virtually to the entire population. Sometimes may be used for well-known brands not quite so commonly accepted.

Housewife time   On radio, the time between the morning and afternoon Drive times.

Human resources   A term which is now mostly used in place of 'personnel'.

Hype   Short for hyperbole – an exaggeration.

Hypermarket   Larger self-service unit with minimum sales area of 2500 square metres offering an assortment of food and non-food merchandise at popular prices; often provides extensive parking facilities and associated with out-of-town shopping; often called superstores but to be distinguished from discount houses. Operation varies between retailer providing a number of shopping departments or, more usually, a site operation leasing space to different kinds of retail concerns.

Hypertext   One of the most modern techniques used to allow people to 'navigate' through an electronic document. The hypertext links are permanent internal electronic ties which facilitate access to most needed data items.

Hypnoidal trance   Bordering on sleep, may appear whilst watching or listening to broadcasts. Considered a prime time to achieve the placebo effect, the power of suggestion.

Hypothesis testing   Determining the correctness of assumed parameters, usually by sampling techniques.

I

IBM-compatible A computer which can use hardware and software designed for the IBM PC.

IBM PC (International Business Machines Personal Computer) Single-user personal computers (PCs) manufactured by IBM and based on the Intel family of microprocessors. IBM PCs and compatible models from other vendors are the most widely used computer systems in the world.

IC (Integrated circuit) A single semi-conductor comprising an electronic circuit and all its constituent components.

Iceberg principle Psychological concept suggesting human personality is similar in appearance to that of an iceberg, with innate desires hidden deep down under the surface. Advertisers recognize that influencing people to move in any given direction frequently demands an appeal to their less apparent desires.

Icon A graphical on-screen representation of a software program, function, menu item, hardware peripheral, etc., used extensively in GUI applications (e.g. the icon for the 'File Manager' utility in Microsoft Windows is a 3-D representation of an office filing cabinet).

Identification Establishing common relationship between factors.

Illuminated interior panels Small posters placed above the windows of a double decker bus, and illuminated.

Illuminated posters Translucent posters lit from behind, to be seen at airports, hotels, shopping precincts, etc.

Illustration Picture, painting, drawing or other visual element used in an advertisement or publication in order to enhance its effectiveness in terms of informing and motivating. Further, it integrates with the copy in order to add to the attention value and to provide an integrated message. *See* Visual *and* Scamp.

144

ILR (Independent Local Radio)   General term referring to commercial radio stations.

Image   Composite mental picture formed by people about an organization or its products, e.g. brand image, conception of a product in the market place.

Image advertising   In product promotion this activity is more concerned with the perception of the product rather than its specific benefits or attributes, i.e. enhancing its brand image. Its use, however, is more commonly applied to the organization where its purpose is to establish and strengthen the corporate image or reputation. As such, it is a sub-set of public relations. Also referred to as Corporate advertising, Prestige advertising, or Institutional advertising, which *see*.

Image audit   A methodical assessment of the perception of a company by isolating every message source and applying the question 'What impression would this give of the company? Good, bad or neutral. Each message source can be weighted according to its importance in company/brand imagery. *See* Message source.

IMF   *See* International Monetary Fund.

Impact   Force with which an advertising or promotional message registers in a person's mind.

Impactaplan   *See* Preselected campaign (PSC).

Impacts   The number of exposures of a particular advertisement to a target audience.

Implementation   Putting into practice all the tactics outlined in the marketing or marketing communications plan, having regard to resource limitations and to the timescale involved.

Implied condition of sale   Part of the Sale of Goods Act 1979, giving parties to a sale their rights and duties.

Import   Goods or services from a foreign country.

Import duty Tax levied on imported goods.

Import quota Restriction on the quantity of goods which are permitted to be imported.

Imposition The number of pages on a printing press e.g. 8, 12, or 16, such that they are correctly positioned when cut and bound.

Impression cover Number of insertions it takes to cover the required percentage of population actually seeing the advertisement or commercial.

Imprint Sign, symbol or code used in print work to identify such factors as print quantity, date, supplier or other such information.

Imprinting Attitudes and beliefs, left in the subconscious during childhood, conditioning behaviour in adulthood.

Impulse goods Products which are purchased on the spur of the moment without any previous consideration.

Impulse purchase One made without careful prior consideration, i.e. on the spur of the moment or even in contradiction to normal buying behaviour and sometimes without apparent rational or logical justification.

Imputed costs Sum of opportunity costs for economic resources employed in an organization.

In-bound telemarketing A system set up to receive and process incoming telephone calls, usually in response to an advertising or other promotional campaign. Increasingly, the procedure is being automated with an answering machine which instructs callers to take further action to receive the service they require. Customers have been known to be highly critical of the latter practice with its lack of personal or human contact. *See also* Out-bound telemarketing.

In-flight magazine Periodical published by airlines for the benefit of passengers.

In-home media All those media which are seen in the home, such as newspapers, magazines, television and radio, as against posters and exhibitions, for instance.

In-home placement Pre-testing a product by putting out a number to customers who use or try it and report back their experiences.

In-home use test In which a number of products are placed in a sample of typical homes for people to try out, evaluate and report back. A form of pre-product testing.

In-house Activities conducted within the business as against putting them out to a specialist supplier, e.g. producing one's own advertising rather than using an advertising agency.

In-pack premium Gift offer contained within a pack, as opposed to appearing on the outside of the container, in the media or within the sales outlet.

In-pro A reproduced illustration, enlarged or reduced in proportion to the original.

In-store interview One of a number of research interviewing techniques in which a respondent is questioned in a shopping situation.

In-store promotion Promotional activity located within a sales outlet.

In-theatre research A market research activity in which people are assembled in a hall, room or theatre in order to obtain their reaction to a proposed commercial or other advertisement. *See also* Hall test.

Incentive marketing Function of providing special additional reasons for making a purchase, such as tactical pricing, competitions, premium offers, trading stamps. At one time, known as consumer promotions. In recent years, has assumed a major importance in marketing activity.

Incentive/reusable packs Promotional device offering attractive containers available for some subsequent use by the consumer. Frequently encountered in food and drink products.

Income Flow of payments accruing to an individual or organization during a stated period of time. Also known as revenue and usually contrasted with expenditures in the same period for budgetary or accounting purposes.

Income distribution National income divided among households to produce an average, useful for comparison with other markets.

Income velocity of circulation Measurement of the rate at which money is circulating through an economy.

Incremental demands Additional costs or time to be consumed as the result of additional activity, but where part of the additional costs are absorbed by existing facilities or manpower.

Indent To commence a line of type at a 'distance in' from the left hand margin.

Independent local radio *See* ILR.

Independent retailer A shop which is owned by one person or company, i.e., not part of a chain.

Independent variable Variable subject to chance or choice factors which has an observed causal effect upon the behaviour of other variables.

Indexing Statistical term describing a method of standardizing the base for comparative data in a time series, usually equating the initial measure to 100 and then expressing all other data in exact relation to that base, e.g. the index of wholesale prices in any year by comparison with a base year of 100 might stand at 92 or 108 to indicate a fall or rise of 8 per cent respectively.

Indirect costs Any expenditure in a business other than that incurred directly by a specific cost unit.

Industrial advertising Advertising of products or services to industrial, commercial or business organizations. Usually relates to industrial or technical products but essentially refers to any purchase of goods or services which might be made by any such organization to distinguish it from advertising directed at consumer markets.

Industrial buying behaviour The elements which comprise the factors and motivations which go into organizational purchasing. *See also* Decision-making unit, Buying motives, *and* Buy classes.

Industrial goods Usually refers to such products as machinery, manufacturing plant or raw materials. Essentially, they are goods sold to industry as opposed to consumers.

Industrial marketing *See* Business-to-business marketing.

Industrial selling Selling to industry for industrial consumption, e.g. catering or fuel products, but more usually goods required for further production, e.g. raw materials and machinery.

Inelastic demand *See* Elasticity of demand.

Inertia Resistance to change in individuals and/or organizations; considered one of the major problems confronting marketing effort.

Inertia selling Goods delivered to a prospect upon a sale-or-return basis without the previous consent or knowledge of the prospect. Legally, the recipient is not obliged to retain or pay for such goods and has the right of disposal in UK if reasonable notice is first given to the sender.

Inferior goods (1) Relative term denoting goods the demand for which tends to fall as incomes of their purchasers rise. (2) Descriptive term relating to goods not of a required standard.

Inflation An economic phenomenon in which decreasing purchasing power of a currency is caused by a persistent tendency of prices to rise, often sharply. Compare with deflation.

Inflationary spiral An upward trend in prices which may have been caused by an increase in wages and/or may be the cause of such increases.

Influencer An important member of the Decision making unit, which *see*. Any person within an organization, or, indeed, a family unit, who can affect the outcome of a purchasing decision.

Infomercial A paid-for television programme purporting to be a genuine station programme. Its use is restricted to certain countries including the USA, but not the UK. Similar in practice to an Advertorial, which *see*.

Informal group Association of individuals brought together by common association, without any formal organizational structure but not necessarily lacking leadership. Elton Mayo's researches in the USA uncovered the existence of many such groups within the industrial community.

Informant Person answering or supplying answers to research questions. *See* Respondent.

Information super highway The name coined by US Vice-President Al Gore in the early 1990s for the then emerging high-speed global communications network capable of carrying voice, data, video and other services around the world. Ultimately these services will be accessible in the home via TV 'set-top boxes' or suitably equipped computers.

Information system *See* IS.

Information technology *See* IT.

Informational advertising Basic style of advertising based on dissemination of product or service information.

Infrastructure Basic support services for computing.

Initial sale First time purchase by a customer who then becomes a prospect for repeat purchase.

Ink-jet printer A type of printer which utilizes an electrostatic ink spray to form an image on the paper.

Ink-jet printing A printing process in which there is no contact between the printing head and the paper being printed. Based upon a computer controlled system.

Inland waterways Network of canals, rivers, and locks intended for conveyance of goods but, due to the competition of faster means of transport, is often used nowadays for pleasure craft and the provision of marinas.

Inner pack One of a number of packs which are then stored in multiple containers, e.g. twenty individual cartons of cigarettes might be wrapped as a unit, a number of which are then packed in a fibreboard case.

Innovation Introduction of new thoughts, policies, products, markets, distribution, merchandising or other deliberate change. Given that, all things being equal, all products have a life cycle which dictates that, at some point, their usefulness will decline, innovation is an essential ingredient to long-term development of commercial enterprise and its absence must lead to the decline of the enterprise itself.

Input The transfer of data or information into a computer memory from an external peripheral device (e.g. a terminal).

Inquiry The initial request from a prospective buyer or user for information, often following some form of advertising or sales promotion, usually with a particular purchase in mind or consideration. *See* Sales lead.

Inquiry test Method of testing advertisements or media by comparing the number of inquiries received. *See* Cost per inquiry.

Insert Piece of sales promotional material placed into the pages of a publication, either loosely or bound in. Sometimes encountered as 'inset' but this usage is not recommended since 'inset' more usually refers to the insertion of a separate photograph or chart within an overall illustration.

Insertion weights Used for weighting advertising expenditure; means of varying expenditure according to the impression value of alternative publications. It reflects the likelihood of an advertisement being seen.

Inside covers Two so called premium positions in a magazine, namely, inside back and inside front. Usually an extra charge is made though there is very little evidence, for instance page traffic data, to demonstrate any advertising superiority.

Instalment The means by which goods are paid for over a period of time rather than a lump sum. Has the effect of being perceived as a lower financial outlay.

Instant Term frequently applied to preprepared products of high convenience value, especially foodstuffs.

Instinct Innate, unlearned, unchangeable behaviour in response to the stimuli of a normal environment, such responses being normal to a species.

Institutional advertising *See* Corporate advertising, to which it is very similar. Institutional advertising, however, refers especially to advertising undertaken for whole industries rather than to individual corporations, e.g. Eat More Fruit.

Institutional market   Commonly regarded as those organizations which have people in their care, e.g. hospitals, schools, churches and prisons.

Intaglio   Printing from a depressed surface.

Integrated circuit   *See* IC.

Integrated marketing   The bringing together of all marketing communications so as to have common or complementary messages, themes, visual identity, response mechanisms and timing. Also, to interrelate with the sales force and other elements in the marketing plan. The rationale is that by so doing, the outcome will be synergistic.

Integrated marketing communications   Where each of the media being used in a campaign is co-ordinated in time, message and graphics, and so results in a synergistic overall effect.

Integration   A strategy aimed at increasing profit and/or sales turnover and/or market share by acquiring other companies in related fields. There are three forms of integration: backward integration whereby a company acquires one or more of its suppliers; forward integration in which some part of the distribution is taken over; and, finally, the most common form – horizontal integration – in which acquisition of some of the competition takes place. *See* Acquisition *and* Diversification.

Intensive interview   Technique used in marketing research to endeavour to formulate a true pattern of human behaviour by a process of continued patient probing into beliefs and desires.

Intensive selling   Selling a greater volume to present customers through energetic promotional drive.

Interactive television   A means by which goods may be purchased or information obtained directly from the home by means of video and computer/telecommunications technology.

Intercept interview A common form of research in which an interviewer stops people, either at random or based upon some predetermined criteria, in order to ask questions. Locations are chosen to be appropriate to the desired market segment and so might range from a shopping mall to an airport; or holiday beach to an industrial exhibition.

Interface (1) Meeting between two or more parties whose differing interests have in some way to be reconciled. (2) The point at which two computer systems, or elements of a system, meet, allowing connection and exchange of data.

Interfirm comparisons Service pioneered in the UK by the British Institute of Management in which information is mutually exchanged between firms, usually in the same business, upon a confidential basis, with a view to establishing objective, practical criteria against which to evaluate comparative levels of activity and performance.

Interleaves Sheets of paper placed between printed paper in order to prevent wet ink being set-off or transferred to the adjoining sheet. *See* Set-off.

Intermedia comparisons Comparing one medium against another or others according to cost, characteristics of the audience, and the atmosphere of the audience. *See* Intramedia comparisons.

Internal communications A developing public relations activity concerned with informing and motivating existing employees, sometimes referred to as Employee communications. Also part of the growing discipline of Internal marketing, which *see*.

Internal house magazine *See* House magazine.

Internal image audit An assessment by one's own members of staff of the perceptions they feel outside people (e.g. customers) have of the company. An internal audit may well be followed by an external one. *See* Image audit.

Internal marketing In which all employees are regarded as being in marketing, the only difference being as to whether they are in customer facing positions, or providing a service to those who are. An essential ingredient to Relationship marketing, which *see*.

International When referring to a Company, indicates that it not only trades in a number of countries but also has bases in them, either wholly or partly owned. *See also* Multinational.

International marketing Conducting marketing operation simultaneously in a number of countries but with some degree of co-ordination.

International Monetary Fund An institution arising from the Bretton Woods Agreement in 1944, the fund being established from 1946. Its primary object is to maintain and stabilize international rates of exchange. It is also expected to provide facilities for arranging multilateral clearing systems and to help to eliminate restrictions on international trade. The IMF is often used by countries as a world bank, particularly when facing balance of payment difficulties, each country having drawing rights against present and anticipated contributions to the fund.

Internet A world-wide collection of interlinked computer networks providing its subscribers with E-mail, on-line databases and other information services (e.g. World Wide Web).

Interpolation Mathematical term referring to the technique of judging a value or values between known value points. More generally, it may be used to describe the process of drawing conclusions from known data.

Interval sample *See* Random sample.

Interview (1) Contact between parties, either face-to-face or through a communications medium, e.g. telephonic or postal means. (2) Market research interviewer obtaining information. (3) Sales-people giving information and obtaining data as basis for a sales transaction.

Interviewer Person who administers an interview with a respondent in a market research programme: usually one-to-one.

Interviewer bias A situation in which an interviewer derives an inaccurate response from an interviewee as a result of the way in which questions are asked, by leading or explaining in some way, or non-verbal signals, such as body language. Also by influencing respondent selection so as to misrepresent the target group.

Intra-firm data Company internal costing and statistics, basis of budgetary control and decision-making.

Intramedia comparisons Comparing publications or channels one against another or others within the same medium. *See* Intermedia comparisons.

Intransient Applies to messages transmitted and capable of retention, such as those within newspapers or magazines. Television and/or radio messages are transient, i.e. transitory, and, although the meaning or content of the communication may be retained, it will be a matter of memory or notation rather than sight of the original message. (This distinction may possibly become obsolete with the spread of techniques of audio/video recording.)

Introductory offer Special incentive offered to induce trial purchases on the launch of a product or service.

Inventory (1) Complete detail of a company's assets. (2) Complete detail of values of raw materials, work in progress, and finished goods. (3) Frequently used as synonymous with stock.

Inverse demand pattern In which the usually accepted laws of supply and demand do not apply. As price increases so does demand.

Investor relations A deliberate and planned programme of activities intended to strengthen relationships with, and perceptions of, shareholders and prospects, analysts, and other financial advisers such as accountants and banks. Can be regarded as synonymous with financial relations though some would hold that the latter covers a wider range of publics.

Invisible exports Items such as financial services, included in the current balance of payments, that are not physically tangible as exports.

Invisible trade Earnings from overseas for the provision of services to people living abroad, including foreigners and revenue from investments in foreign enterprises.

Invitation to treat Retailers putting goods on show in shop windows or display cabinets are inviting people to make an offer – the retailer is not, as is popularly believed, making any offer. Customers make the offer and, by so doing, enable the shop-owner to accept. The term is a legal expression for this principle which, of course, applies equally to advertisements and to the use of illustrated catalogues as sales media.

Invoice Document listing the charges being set against a buyer in consideration of goods or services supplied. A bill.

Invoice discount Obtaining credit on the security of book debts (money owed) at a discount. Applies to companies with money tied up with debtors, especially finance houses.

I/O (Input/output) A combination of input and output, particularly prevalent in computer error messages, e.g. 'I/O error' where problems exist between a processor and one or more of its peripheral devices.

IR *See* Investor relations.

IS (Information system) An interrelation of procedures, processes and operations which combine to produce a defined objective. An information system need not be computer-based, but the term is generally used where computerization is a contributory element of the system. A typical example of an information system would be a payroll system.

Island display Self-standing unit in a retail outlet, typically a supermarket, in which goods are presented in an eye-catching way in order to attract extra sales.

Island position Advertisement surrounded entirely by editorial or margin. Also known as Solus position.

Island site   Exhibition stand surrounded on all four sides by gangways.

ISO Paper sizes   International metric paper sizes for printing paper and board. The most common size being A4 which is the accepted format for business stationery, brochures and booklets.

Issue advertising   *See* Advocacy advertising.

Issue life   Period between publication dates. A publication's life is said to have terminated once a subsequent issue of the same name has been released. Refers specifically to newspaper and magazine *advertising*; of course, their text matter may be retained and subsequently consulted.

Issue readership (average)   Number of readers, on average, who read a publication.

Issues   Internal and external factors which might increase or decrease the likelihood of achieving the objectives of a marketing, or marketing communications plan.

Issues management   The identification of issues, which affect an organization in PR terms, and preparing a plan of action to manage them to the best advantage. *See* Crisis management.

IT (Information technology)   Strictly speaking a sub-set of an information system where such a system relies on computer-based processes, but is generally used as a portmanteau phrase covering the production of information by computerized data processing techniques.

Italics   Style of typography in which a particular typeface is given a *slant* to the right, and sometimes a finer stroke, in order to give emphasis.

J

Jar (1) A wide mouthed container, usually of glass, stoneware, or plastic (BS 3170). (2) Glass container usually for high viscosity materials such as pastes and greases.

Jerque note Certificate issued by Customs when they are satisfied that cargo is in order.

Jiffy bags Lightweight padded envelopes to give extra protection to the enclosed goods.

Jingle Short tune to which the advertising message of a television, radio, or cinema commercial is sung. Not necessarily an original tune since often different words are sung to an already familiar tune.

JIT *See* Just-in-time.

Job One of the oldest computer terms used to describe a task that you want a computer, usually a mainframe, to do.

Job evaluation Determination of the value of a job in relative or absolute terms, usually with a view to fixing the rate of pay, but also has a motivation aspect.

Job selling (1) Disposing of unwanted remainders in bulk and at a low price. (2) Selling units, usually capital equipment produced in low volume, against limited demand and established specification.

Job sheet Typically used in an advertising agency in order to progress a given client assignment for both production purposes and for charging out. Often used with a job bag which contains material in connection with the project.

Job specification Definition of tasks to be undertaken in relation to a specific job category. Also includes responsibilities and functions in connection with other activities within an organization.

Joint venture   In which two or more companies collaborate in a common enterprise, e.g. to join forces in attacking a particular overseas market.

Jollies   Jet-setting Oldies with Lots of Loot.

Journey cycle   *See* Calling cycle.

Journey planning   Organizing the salesperson's route, rate(s) of call, and customer priority rating so as to make his/her selling as cost effective as possible. *See* Call rate.

Judgement sample   Group selected without use of statistical methods in order to obtain its views and ideas. Usually comprises the more important figures in a particular sector. (A major constituent of the Delphi method of forecasting – *see* Forecasting.)

Jumbo pack   Large economy pack of consumable products, e.g. detergents, beer, wine, coffee.

Junk mail   Unsolicited mail.

Just-in-time (JIT)   An arrangement between a supplier and a customer whereby deliveries of a product are timed precisely to coincide with the need for that product. Saves unnecessary capital tied up in stock waiting to be used. Such an arrangement means that the two companies involved have, in effect, a Partnership, which *see*.

Justify   To adjust the position of words on a printed page so that the left or the right hand margin is regular (BS 3527).

K

KD Knock down which *see*.

Keen price Low price. *See* Competitive price.

Kerbside conferences Post-interview discussion between a salesperson and his/her sales supervisor, involving analysis of selling method, performance and achievement.

Key factors Essential elements of a given marketing or other situation, i.e. those factors which are crucial to achieving a specified goal.

Key prospects Group of buyers within a market who hold the greatest proportionate potential purchasing power.

Keyed advertisement Advertisement designed to cause an enquirer to indicate the source of his/her information, for instance by including a code number or a particular 'department' within the return address.

Keyline Line drawing showing in outline the positioning of all the visual elements of an advertisement or other promotional piece. Alternatively, on an overlay to show where some extra treatment is required, e.g. a second colour. *See* Overlay.

Kickback Secret commission which is illegal, paid to a person who helps to expedite a business transaction, e.g. a government employee in relation to an official contract.

Kill Action of media in deciding not to carry an available story or news item.

Kilobyte A thousand bytes.

Kiosk A free-standing unit, usually in a retail store, which contains promotional material or selling information. May or may not be staffed. Increasingly kiosks are providing video technology to enable orders to be placed directly, and for further information to be accessed.

KISS principle (Keep It Simple Stupid)   Term used to apply to persons who are verbose, garrulous, or ambiguous.

Kitemark   Registered symbol of the British Standards Institution.

Knockdown (KD)   (1) Goods which are supplied in unassembled form but with all the components and instructions necessary for their completion. Has particular application to furniture, mail order and certain export shipments. (2) Taking down an exhibition stand at the end of a show.

Knocking competition   Deriding the quality of competitors' products or services.

Knocking copy   Advertisement copy which deliberately exposes competitive products to adverse comparison(s).

Kraft board   Paperboard noted for its strength and water-resistant characteristics, manufactured from bleached or unbleached sulphite wood pulp. Main use is in packaging.

Kraft paper   Paper, usually brown, and noted for its strength. Much used in packaging.

L

Label   Card, tag, patch or other attachment to a product or package in order to give it a particular identity.

Labour costs   That part of the cost of a product which is paid to the workforce.

Labour-intensive   A production process with a large involvement of labour as against capital equipment.

Ladder of customer loyalty Seven steps towards the ultimate customer: Suspect, Prospect, Customer, Client, Supporter, Advocate and Partnership. *See* elsewhere for definitions.

Laid paper High quality paper characterized by parallel watermark lines.

Laissez faire Philosophy in which it is held that governmental involvement in business should be kept to a minimum, consistent with a basic level of legal protection regarding breaches of contract, safety measures and fair dealing.

Lame duck A business which is in financial difficulties.

Laminate (1) Two or more sheets of material bonded together either to produce simply a thicker, stronger medium, or, where different materials are laminated, to combine various desired properties. An example of the latter would be a foil-laminated board which provides a decorative finish with a rigid base. (2) Thin clear film applied by heat to printed brochures, etc., to protect surface or to give a glossy or matt finish.

LAN (Local area network) A physical installation of special computer cabling which allows many computers in the same local area (office block) to use and share information.

Lanchester theory Known also as Lanchester's Square Law in which the number of incidences, contacts or events has a greater outcome than the sum of the parts: nearer to the square, e.g. the effectiveness of a committee decreases as the square of the number of members. Similarly, if one company has a sales call rate of four times a month, and a competitor of eight times, the effect is considerably more than double.

Landscape Describes an illustration or piece of print where the width is greater than its height.

Laptop computer A portable personal computer of a size suitable to rest comfortably on a user's lap.

Laser Acronym for 'Light Amplification by Stimulated Emission of Radiation'.

Laser personalization In reproduction, a method of producing personalization and text in one pass.

Laser printer A printer which uses laser technology to produce a high-resolution image on paper.

Last in first out (LIFO) Principle frequency used by trade union negotiators considering redundancy plans.

Latent demand Made up of people unaware of a product's existence or its beneficial advantage.

Lateral diversification Company entering a new area of business activity not related to its present field, e.g. brewers entering field of drugs (antibiotics). Compare with vertical integration.

Launch To introduce a new product or service on to the market with some special campaign or activity.

Laundromat Mechanically operated laundry using vending machines and often operating as part of a franchising operation or alternatively by a concessionaire arrangement.

Law of demand The theory that the higher the price, the lower the demand and vice versa. With some goods, e.g. luxuries, the very opposite happens; also with any other goods or service where a pre-purchase evaluation is difficult. In this case, price is taken as a measure of quality, e.g. perfume or a seminar. *See* Demand.

Law of diminishing returns Economic 'law' which states that, while extra units of input critically increase output, perhaps more than proportionately, the rate of return will flatten out, increasing by steadily smaller amounts until ultimately more units of the same kind will have a negative effect. For example, that £X spent on advertising may bring a return of £Y in sales, but twice the amount spent (£2X), may bring only £1.5Y; the *rate* of return has fallen even though the overall amount of return has increased.

Law of supply and demand   Refers to the interrelation between demand, supply and price. As demand increases a higher price can be charged which in turn will encourage an increase in supply. Similarly an increase in supply will tend to depress prices. In marketing practice this law has to be viewed with caution since in certain cases a high price is taken as being indicative of high quality, in which case an unduly low price may lead to a low demand.

Layout   Accurate position guide of an advertisement or piece of literature showing the location of each visual element in relation to the other in order to permit review before printing commences. *See* Visual.

LCD (Liquid crystal display)   A display technology mainly used on screens for portable PCs because of their low power consumption and flat design.

Lead   Selling opportunity where an interest in purchasing has already been established. (Pronounced 'leed'.)

Lead generation   An activity designed to obtain names and addresses of potential customers. In the past, a function of the sales force. Nowadays taken over by marketing communications. *See* Response mechanisms.

Lead time   Gap between initiating an idea and its realization or achievement. *See* Gestation period.

Leader   Leading article in a publication; normally a newspaper's formal view of the events of the day.

Leaders   A line of dots, dashes, or other typographical characters used in lists, tables, etc., to guide the eye across the space from one item to the next.

Leading   In letterpress printing, putting space into text or typematter usually between lines. This is achieved by locking lead blocks into the printing forme. (Pronounced 'ledding'.)

Leading question (1) Particularly pointed question suggesting further unrevealed particulars. (2) Question in market research suggesting a particular answer is sought – otherwise known as *loading* a question.

Leaf A single sheet of paper.

Leaflet Printed piece of paper, single or folded-over to make four pages. It can be stitched with additional sheets to make into more pages. Term is, however, usually applied to a publication with no more than twelve pages, i.e. three folded sheets. *See* Brochure.

Leasing Practice in business whereby a firm may, for a continuing consideration, obtain the use of a piece of equipment or other plant without purchasing it. Of particular interest where new technology is likely to lead to premature obsolescence.

Least squares Statistical technique for identifying best fitting trend line through a collection of non-linear data points.

Legal tender Form of money which is acceptable in legal settlement of a debt. In UK, Bank of England notes of any denomination up to any amount and 'silver' up to £2.

Legend Title or description of an illustration. *See* Caption.

Letter of credit Document issued by a bank supporting a transaction, usually for foreign trade. A stronger guarantee is provided by the so-called 'irrevocable' letter of credit.

Letter of indemnity Document guaranteeing to cover another party against loss or default.

Letter of intent A written communication confirming that a certain agreed course of action is going to take place, or at least it is the intention that it should do so.

Letter spacing Insertion of space between the letters of a word in order to make it more legible, to stand out, or to take up extra space in order to 'justify' a line of type.

Letterbox marketing   Hand distribution of promotional material with or without free local newspapers.

Letterhead   Formal printed stationery in which the name of a company is printed at the top of the paper, often in a characteristic 'house style'. Such stationery will also include address, telephone and fax numbers, and often names of directors, logotypes, symbols, slogans and other matter.

Letterpress   Obsolescent form of commercial printing. Consists of raised printing surfaces bearing characters upon which ink is deposited and subsequently transferred to paper.

Leverage   Synonym for Gearing, i.e. ratio of debt to equity.

Library music   Recordings of music for hire to build into television or radio commercials.

Library shot   Photograph from outside agency which holds stocks of frequently required scenes, e.g. aircraft, ships, resorts, etc.

Licensee   A person or organization which is authorized to undertake certain business transactions 'under licence'.

Licensing   Legal arrangement transferring the rights to manufacture, or to market a product. Such an arrangement, also known as franchising, is usually formalized by contract in which there is a consideration, perhaps in the form of a regular fee, or of a commission or royalty. For the licensing company, it represents a means of expanding demand from new markets, without incurring a high speculative investment. For the licensee, it reduces the need to generate new product development, facilitates lower setting up and operating costs and thereby diminishes the degree of business risk.

Licensor   The holder of a patent or some other such exclusive right, and who assigns to a third party the right to make use of it.

Lien   Right of seller to hold goods in possession when the price is not paid, even when not the owner.

167

Life cycle Descriptive term for the stage of life, of childhood, teenage, young marrieds with children, middle age and retirement. Mostly used in market research.

Life cycle analysis Applying quantitative techniques to product life cycle in an attempt to predict future trends. Often involves study of deviations from earlier projections.

Life cycle (Product life cycle) Term relating to a generally accepted hypothesis that all products are subject to a pattern of demand which after it starts, grows, stabilizes for a period, then tends to decline and finally disappear. Whilst demand curves differ in rates of change, shape and time span, the life cycle contention is that all products have both a beginning and an end. This dictates the need for new product development; the order of time scale determines the intensity with which such development takes place.

Life cycle profiling Monitoring progress of different products within the range so as to ensure adequate provision of new products to replace those about to enter decline.

Life style Way of living, in the broadest sense, of a society or segment of that society. Includes both work and leisure, eating, drinking, dress, patterns of behaviour and allocation of income. *See* Family life style.

Lifetime customer A concept whereby one evaluates a customer in terms of the likely business to accrue both now and in the future. An intrinsic component of relationship marketing.

Light pen A light-sensitive device for 'reading' a bar code.

Light reader People whose reading of periodicals and publications are below average. *See also* Light viewer.

Light viewers People whose television viewing is below average.

Line block Printing block for reproducing line illustrations. Face of metal is solid, without any halftone or screen.

Line chart Two-dimensional diagram showing relationship between two different sets of data.

Line drawing Pictorial illustration in solid lines only, without any tones.

Line manager Functional head, with powers of command and carrying executive responsibility as compared with staff appointments with merely advisory powers.

Lineage Method of charging for classified advertising by the line.

Linear programming Any procedure for locating the maximum or minimum of a linear function of variables which are subject to linear constraints and inequalities (BS 3527).

Lickert scale A system in market research in which respondents are asked to indicate their perceptions of the importance and then the strength of feelings about a given issue.

Liquid crystal display *See* LCD.

Liquidation Legal process bringing the life of a company to an end.

Liquidity Extent to which a company has available cash resources to meet its obligations.

List *See* Mailing list.

List broker Organization or individual supplying on commission mailing lists of specific categories of people representing markets or segments of a market, e.g. teachers, garage owners, doctors.

List cleaning The practice of removing incorrect or out-of-date names from a mailing list. Can only be achieved with any certainty by telephoning each name on the list.

List exchange In which two non-competing companies make use of one another's mailing lists. Maybe selling parallel products to the same market.

List manager Person who looks after, edits and updates a mailing list.

List price The basic, recommended or retail price published by the supplier, without allowance for any possible discounts.

List rental The means of obtaining access to an outside mailing list. Usually on a one-off basis for which a fee is charged, and which must be used through a recognized mailing house. Rented lists are expected to contain a number of Sleepers or Seeds, which *see*.

List sample A representative number of names taken from a mailing list and used for a test mailing prior to the main campaign.

Literal Typographical error requiring correction before printing commences.

Lithography Form of printing process from a flat as opposed to a raised surface. Ink impression is obtained by chemical treatment of surface such that certain areas retain ink whilst others reject it.

Litter bin advertising In which litter bins are partly or wholly paid for by charging a fee for the use of the sides for advertising.

Live customers Active customers who are still trading and likely to continue trading with any particular company.

Live programme Performance and broadcast transmitted simultaneously.

Livery Distinctive dress or appearance of staff, equipment and communications of a particular company. *See* House style.

Loaded question *See* Leading question.

Local area network *See* LAN.

Local press Local newspapers, usually covering a borough or rural district. Published once or twice a week. *See* Provincial press.

Location   Real-life setting for still or motion photography or for television filming, as opposed to an artificial setting.

Lock-up premises   Building, such as a shop, which has no living accommodation, and thus has to be 'locked up' each night.

Log in/out   The act of the user signing on to and off from a computer session. A common feature of multi-user systems, logging in usually requires the user to enter a user name or ID recognizable by the computer, sometimes accompanied by a password, before access is granted by the system.

Logistics   Term borrowed from the military, describing the science and practice of estimating the likely flows and timings of company resources for any particular project or campaign and providing the means to achieve them. Primarily used in physical distribution management and the control of materials transfer and stock holdings.

Logotype   Commonly used to describe a company symbol, badge or name style.

Long-range plan   Quantitative plan of development for the future, usually at least five years. *See* Corporate planning.

Loose inserts   Advertisements distributed separately with a publication, and usually inserted loosely within its pages. *See* Insert.

Lorenz distribution   In which the majority of purchases of a product are made by a relatively few customers, e.g. aircraft components.

Loss leader   Product offered at cost price or less to increase store traffic.

Lost order reports   Reports explaining why particular orders – usually contracts – have not been obtained or renewed.

Lottery   Giving away prizes chosen by chance or by lot.

Low involvement products   *See* Impulse goods.

Low pressure selling   Concentration on winning customers' confidence and respect for long-term gains rather than gaining one particular order. Sometimes known as soft selling.

Lower case   Printing convention designating small letters, as against capital letters, which are referred to as upper case.

Loyalty factor   Supposition that the more a periodical is read the more likely it is that its readers will pay attention to its contents.

Loyalty marketing   An extension of Brand loyalty (which *see*) in which some additional incentive is offered for doing business with a given supplier, such as joining a club and obtaining some financial benefit as a result.

M

Machine proof   Proof taken directly from the printing machine for immediate checking.

Machine readable code   *See* Bar code.

Macintosh   Not a raincoat but one of the first 'user friendly' personal computers which utilised graphical user interfaces. Main rival to IBM PC and clones.

Macro marketing   Overview of society's needs in the interplay of marketing actions within a country's economy. *See also* Micro marketing.

Macro media   *See* Mass media.

Magazine   (1) Periodical, usually published weekly or monthly, and catering for special interest groups. (2) Container used to feed supplies into a mechanism, e.g. slide-projector.

Magnetic film   Generic term for film coated with substance capable of retaining magnetic variations transferred to it by a magnetic head on a recorder. Used for the sound or audio input for a film, for example.

Magnetic sound track   Sound track recorded on magnetic tape, in much the same way as on a domestic tape recorder.

Magnetic tape   Usually plastic strip coated with magnetic recording medium. *See* Magnetic film.

Mail drop   Circular distribution by hand.

Mail-in   Gift offer to be claimed through the post.

Mail-in premium   Awarding a gift as a result of a consumer sending in an application, usually requiring proof of purchase.

Mail-merge   To merge copy (such as a 'form letter') with data and mailing lists so as to personalize each item of the output.

Mail order   Distribution channel. Customers buy direct by post either in response to an advertisement or from a sales promotional catalogue. Deliveries are made through the mail, by carrier direct from warehouse or factory, or sometimes through a local agent.

Mailbox   The repository for messages exchanged over an electronic mail (E-mail) system.

Mailing list   Classified list of names and addresses suitable for distributing mailing shots. May be purchased or built up over time but requires careful maintenance to keep in an up-to-date condition.

Mailing piece   Letter, leaflet or other article sent through the post on a widespread basis. *See* Direct mail.

Mailing shot   Single mailing operation. Two mailings to the same list would be referred to as a two-shot campaign. *See* Direct mail shot.

Mailsort   A system whereby a discount is obtained for a mailing provided the mailing pieces are sorted into specific areas.

Mainframe computer   Originally a computer housed within a large, often room-sized chassis (mainframe) but has come to denote very powerful and high-capacity machines designed for heavy 'number crunching' and batch-processing within computing departments rather than real-time use by ordinary users.

Make-good   Repeating advertisement without charge, or refunding fee, due to error in advertisement as published.

Make-ready   Preparation of printing machine, in particular of the forme in letterpress printing.

Make-up   Arrangement of type and plates in page form for advertising.

Man profile   Specification of human characteristics, experience and training suited to the satisfactory performance of a particular job function. Usually formulated after the production of a job specification which similarly specifies the duties to be carried out.

Management   (1) The owners, or directors, of an organization. (2) The generic (and still to a degree controversial) term employed to designate those executive tasks in a business which ensure that diverse resources are utilized in such a way that preplanned economic performances are achieved. Commonly regarded as comprising the interlocking activities of planning, organizing, staffing, directing, controlling and co-ordination, using all liaison and communications resources available for these ends.

Management audit   Systematic assessment of all management functions and techniques to establish the current level of effectiveness, and to lay down standards for future performance.

Management by exception Management technique based upon the comparison of performance with set budgets or targets which enjoins action only when large enough variations are recorded.

Management by objectives System whereby each management function is required to define the objectives it is set to achieve. Such objectives are designed to inter-relate for maximum efficiency, and require an effective feedback system to enable management to be aware of progress and to exercise adequate control.

Management development Deliberate formulation of plans to train staff and encourage them to acquire new skills in order to provide an organization with future executives, whilst at the same time giving staff a sense of purpose.

Management information system Software programs deliberately designed to provide managers with the information they need to make decisions.

Manifest Detailed list of a ship's cargo. This is sent to Customs officials within six days of clearance outwards.

Manual Printed document (of any number of pages) usually containing specific instructions, e.g. sales manual, operating or service manual, relative both to products and services as well as company policies, regulations and practices.

Manufacturer's agent Freelance sales agent employed by one or more manufacturers, usually on a 'commission on sales' basis, because of established connections in a particular market.

Manufacturer's brand A symbol or a name indicative of the manufacturing company, as against Private brand or Own label, which *see*.

Manufacturers' recommended price The price at which the manufacturer suggests the retailer should sell the product. *See* Resale price maintenance.

175

Manuscript   Final draft of a written document as submitted to a publisher for typesetting and subsequent reproduction. Abbreviation MS.

Mapping   *See* Perceptual mapping.

Marcom   Popularly used abbreviation for Marketing communications, which *see*.

Margin   Normally the mark-up given to the cost price of a product by distributors to cover their own costs and include some level of profit. Is sometimes referred to as the difference between the arbitrary cost of a product and the actual selling price.

Marginal cost   Difference in costs between producing X units for sale, and X + 1 units for sale. Marginal revenue is the increment in revenue when one more unit is sold. In some firms at some times, marginal cost may be negligible and therefore, when an extra unit is sold, a greater than proportional profit is made. Alternatively, marginal costs may be high, e.g. when maximum output is already achieved. At such times additional sales may have the effect of reducing profit levels.

Marginal costing   Pricing of additional sales on the basis of merely the direct costs, leaving overheads to be recovered from existing sales.

Marginal utility   Amount of increased satisfaction gained from one additional purchase. In some cases, the one additional purchase may outweigh the satisfaction gained from numerous previous purchases. For example, buying the final club to complete a set of golf clubs may bring greater satisfaction than all the previous clubs; indeed a higher price may even be considered to ensure having the complete set.

Mark-down   To reduce price below normal as in a sale.

Mark-up   (1) Amount added to a purchase price to provide a selling price. *See* Margin. (2) To give typographical details in the form of a layout, also called a Type mark-up.

Marked proof Printer's proof upon which corrections have been marked.

Market (1) Group of persons and/or organizations identified through a common need and with resources to satisfy that need. (2) Place where buyers and sellers gather to do business. (3) To market; to indulge in trade, i.e. buying and selling for pecuniary advantage.

Market acceptance Condition in which a product satisfies a sufficient proportion of the market to continue production and possibly increase it.

Market attrition Gradual wearing away of brand loyalty over time especially in the absence of promotional stimulus.

Market connection Extent of brand or company acceptance in the market place. Often believed to be a company's major business asset.

Market coverage Measurement of extent to which advertising media reach target audiences. The same calculations may be applied to estimate: (1) the extent to which sales forces cater for all prospective customers; and (2) sales outlets are supplying for all available custom.

Market development *See* Product portfolio.

Market ecology Study of cultural, political, economic, and social environments of a country together with the effect these have on business methods and trading policy.

Market indicators (1) Evidence of shifts in market profiles; may come from monitoring system or research findings. (2) Conclusions from trend analysis suggesting future changes are possible.

Market intelligence Information, and the network for securing it, as related to a company's markets.

Market leader Brand or product securing the greatest proportion of total sales within its field. May sometimes refer to the company marketing the brand or product concerned.

Market niche   Taking a market segment and producing an even narrower target market where the competition is not likely to be so strong. *See* Segmentation.

Market overt   Refers to an accepted convention whereby sellers of goods which are exposed in bulk, and part of normal stock in trade, may pass a good title for goods, irrespective of the title of the seller.

Market penetration   The act of a newcomer (firm or product) to an existing market. Also obtaining increased market share for a product with no change in the target market. *See* Penetration.

Market place   Figurative; applies to any or all places where trading takes place.

Market position   Ranking in sales volume relative to other suppliers.

Market potential   Estimated size of total present or future market. Alternatively, the maximum share of a market which can be reasonably achieved during a defined period.

Market price   Price ruling for a commodity in the market place. Stated by economists as the value which a purchaser places upon a product or service to satisfy his/her need. Related to the Law of Marginal Utility.

Market profile   Facts about members of a particular market group sufficient to identify such members.

Market reach   Total number of prospects it is possible to reach through a given campaign.

Market recognition   Universal awareness for a brand or product, often measured in percentage sales.

Market research   Process of making investigations into the characteristics of given markets, e.g. location, size, growth potential and observed attitudes. *See* Marketing research.

Market sales potential   Calculation of cumulative sales value potential of a pre-determined market, taking into account different purchasing scales of preference.

Market segmentation   The theory and practice of dividing a market into definable groups, usually to improve marketing performance. Frequently different segments of a market have individual behaviour patterns and require a different approach for success to be achieved. *See* Segmentation.

Market share   Percentage measure of the share obtained by an individual company from the total market available. Usually calculated upon a national basis but some international measures are in use.

Market testing   The penultimate stage in the development and launch of a new product in which samples or prototypes are put out with customers for their reaction, and in which various promotional techniques are tried. *See* Test marketing.

Market target selection   Choosing a particular market segment for promotion and penetration often based on gap analysis.

Market trend   Direction of developments in a market.

Market value   Price at which the market values a product at any given point in time.

Market weight   Used for weighting advertising expenditure; means of varying expenditure according to the pattern of consumption by different market groups.

Marketing   Marketing is still the subject of much misunderstanding, for it is not just a phenomenon of the twentieth century but a whole family of phenomena. The 'father' arose many centuries ago at the very beginning of trading, when merchants recognized the commercial advantages of supplying the food and clothing people needed, leaving others to minister to the needs of their souls. The 'mother' may be seen as a characteristic of the nineteenth and twentieth centuries. Using the fast-developing network of communications systems, the activities of marketing, the so-called marketing mix, joined with the already traditional 'concept of marketing' giving rise to the large family of today. It is in fact the confusion in identifying such offspring that antagonizes most non-marketing executives. For, although they spring from the same seed and share the same philosophies, the branches of the marketing family tree have reached different degrees of maturity and, like all children, have formed their own unique characteristics. So the practice of marketing in each branch of the family shows a markedly different profile. The branches are: Consumer goods marketing, Industrial goods marketing, Services marketing, International marketing, and Mini-marketing. Each of these areas of marketing practice has used the principles most applicable to its own marketing – true market orientation. It follows that various definitions of marketing tend to show the significance of one particular aspect, according to the branch in which the emphasis has been placed. Clearly, there are many definitions each of importance, yet different in substance. Two of these which endeavour to cover all facets of the subject are listed below for general guidance, though they here represent hundreds of attempts to provide a satisfactory explanation:

(1) The management process responsible for identifying, anticipating and satisfying customer requirements profitably. (Chartered Institute of Marketing definition 1996.)

(2) Marketing starts in the market place with the identification of the customers' needs and wants. It then moves on to determining a means of satisfying these needs, and of promoting, selling and supplying a satisfaction. The principal marketing functions might be defined as Marketing Information and Research, Product Planning, Pricing, Advertising and Promotion, Sales and Distribution. (*Industrial Marketing Communications*, Norman Hart, 1993.)

Whatever the definition it is clear that marketing is a positive business activity which establishes, develops, and satisfies both customer needs and wants. It is an intercommunications link provided by suppliers with a view to matching adequate supply with realistic demand, the reward for which is the operation of a profitable undertaking. It involves groups of commercial activities in contact with customers, and a concept permitting every critical business decision to be taken allowing for its present and future impact upon customers and society.

180

Marketing audit   The assessment of a company's market place including its size, the competitors' strengths and weaknesses, distribution channels, and the company's present marketing activities and the relating of them to what it should be doing.

Marketing budget   The advance allocation of finance to each of the various marketing functions, e.g. research, sales, or advertising. A number of techniques are used to arrive at a budget, the most common and logical of which is related to the marketing objectives. *See* Task method *and* Budget.

Marketing chain   Composed of essential links between all marketing activities.

Marketing channels   The means by which goods are distributed to the ultimate customers. These obviously take in retailers, wholesalers, subsidiaries, and agents. *See* Distribution network.

Marketing communications channel   Means by which firms are able to communicate with their customers, e.g. press advertising.

Marketing communications manager   An increasingly popular title replacing advertising or publicity manager. Includes all non-face-to-face communications.

Marketing communications mix   Group of channels available for communication with buyers and prospects.

Marketing communications objectives   There are many specific objectives, the principal ones being to gain attention for a product or service, to secure and strengthen perception, and to generate sales leads. In consumer marketing, the process goes further into changing behavioural intent, and then on to behaviour, i.e. sales. In business marketing, behavioural intent and behaviour are affected by other factors outside the marketing communications remit, e.g. the sales force. But all communications are affected by price and product, and so can be measured only in perceptual terms and not sales. A vital element of the objectives is that they should be quantified in order that their achievement can be measured.

Marketing communications plan This breaks down into ten chapters: Objectives, Issues, Strategy, Target audiences, Messages, Media, Timetable, Budget, Measurement, Resources.

Marketing concept Philosophy underlying the application of marketing thought to the operation of a business in all its various activities.

Marketing driven company In which an organization's operations are centred around the customer's wants, needs and requirements. *See* Marketing concept.

Marketing function (1) An all-embracing term covering every contributory factor in the marketing process. (2) Considered to be the responsibility of marketing management.

Marketing information Data and news relevant to a marketing operation.

Marketing intelligence Information or data being gathered or used to aid decision-making or to monitor earlier decisions.

Marketing management Functional and personnel organization within the framework of a marketing plan. Optimum use is made of internal and external people, together with all the other marketing functions.

Marketing manager Person responsible for formulating, planning, executing and evaluating the marketing function. Increasingly, and rightly, this responsibility is under the control of a marketing director who has overall responsibility including the whole selling operation.

Marketing mix Planned mixture of the elements of marketing in a marketing plan. The aim is to combine them in such a way as to achieve the greatest effect at minimum cost. *See* Four Ps.

Marketing models Simulation of total marketing environment, usually built into a computer. Possible to in-feed alternative proposals and obtain likely outcomes.

Marketing myopia   A term attributed to Theodore Levitt which centres on the strategic question 'What business are we in?' The key to answering this question is to examine what the customer is buying as against what are we selling. For instance, in journal advertising sales, the space sales person may be selling space whereas the advertiser is buying audiences. Similarly, railways *vis-à-vis* transport, cinema *vis-à-vis* entertainment.

Marketing objective   Where an organization aims to be in the market place within a specified time. This may be broken down into products and territories coupled with sales turnover figures and market share.

Marketing orientation   Used to describe concerns which seek to identify and quantify customer requirements and to plan output and profitability accordingly. *See* Production orientation.

Marketing plan   Written plan, usually comprehensive, describing all activities involved in achieving a particular marketing objective, and their relationship to one another in both time and magnitude. Will include short- and long-term sales forecasts, production and profit targets, pricing policy, promotional and selling strategy, staffing requirements, as well as the selected marketing mix and expense budgets.

Marketing research   Any research activity which provides information relating to marketing operations. Whilst the term embraces conventional market research, motivation studies, advertisement attention value, packaging effectiveness, logistics, and media research are also included, as well as analysis of internal and external statistics of relevance.

Marketing services   Term sometimes used to cover all marketing activities in a company other than the sales function, e.g. marketing research, advertising and public relations.

Marketing services manager   Person with responsibility for all the services required by the marketing function. Commonly these include research, advertising and promotion, and sometimes planning and public relations.

Marketing strategy A statement in very general terms of how the marketing objective is to be achieved, e.g. by acquiring a competitive company, by price reductions, by product improvement, or by intensive advertising. The strategy becomes the basis of the marketing plan. *See* Marketing plan.

Marketing tools Activities, processes and techniques used for implementing marketing strategies or tactics.

Marketing upweight discounts Price concessions given to advertisers who are prepared to spend a more than proportional amount in any one or more television areas. Also known as Booster packages.

Markov chain Mathematical term describing a series of events in which each event is dependent upon the outcome of the previous event for its own particular result.

Marque Identifying name, symbol or graphic design giving a product a certain image. *See* Brand.

Married print Visual and sound track made separately are 'married' by printing the two films onto one track.

Mask Frame, usually rectangular, used to cover those parts of an illustration which are not required to be reproduced, e.g. cropping of a photograph for this purpose.

Mass advertising Using the mass media to reach markets.

Mass communications Delivery of message to target audience utilizing mass media such as national press and television.

Mass market Large homogeneous market for consumer products.

Mass media Principally, television, radio and newspapers, i.e. those channels of communication which reach a very large market.

Master sample Assembly of sampling points maintained by a number of research establishments and used as a basis for final selection of samples. This practice eliminates the expensive selection processes which would otherwise be required each time a survey or research study is commissioned.

Masthead Main heading or title at the top of a newspaper or magazine.

Matched sample Describes a technique wherein two or more samples with matching characteristics are used to provide realistic comparisons on different test subjects.

Matching in Inserting a name, address and salutation plus other personalization into a pre-printed item using the same typeface.

Maths co-processor A chip which can be added to a computer to increase the speed at which it deals with mathematical computation.

Matrix (1) Paper or plastic mould from which duplicate printing blocks are produced. (2) Horizontal and vertical lines or columns used for establishing relationships between sets of data.

Matt Surface of material which is smooth, or even rough, as opposed to glossy.

Matter Type or copy in print or gathered together for printing purposes. *See also* Editorial matter.

Maturity stage That stage in the life of a product in which demand flattens out prior to eventual decline. *See* Life cycle.

Maximal awareness Point at which a consumer becomes sufficiently conscious of an advertising message to react favourably, if he/she is going to react at all.

Maximum brand exposure   Full communication activity, with extensive product distribution and retail promotion.

MBO   (1) Management buy-out. (2) Management by objectives, which *see*

Mean   Arithmetic average where a total of distinct values is related to the number and distribution of each value to arrive at a figure intended to be representative of all the values. *See* Average.

Mean audit date   Date at which the average shop in a retail audit sample was visited for the purpose of a particular report.

Measure   In printing, length of line to which type is set.

Measurement   That part of a marketing or marketing communications plan which assesses the extent to which the objectives have been achieved. Commonly, such measurements are taken whilst the campaign is in progress (tracking) as well as at the end. This is to provide the opportunity of making changes in good time to affect the overall outcome of the campaign.

Measures of central tendency   Term used in statistical method to describe the various forms of average, based on the tendency of quantitative data to cluster around some middle value or values in sets of variable values.

Measures of dispersion   *See* Dispersion.

Mechanical art   *See* Artwork.

Mechanical binding   A means of holding together a number of sheets of paper by some special device such as spiral wire or plastic comb.

Mechanical data   Information relating to magazines or news-papers concerning page size, column width and other matters relating to physical reproduction.

Mechanical sales talk   Continual use of trite expressions or cliches; often contained within the company sales or technical literature. Hence, sometimes described as 'canned' talk or presentation.

Mechanical tint   Fine dotted screen on artwork which shows up in print as a grey tone. Various gradations of grey are obtainable depending on the fineness of the screen.

Media   Plural of Medium.

Media affinity scores   A quantitative measurement of people's reaction to advertisements in a particular medium. Examples include 'I read' ('Read most' score), 'I like' (a positive perception), length of time reading, etc. A measure of the affinity of a customer towards a medium.

Media analyst   Advertising agency worker (usually) employed to maintain and collate media statistics.

Media broker   Independent agency, usually dealing exclusively with buying space or time in the media on behalf of a client. May or may not include media planning or other support services.

Media budget   Amount of advertising appropriation allocated to media advertising, classified by medium, vehicle and time periods.

Media buyer   Executive in an advertising agency, responsible for timely and economical purchasing of media time and space (readership or audience) to discharge the requirements of a client's media schedule.

Media buying service   A specialized advertising agency which concentrates on the buying of media and maybe also its planning. Also referred to as Media broker, which *see.*

Media commission Commission allowed by publishers and television contractors to 'recognized' advertising agencies in consideration of the space or time they book on behalf of their clients. *See* Recognition.

Media coverage *See* Coverage.

Media evaluation Consideration of alternative media prior to selection, to determine the significance of both qualitative and quantitative factors relevant to advertising objectives.

Media independent Organization providing a planning and buying service in relation to all types of media but not usually offering related facilities normally expected from a full-service advertising agency, such as creative design and campaign planning. *See* Media broker.

Media mix Explanation of amount of advertising appropriation allocated to each medium within the media budget.

Media owners Publishers and contractors supplying media, including press, cinema, TV and radio broadcasting, and posters available for carrying advertising. More broadly, those offering any channel of communication which can be used for advertising purposes.

Media plan That part of the marketing communications plan which gives the rationale for media choice together with the tactical details of its implementation.

Media planner Executive in an advertising agency responsible for formulating plans involving all types of media in such a way as to enable a client to reach out to his/her potential market(s) with maximum efficiency and minimum expense.

Media relations *See* Press relations.

Media representative Sales person selling space or airtime. often referred to as space salesman or woman.

Media research   Investigation and analysis of media, comprising: (1) Media characteristics; (2) Qualitative factors; (3) Quantitative factors; (4) Cost factors; (5) Mechanical data. In practice, is largely concerned with readership, audience and circulation data.

Media schedule   Chart drawn up by an advertiser, usually with the aid of an advertising agency, setting out the media to be used in a campaign indicating the weight, timing and cost of each item.

Media selection   Deciding which are the appropriate media to achieve advertising objectives in line with media strategy and evaluation. Will normally be based on most cost-effective communication to pre-determined target audiences.

Media strategy   Amount of advertising appropriation defined by its purposes and allocated to the factors of impact, coverage, frequency and duration.

Media training   In which company spokespersons, usually senior management, are given advice on how to conduct themselves in a media interview, whether face-to-face in television, radio, print, or by telephone. The procedure usually involves a simulated interview, maybe with an ex-journalist, and a video recording which is then played back for a critique.

Media-weight   Used for weighting advertising expenditure; means of varying expenditure or actual decision criteria according to the value of particular media characteristics, especially the qualitative factors. It reflects the effectiveness with which an advertisement will work in a particular medium or publication.

Median   Midpoint of a series of numerical data. Often referred to as a kind of average. Observed by inspection, e.g. 4, 7, 13, 16, 20; median is 13. Where the number of items in a series is even, interpolation may be used.

Medium   Channel of communication, e.g. press organ, television station, exhibition or direct mail. Plural form is media, often used to refer specifically to periodical publications. *See* Advertising medium. *See also* Mass media.

Megabyte   A million bytes.

Memory   The area of a computer where programs and data are manipulated or stored.

Memory decay   Erosion of memory, usually of conviction, over a period of time; affects a buyer's loyalty towards a particular brand choice.

Memory lapse   Breaking from regular or habitual purchase through forgetfulness. Natural phenomenon, which happening regularly causes a significant amount of lost sales; hence much advertising expenditure on established brands is devoted to 'reminder' advertising.

Menu   A software-based list providing the user with a selection of functions, programs, etc.

Merchandise   Goods which are offered for sale.

Merchandising   All activity directed towards selling goods once they have reached the point-of-sale, e.g. packaging, display, pricing, special offers. May be carried out by supplier's salespeople, store staff or jointly operated.

Merchantable quality   Implied condition that a reasonable person would, after examination, accept goods as satisfactory to complete a contract for their purchase or sale.

Merge-purge   In which two or more mailing lists are put together in such a way that duplicates are identified and eliminated.

Merger   Amalgamation of two or more organizations with the object of growth, possibly to improve spending efficiency or to improve market performance but also to absorb competition. Mergers may be referred in UK to the Monopolies Commission for approval and are now increasingly affected by EU regulations concerned with practices in restraint of trade.

190

Merit rating   Practice of ranking salespeople or other employees for payment or advancement according to their observed ability or achievement.

Message source   The base or origination of any marketing signal which results in a product or company message being received. Equally important to monitor negative messages (e.g., badly designed letterheading, poor appearance of sales staff) as well as positive ones (e.g., favourable interview of chairman on TV, or unsolicited praise by a customer). Message sources can be analysed in four categories: 1 Active message sources such as advertising, direct mail; 2 Outside message sources, e.g. comments by influential journalists; 3 People message sources, e.g. the impression created by the switchboard operator; 4 Passive message sources, e.g. company name, appearance of the factory.

Messages   The propositions to be put to a target audience as part of the marketing communications plan. It is important that these be prioritized, and tailored specifically to a particular market segment. They may arise out of product attributes, but will then be converted into customer benefits. *See also* Unique selling proposition, *and* Single selling proposition.

Meta marketing   Method of studying marketing and its relationship to every aspect of human life, so establishing a body of knowledge, based on experience of and with every facet of human personalities and life styles. Usually ascribed to Philip Kotler (USA).

Methodology   Strictly relating to the basis of a research design application and analysis. Commonly used as a synonym for 'method', but more properly should apply to a set of methods.

MG paper   Machine-glazed paper commonly used for printing bags and wrappers.

Micro marketing   Meeting the needs of the individual firm in terms of its objectives and its actions to achieve them. *See also* Macro marketing.

Microchip   *See* IC.

Microprocessor *See* IC.

Microsegmentation To select the high-value/low-value prospects in order of size, e.g. segments or niches.

Migration (1) Switching from one television channel to another; may occur as a reaction to television commercials. (2) Switching attention from a feature or news item in the press to an advertisement.

Mileage Measure of reaction gained from a media communication.

Milline rate Unit for comparing newspaper advertising rates in relation to circulation.

Minicomputer Traditionally the step between a PC (or microcomputer) and a mainframe computer, although with improvements in computer performance the distinction has become blurred as the computing power of a PC can now overreach that of a minicomputer (and similarly a minicomputer can outstrip a mainframe).

Minimil Lowest milline rate or an average of the lowest milline rates.

Minor Person not eligible to sign binding contracts, not having reached a majority (eighteen years in UK).

Minority viewers Audiences for specialised television programmes, such as any of those shown on Channel Four. *See also* Light viewers.

MIS Marketing information service.

Misrepresentation Inducing another party to engage in a contract upon the basis of false or inadequate information.

Mission Prime function of an organization or business; relates mostly to the desired market reputation.

Mission budgets   Costs to be incurred to achieve business mission. *See* Mission.

Mission costing   Detailed cost analysis of a particular mission or objective.

Mission statement   A carefully drawn up statement by an organization of 'what we are, and what we aim to do', i.e., 'our unique ethical stance and strategic objectives'.

Missionary salesperson   Salesperson calling, for example, upon a doctor, who is not a purchasing agent, so as to promote goodwill in an effort to stimulate sales through prescriptions to a third party, the patient, who is supplied by a chemist. *See* Propaganda selling.

Mixed economy   National economy with elements of both publicly-owned industries and private enterprise industries, operating side-by-side. Public undertakings enjoy a large measure of monopoly power, protected by law, whereas private monopolies are banned or restricted.

Mixed media   Using more than one medium in any advertising campaign. Most often used where more than one advertising objective has been set for the campaign.

MLM   *See* Multi-level marketing.

Mobile   Sales promotion device to hang from ceiling of a supermarket for instance, in order to attract the attention of shoppers to a particular brand.

Mobile advertising   Posters on vehicles, or painting directly on to vehicles, e.g. taxis, buses, trains and aircraft.

Mobility Freedom with which labour, or other resources, move to other uses in an economy.

Mock auctions Under the Mock Auctions Act 1961, it is a criminal offence to assist, promote, or conduct a public sale passing as an auction where the highest bid does not prevail.

Mock-up Facsimile of package or product for use in photography for television or other visual display form. *See* Dummy.

Mode Most commonly recurring value(s) in any recorded numerical data. Such clusters are often referred to as averages and may sometimes be more representative of the data than the arithmetic mean.

Model (1) Mathematical representation of real life situation. (2) Person used to illustrate an advertisement. (3) Reproduction on a small scale.

Modem (MOdulator/DEModulator) An electronic device enabling a computer to transmit data over a communications line (e.g. telephone line).

Modification In product development, to change a product or its presentation in order to effect improvement in performance, characteristics, acceptability, manufacturing procedure, or profitability.

Modified re-buy *See* Buy classes.

Monadic Single product test. Used as a test of acceptance or validity as an alternative to a comparative assessment.

Money Any acceptable means of settling debts as an established practice within a nation or group of nations. *See* Legal tender.

Money-off pack *See* Flash pack.

Monitor To check performance at regular intervals in relation to pre-established norms.

Monopolistic competition State said by economists to exist when a restricted number of firms compete not so much by price and performance as by competitive promotional outlays. Products are thus differentiated in the market place by the amount of pressure generated upon demand rather than by any significant differences between them.

Monopoly (1) Sole producer or supplier to person or organization of a commodity or service. (2) In UK, private companies are referred to the Monopolies Commission if they account for more than a percentage of the total national output of their product. This proportion was reduced by law to 25 per cent from 1975. Publicly-owned (nationalized) industries are exempted from such provisions.

Monopoly advertising In which all the available advertising space is allocated to one advertiser exclusively.

Monopsony Occurs where only one sales outlet operates for a range of similar competing products. Significant in countries where certain essential industries have been nationalized.

Montage (1) Showing of rapid succession of scenes in television filming. (2) Bringing together into one illustration a number of different artistic materials.

Monthly A magazine or journal published on a monthly basis which usually has an earlier copy date than weeklies or dailies, e.g. first of the month preceding publication date.

Mood advertising Advertising which is deliberately aimed at putting potential customers into a frame of mind conducive to acceptance of the product.

Mood conditioning Creation of atmosphere conducive to favourable reactions either in advertisement or in retail outlet.

Morale Attitude of mind induced by surrounding conditions and considerations. Psychological state which may react, positively or negatively, to management efforts to improve.

Mores   Customs and behaviour which is the norm of a particular society. *See* Culture.

Morphological analysis   Three dimensional analysis to suggest market segments most likely to produce profit opportunity. Three dimensions may be a) overseas countries, b) industrial classification, c) product or service group.

Motherboard   The circuit board used by the central processing unit to communicate with its peripheral devices (e.g. hard disk drive).

Motivation   Psychological stimulus behind the acts or courses of action adopted by individuals or groups of individuals. Applied in marketing both to individual and organizational activities as well as to consumer and user behaviour.

Motivational research   Study of psychological reasons underlying human behaviour particularly in relation to buying situations. *See* Group discussion.

Mould   *See* Matrix.

Mouse   A generic term for a device used to control cursor movements and select programs, menu items, etc., in a GUI environment. A traditional mouse consists of a palm-sized instrument connected to the computer by a wire resembling a mouse tail, hence the name. Mice can come in various shapes and forms, usually as a result of different manufacturers producing variations on a common design (e.g. 'Ballpoint', 'MousePoint', 'Trackball') but their basic function is usually the same.

Moving average   Statistical technique used for reducing the significance of wide seasonal or other variations. Moves forward on a periodical basis, (e.g. every week or month by adding the most recent data and dropping the oldest). A smoothing technique to permit longer term trends to be more clearly discerned. *See* Exponential smoothing.

MS   *See* Manuscript.

MS-DOS (Microsoft Disk Operating System) Microsoft Corporation's own version of DOS.

MTBF (Mean time between failures) MTBF is a benchmark for hardware or general system reliability and denotes the ratio of time in a given period to the number of hardware or system failures in that same period.

Multibrand strategy Where a company is marketing several brands within a single product category, e.g. Unilever or Proctor and Gamble, and their various washing detergents.

Multiclient survey Marketing research study financed by a collection of interested organizations.

Multidimensional scaling A research practice in which degrees of respondents' attitudes are quantified on an arithmetic scale, e.g. 1, 2, 3, 4 and 5, where 5 might represent complete satisfaction with a product and 1 only minimal satisfaction. With a scale of +5 to –5 complete opposites can be returned, e.g. completely agree, completely disagree.

Multilateral trade Business transactions which are conducted across a number of countries.

Multilevel marketing A form of network marketing in which there are a number of levels of distribution, each one passing goods on to the next. The senior distributors split their commission with the 'down-line' distributors.

Multimedia The communication technology that will revolutionize marketing. It combines text, video, sound and graphics for presentations and fully interactive electronic communications.

Multimedia advertising Using a number of complementary media channels to increase coverage, awareness, or credibility.

Multinational Usually applied to companies conducting major business in a number of countries by means of their own local or indigenous manufacturing and/or marketing organizations. *See also* Transnational and International.

Multiple Group of shops with similar merchandise and image and controlled by a single firm.

Multiple choice question In research, a system whereby a respondent is offered the alternative of several possible answers, already formulated, and in which he indicates which comes closest to his point of view.

Multiple correlation Marketing research tool used to measure the effect of several independent variables on one dependent variable. *See* Independent and Dependent variable.

Multiple readership More than one reader per issue, usually involving secondary and tertiary readers. In trade and technical press, can amount to double figures for each copy.

Multiple unit pricing Pricing technique, involving a number of identical items in one pack. Significant, since the introduction of multiple unit packaging encourages consumers to buy more than they need immediately.

Multiplexer A device which allows the splitting of a single communications line or channel into various sub-channels. A common use of a multiplexer is to connect several terminals and/or printers to a single connection at the computer, and effectively merge and unscramble the data and instructions being sent up and down the line.

Multiplier (1) Keynes' term for the phenomenon of a total increase in national income being several times greater than an initial injection of investment in a community. (2) Ratio in investment designed to produce a given increase in employment.

Multiproduct strategy The use of the same brand name across a range of different products.

Multisegmented operations Large commercial organization with numerous product or service groups serving a wide range of countries and industry groupings.

Multistage sample Sample assembled by combining proportionate numbers of respondents of different characteristics represented in a universe. Selection is random within each category. Satisfactorily combines the benefits of both quota and random sampling.

Multitasking An operating system feature allowing sharing of a single processor between several independent jobs. At user level a computer can therefore carry out several jobs simultaneously, such as printing a document while a user composes and sends E-mail.

Multithreading Akin to multi-tasking but differs in that the 'threads', or instructions, issued by the various software programs are more closely shared resulting in a faster and more flexible and efficient multi-tasking environment for the user.

Multivariate Many variables, making decisions complex. Description used mainly in life-style analysis.

Multivariate analysis Technique used for assessing the extent to which variables cause a number of differences in subsequent behaviour patterns.

Murphy's law If anything at all can go wrong, then it will go wrong. *See* Sod's law.

Must Editorial item which it is considered essential should appear.

MUX *See* Multiplexer.

N

Narrowcasting Channeling messages into electronic medium in such a way as to reach small well-defined specialist audiences, e.g. with cable television. Opposite to broadcasting.

National account Customer of major 'national' importance, often with several locations throughout a country. May or may not operate a central purchasing operation. Sometimes handled on a national basis by one executive or manager.

National brand A brand available throughout the country as against in just one region.

National campaign Marketing operation covering the entire country.

National press Newspapers, daily or Sunday, distributed throughout the country but not necessarily enjoying a mass circulation.

National Readership Survey *See* NRS.

Natural break Requirement in broadcast media that commercial breaks occur only between normal gaps in the continuity of programmes. Almost impossible to achieve in a network involving many different programmes being broadcast simultaneously to different geographical regions, and so operates in principle rather than being applied rigidly. *See* Break.

Neck hanger A device fixed around the neck of a bottle and used for sales promotional purposes, e.g. a competition.

Need Object, service or resource which is necessary for a person's survival, well-being or comfort. Not to be confused with Want, which *see* elsewhere. E.g. a person may need a surgical operation but can hardly be said to want it. Equally, one may want an extra helping of a delicious meal, yet not need it.

Need-arousal Stimulating people and motivating them to seek satisfaction from suggested sources, those offering a high probability of gratification.

Negative currency Giving something away in negotiations.

Negative demand Actual avoidance of a product; refusal even to consider a purchase.

Negative line art A piece of artwork upon which the typesetting and illustrations are reversed out, white upon black. Arguably more distinctive but less legible than black upon white.

Negative option The procedure in a direct marketing campaign whereby some action will be taken by the supplier unless the customer indicates proactively that such action is not required, e.g. with a book club, the next month's edition will be sent unless the member informs the club that the book is not wanted. *See* Positive option.

Negative setting Reversed type setting, white upon black. Has a tendency for smaller letters to fill in. Legibility is reduced with white upon a colour.

Negotiations Seeking agreement on mutually acceptable terms prior to concluding a trading agreement.

Neighbourhood classification Market segmentation based upon the locality of prospects. *See* ACORN.

Net audience Number of unduplicated homes, readers or viewers, etc., also known as net readership.

Net cover Percentage of the target audience receiving at least one exposure to a commercial or advertisement. *See also* Gross cover, Coverage, Four plus, Effective cover.

Net paid circulation Part of total circulation paid for by readers, i.e. after deduction of free or complimentary copies and of unbought copies published.

Net present value The present value of an investment after taking account of future financial returns, having regard to inflation.

Net price Final price after all discounts and allowances have been deducted.

Net profit Gross profit minus operating and selling costs.

Net rate Publisher's rates after deduction of agency commission.

Net reach Number of people who will have at least one opportunity to see an advertisement after allowing for duplication of readership between issues and between publication.

Net weight Total weight of a product minus any packaging.

Netting Plastic netting extruded as a continuous cylinder and chopped into single units which are used to hold units of merchandise and to enhance their display. Frequently used for fruit or vegetable display in self-service stores.

Network (1) Television or radio stations linked together for transmitting identical programmes simultaneously. Refers also to the facility by which programmes may be retransmitted by other TV regions, and thus similar to syndicated press features. (2) A series of workstations and computers linked by communications circuits allowing the sharing of data and/or machine resources.

Network analysis Breaking down a complex project into component requirements and recording these in a diagramatic form which incorporates a critical time scale, so that planning and control can be effected in the most expedient manner.

Network marketing A new term to cover what was previously known as 'Pyramid selling' (which *see*), and comprising the building up of one's acquaintances, friends and relations as a first base of prospects. One then looks for their contacts, whilst all the time looking out for suitable agents to take on selling on a commission basis.

Networking The deliberate action by a person to make contact with other people having similar characteristics, interests, or other common features. Preferably face-to-face, and one-to-one.

Never-never Vernacular for buying on credit; somewhat dated.

New   Word often applied to indicate a novel market opportunity. Newness may vary from very slight to very large, the risk factors increasing with the actual amount of innovation, so that many 'new' products fail to achieve market acceptance.

New buy   *See* Buy classes.

New product development   A function of marketing involving the concept of a new product to satisfy a consumer requirement followed by R&D, design, prototype, consumer testing, test market, and campaign launch.

News agency   A company which obtains news and then distributes it for a price to subscribing organizations which may include newspapers, magazines, radio and television.

News conference   Meeting set up by a company or organization to announce an item of news which they regard as being of significant importance. Is usually directed at journalists but can well include other interested target audiences. *See* Press reception.

News release   *See* Press release.

Newsletter   A simple publication containing news about an organization, its people, and its products and sent periodically to such interested parties as customers, prospects, dealers and, sometimes, to internal audiences. *See* House magazine.

Newspaper   Periodical published daily or weekly and containing news, features, reports, together with advertisements.

Newsprint   Coarse paper from which newspapers are commonly produced.

Next-to-reading matter   Advertisement position immediately adjacent to editorial. *See* Facing matter.

Niche marketing   Directing marketing activities into a market segment or niche.

Nielsen index Retail audit of brands within pre-determined groups, classified by geographical area within regular time periods. Standard format is available to subscribers in large and steadily increasing number of countries. *See* Retail audit.

Nixie Returned mailing shots due to addressee having moved or the address being incorrect.

Noise Term used in communication theory to indicate an undesirable extraneous input which interferes with the primary message signal.

Nominal price Face value of an item, often used to indicate a minor charge being made for something of greater economic value.

Non-durable goods Products which are consumed within a short space of time, e.g. FMCG.

Non-luxury goods Necessities.

Non-price competition Price is not considered a significant factor in consumer's decision-making. Concentration of competitive activity into sectors other than price, such an incentive marketing, packaging and image advertising.

Non-profit marketing Simply stated, this is the application of marketing techniques by organizations which are non-profit making. *See* Social marketing.

Non-response bias In a piece of research there may be a bias due to certain intended respondents being unavailable or unwilling to be questioned. Thus the sample may become unrepresentative. *See* Sampling error.

Normal distribution Statistical term central to sampling theory. On a line chart, it shows the point at which the mean, mode, and median averages share the same value and has a characteristic bell-shaped profile. Standard deviation is calculated upon a formula derived from this distribution, enabling the confidence level (e.g. 95 per cent) within which results are confined to be stated. In the example given, this would be accuracy defined to within ±5 per cent.

Normal frequency curve   Pattern of distribution of values encountered frequently in statistical analysis where the mean, mode, and median values are identical or very close together. The curve is symmetrical, bell-shaped, and the average value lies at the peak of the curve. *See* Frequency curve and Dispersion.

Notebook computer   A computer of a size comparable to an A4-sized notebook (or even smaller, but stopping short of 'palm' sized).

Noting   Term used in advertisement research. Indicates that a reader's attention was drawn to an advertisement when first looking through the newspaper or magazine in which it appeared, though not necessarily that he/she read, fully understood or acted upon this stimulus.

Noting score   Average number of readers found to have noted a specific advertisement or editorial item expressed as a percentage of total readership.

Novelty   A promotional item which is novel; usually embodying the name or logo of the company issuing it, and mostly cheap, i.e., a give-away.

NPD   *See* New product development.

NRS   A survey conducted to determine the readership of major national newspapers and consumer magazines in the UK by National Readership Surveys Limited, a company limited by guarantee.

Numerical concentration   Selection of the most economic or effective media based on readership figures which most closely match those of the chosen target audience, after duplication and wasted readership have been eliminated.

O

Objection, overcoming   Anticipating likely forms of sales resistance, reacting to an objection and providing real or, at least, plausible answers. These objections are sometimes, if not frequently, contrived to provide a camouflage for the real reasons which the prospect may not care to disclose to a stranger. Hence the importance of a salesperson's technique in identifying and dealing with the real situation.

Objective   *See* Business objective.

Objective budgeting   Allocating expenditure according to established objectives, rather than arbitrarily or by historical precedence. *See* Task method.

Objective selling   Selling against predetermined aims, e.g. to obtain an interview or a demonstration, where an immediate sale is not always possible.

Observation   Research technique, in which data is collected by researchers witnessing or recording the actual events which take place.

Obsolescence   Indicative of a significant relative decline in a product's usefulness or competitiveness in the market. This occurs when alternative products become available which have a better performance or lower price. The final stage before a product finally becomes obsolete. The phrase 'planned obsolescence' refers to the adoption of a policy of relatively frequent design changes to induce users to renew their equipment more often than would otherwise be the case, e.g. motor cars.

Obsolescent product   Product no longer representing current production.

Obsolete   Out of date. No longer used.

Occupation groups   A form of market segmentation based upon the occupation of the prospective customers. A narrower definition than socio-economic groups, i.e. niche markets.

Oculesics Use or avoidance of eye contact in personal communications.

Odd-even pricing The outcome of a pricing strategy in which a product is priced at a fraction below a whole number, e.g. £4.99 (odd pricing) or the very opposite – rounded off to an even number, e.g. £5.00.

OEM (Original equipment manufacturer) An organization which takes in technologies and combines them into a new and unique product and 'own-brands' them.

Off-card rate Special negotiated price for media advertising, i.e. other than that published in the official rate card.

Off-line The state of a peripheral device, such as a printer or workstation, when it is not under the direct control of the central processing unit.

Off-peak time All airtime segments (television and radio) other than those occurring at peak time. Usually offered at significantly lower rates.

Offensive marketing *See* Conquest strategy.

Offer Legally, the first step in the making of a contract for the sale (or acquisition) of goods.

Offset-litho Offsetting is merely that part of the process by which the image on a litho plate is transferred to a rubber sheet which then prints onto paper, thus avoiding a mirror or reversed reproduction. *See* Lithography.

OHP Overhead projector.

Olfaction Use of aromas or the action of smelling to effect personal communications.

Oligopoly Influence exercised over a market supply by only a small number of independent companies, not necessarily acting in collusion.

Oligopsony An economic state which occurs when there are only a limited number of buyers for products because there are no real alternatives.

Omnibus Continuous survey which is used to cover a number of topics at the same time. Companies offering this facility invite sponsors to commission a limited number of questions which would not alone justify setting up a separate research study.

On-line The state of a peripheral device, such as a printer or workstation, when it is under the direct control of the central processing unit.

On-line database A database provided by an external computer (e.g. server) or organization (e.g. CompuServe) allowing a remote user to connect and interrogate it in real-time.

On-pack Gift or other offer or information printed on the outside surface(s) of packaged goods, particularly relating to premiums or competition entries.

On-pack price reductions Price cut, such as '3p off' printed on pack as a temporary promotional device aimed at securing trial purchases and increasing market penetration.

On-the-air Indication that broadcasting is taking place.

One-stop shopping Facility to provide shoppers with a wide range of goods from one, often covered, shopping centre, usually with parking facilities. Frequently in UK a municipal enterprise as opposed to Hypermarkets and Supermarkets operated by private firms.

One-time use A mailing list which has been rented, but for one-time use only.

One-to-one interview In which one person talks privately to another person, e.g. in a market research operation or with a press interview.

Open-ended question Formulation of question in a field research which allows respondents to provide a reply in their own terms, i.e. uninfluenced by guidance within the questionnaire or upon the part of the interviewer.

Open pricing General circulation of pricing practices with a view to achieving conformity of prices within an industry.

Open system A system conforming to a set of rules and standards enabling it to exchange information with different and sometimes incompatible systems.

Operating budget Amount of money set aside to achieve a particular objective or to finance a functional department's activities.

Operating system The software which controls the operation of the computer hardware and its interface with other resident software programs, for example applications such as word processing software, spreadsheets, etc. There are various kinds of operating system in the market place, such as UNIX and DOS, which in turn are subdivided into commercial variants produced by companies to run on their own necessarily different hardware platforms (e.g. AIX (UNIX), SCO (UNIX), MS-DOS (DOS), DR-DOS (DOS)) but which maintain a common look and feel.

Operational research Application of mathematical processes to operational problems, having the effect of increasing the proportion of factual data, especially its use in helping to resolve questions which are essentially subjective in its absence.

Opinion-formers Categories of people whose attitudes and/or actions are held to be likely to affect those of others.

Opinion poll A means by which the views of the general public are ascertained by questioning a representative sample of people.

Opinion research Gathers together, from a statistical sample of the population, views that are taken to represent those of the entire population.

Opportunity cost   Value of an opportunity to use committed funds in an alternative way.

Opportunity to hear (OTH)   The number of times a listener has the chance to hear a radio commercial. *See* Opportunity to see.

Opportunity to see (OTS)   Average number of exposures experienced by the audience covered by a particular medium.

Optical disc   A mass storage device using laser optical technology, as opposed to magnetic-based metal-oxide coated media such as hard disks, floppy disks and tape. A CD, or compact disc, is a popular example of an optical disc.

Optimal balance   Point at which elements of the marketing mix achieve maximum effectiveness at minimum cost.

Optimum   Theoretical concept for expressing the most cost-effective course of action or level of activity. The many functions in a modern business may well consider their optimum performance to be located at different and contradictory points, thus giving rise to the idea of sub-optimization and trade-off, i.e. accepting something less than the achievement of individual optima to arrive at the best overall result.

Order   Instruction to supply goods or services. *See* Quotation. *See also* Contract.

Order/call ratio   Relationship between the number of orders obtained and the number of calls made to get them over a particular period of operation. Establishes a useful comparative tool for sales efficiency supervision.

Order form   A pre-printed document to facilitate the placing of an order. Used largely in direct marketing, particularly with consumers, where the need for making out one's own order is obviated.

Ordinary position   *See* Run of paper.

Organization and methods   Examination of the structure of an organization, its management and control, its procedures and methods and their comparative efficiency in achieving organizational objectives.

Organizational behaviour   The way in which people behave in an organization, having regard to the corporate hierarchy and corporate culture, and as distinct to consumer behaviour. In marketing, organizational purchasing has been held to be largely objective compared with consumer subjectivity. This has been shown to be invalid since, over and above the objective criteria of product performance, price, delivery and service, motivation is very strong in regard to the fear factor ('No-one was ever fired for purchasing an IBM'), the ego factor ('What will people think about me?'), and the personal relationship ('I enjoy doing business with this company or person'). *See also* Decision making unit.

Organizational purchasing   Relating to any purchase by an organization as opposed to an individual. Often referred to as 'industrial purchasing' but this can be misleading, since it implies machinery or capital plant, whereas the purchasing procedure by an organization can be the same for an electric generator as for a quantity of lemons, for instance with a hotel. *See* Corporate purchasing.

Original   Master artwork for reproduction. *See* Artwork.

Original equipment manufacturer   *See* OEM.

OS/2 Warp   An operating system launched by IBM as a successor to Microsoft's DOS and Windows programs for its own range of PCs.

OTS   *See* Opportunity to see.

Out-bound telemarketing   The proactive use of the telephone in direct marketing. A sales person will initiate calls to prospects in order to generate or qualify sales leads and/or obtain orders. *See also* In-bound telemarketing.

Out-of-town shopping centre A multi-shop complex located out of a town centre and having extensive car parking facilities.

Outdoor advertising Mainly poster and transport advertising, but including illuminated signs and outdoor displays.

Outer pack Container which holds a number of units and whose function usually is one of protection during distribution. It may also be used to carry an advertising message.

Outlet Selling or trading unit.

Output The result of data processing, produced either on a screen, a printer or other magnetic media (such as a floppy disk).

Output budgeting Budgets set for each functional area of the firm but relating specifically to each product or service division; each division is budgeted as a separate organization tied to its own output, but based on its pre-determined business mission.

Outside broadcast Television or radio programme transmitted from a particular location and not from the studio.

Outside message sources *See* Message sources.

Outwork Work which is farmed out to people working at home and thus with reduced overheads.

Over-priced More than most customers would be prepared to pay.

Over-rider An additional discount given to a retailer for achieving extra sales during a given period.

Over-run An additional number of copies printed of a magazine or publication over and above the quantity strictly needed. A contingency to allow for an unexpected demand.

Over the counter Medicines which can be sold direct to the customer without a doctor's prescription, as against 'ethical pharmaceuticals'.

Overcoming objections *See* Objection, overcoming.

Overhead Cost in a business enterprise not directly attributable to specific brands or products. Normally, overheads are recovered by charging a specific amount, often in percentage form, to each unit of sale. In many organizations, an amount for overheads is included in each functional budget.

Overlap Normally refers to those areas of the country which are covered by two or more ITV transmitters.

Overlay Transparent or translucent sheet of paper laid over one piece of artwork carrying further artwork which is to be reproduced in a different colour; or for protection; or to facilitate instructions on how it should be used or modified for production.

Overmatter Excess of type in printing, in relation to the space available.

Overprint Superimpose one negative over another to produce one combined print.

Overselling (1) Persuading distributor or customer to order more goods than they can reasonably handle or consume. (2) Overstating the case for buying a product or service.

Overset Printing term, used when more text is set than is required to fill space available. *See* Overmatter.

Overtrading Transacting more business than working capital will allow to be serviced and thereby producing serious strains upon cash flow, due to the lag in payment by customers subsequent to the placing of orders.

Own label Branding of products by the outlet itself rather than the manufacturer or distributor. Used widely by chain stores and supermarkets for goods usually sold at lower prices than nationally advertised branded alternatives in an effort to maintain customer loyalty.

P

Pack (package, packet) The product of a complete series of packaging operations or a unit consisting of a number of such products (BS 3130).

Package deal The combination of a number of units or range of services into one saleable unit. *See also* Turnkey.

Packaging (1) The art of and the operations involved in the preparation of articles or commodities for carriage, storage, and delivery (BS 3130). (2) Marketing communications channel.

Packing The operations of packaging by which articles or commodities are enveloped in wrapping and/or enclosed in containers or otherwise secured (BS 3130).

Packing case Usually applied to a case constructed of soft timber for the protection of goods in transit, a common precaution in the case of heavy goods and export shipments.

Page description language A computer language used to produce a piece of software which tells a printer how to print a page, e.g. Postscript.

Page exposure *See* Page traffic.

Page proofs Proofs of a leaflet, brochure, magazine or book, taken at the stage when the pages have been made up and used for final review and correction before printing is commenced.

Page rate Price per page for advertising purposes.

Page traffic Number of readers of a particular page in a publication expressed as a percentage of the total readership of that publication. *See* Read most. *See also* Noting.

Pagination Numbering of pages in a printed publication. *See* Folio.

Paid circulation The total number of a periodical printed and despatched to readers on a subscription basis or for sale at a news stand. Validation by the Audit Bureau of Circulation is essential. Not to be confused with Readership. *See also* Controlled circulation.

Paired comparisons In which respondents express a preference to a series of paired products which will usually have differences which are being evaluated.

Pallet Platform, usually of timber, upon which units are stacked, e.g. fibreboard cases, for bulk movement and transportation. Designed to be used in conjunction with fork-lift trucks.

Pamphlet Short, printed but unbound treatise promoting a product, service, organization or idea.

Pan/panning Abbreviation from panorama; slow movement of camera from left to right, or vice versa, across a scene, with camera set-up remaining stationary.

Panel Sample of retail establishments or consumers specially recruited to provide information on buying, media, and consumption habits and sometimes to test potential new products. Requires careful supervision and maintenance to preserve effective data basis.

Panel data Information, usually quantitative, gathered from a group of people specially commissioned to provide a continuous flow; is major source for marketing of consumer goods and services.

Panel testing   Establishing purchasing habits of the population as a whole by having a predetermined group of people record the products they have purchased or used in a given period of time.

Pantone colours   International system of designating colours for printing.

Pantry check   Used in connection with a panel to establish what is available in the home for consumption and as a check upon the veracity of reportage.

Paper   Sheet material manufactured mostly from woodpulp and used in printing and packaging in a variety of grades, e.g. Kraft, a very tough paper for bags and sacks; glassine, a specially processed paper which is grease resistent.

Paper setting   Setting of an advertisement by the printer of a periodical, usually free of charge. *See* Trade setting.

Paper sizes   These in many countries conform to international standards (ISO) of which the most popular is A4 (210 × 297 mm).

Paperboard   Commonly known as cardboard. Comprises a number of layers of wood fibres, sometimes of differing qualities, which are bonded together during their formation on a board machine.

Parallel processing   The simultaneous use of more than one computer or processor, either by working them together or independently under the control of another computer.

Parallel readership   Reduction of the average claim period for readership research, where a second reading event occurs during original claim period so introducing error into estimated average readership figures leading to understatement of readership. *See* Readership replication.

Parameter (1) A quantity whose value specifies or partly specifies the process under consideration or the values of other quantities (BS 3527). (2) A quantity which changes relatively infrequently during a computation; in particular, in a routine, a quantity which may be given a different value each time the routine is used, but which remains unchanged throughout any one routine (BS 3527).

Pareto effect (or law) Operates where a small proportion has a disproportionate effect on the whole. Often used to refer to the so-called 80/20 rule, whereby 20 per cent of customers may take 80 per cent of production and vice versa. More commonly observed in industrial than in consumer goods marketing, though examples can be found in both sectors.

Part-load (1) Goods occupying an unfilled transport vehicle. (2) Part-order or delivery.

Partnership Association of limited number of persons carrying on business together, usually with a profit motive. Particularly associated with small or localized businesses with limited opportunities for expansion, e.g. professional undertakings such as dentists and solicitors. Also, in the 'ladder of customer loyalty' the final stage of customer status in which the buyer and seller operate jointly as partners. JIT might be an example of this.

Partnership pricing An agreed and mutually beneficial pricing strategy between supplier and buyer designed to foster a long-term relationship between the two parties, sharing the risks and rewards jointly and tying the price paid to performance against agreed targets. *See* Business partner.

Party selling Distribution network through selling agents operating from the homes of customers, each of whom, in succession, holds a party for friends offering goods for sale and earning a commission on sales achieved. Popularized in the UK by the American Tupperware organization.

Pass for press Final approval of a publication before printing.

Pass-on readership The number of people reading a publication over and above the primary or original readers. Of particular relevance with trade and technical publications, where the total readership can be as high as ten times the subscribed circulation.

Passing-off Trader leading customers to believe his/her business, services, or goods are those of another by way of product, trade mark, or trade name.

Passive file A listing of those people who have bought from a company but have not made a recent purchase.

Passive message sources *See* Message sources.

Password Literally a combination of unique numbers and letters which when used to enter a computer lets it know it's you! From a security perspective it prevents other people using your data and applications.

Paste-up A piece of finished artwork in which all the various visual components have been fixed, e.g. the illustrations, the headline, and the body copy are all pasted on to a sheet of board. *See* Artwork.

Patent Legal protection for 16 years for any person or organization inventing or devising an improvement in a manufactured article, or in machinery or in methods of making it, when registered at the Patent Office.

Patronage Of consumers, habitual use of particular sources of supply. *See* Testimonial advertisement.

Patterned interview Technique of planned selling where interview is conducted by salespeople according to a predetermined plan.

Pay-back period (1) Time taken to repay development costs of a business venture before profit is earned. (2) Period allowed for repayment of a financial loan.

Pay TV Cable television to a community who pay for the service by subscription.

Payoff Expected return or consideration for providing a service.

PC (personal computer) A general-purpose single-user micro-computer designed to be operated by one person at a time.

PDM *See* Physical distribution management.

Peak time Segment of television airtime, usually the middle part of the evening, where the highest rate is charged and, theoretically, the highest number of people are viewing. Has similar application in radio transmissions.

Peak time band In television advertising, a span of time during which it can be forecast the maximum audience will be viewing. Potentially applicable to radio commercials.

Pedestrian housewife poster Poster measuring 5 feet high and 3 feet 4 inches wide consisting of four double crown sheets. Mounted at street level where it will be seen by most shoppers. Often illuminated.

Pedestrian traffic flow The movement of people along a certain route, e.g. an exhibition corridor, a shopping mall, or a street. Used as a measure in poster advertising to provide the OTS.

Pedlars Door-to-door or street salespeople carrying stock of wares or services for immediate sales on demand.

Peer group Group of people who are perceived as having the same characteristics as oneself, e.g. in status, rank, class, education, standing or merit. Some may regard Peer groups as a category of Opinion-formers (see) and the term has obvious connections with the purchasing behaviour that marketing is concerned to influence.

PEEST Mnemonic for Political, Economic, Environmental, Scientific and Technological. A basis for assessing the effects of external influences on a business. Previously PEST.

Pegged prices Selling prices which are held at a stable level, with the seller absorbing increased costs and possibly subsidised by government action. When undertaken on private initiative, they may enable the seller to win customers from rivals, or at least to maintain market share, especially during periods of inflation. Such an outcome can, however, in no way be guaranteed in all cases.

Penalty clause Clause in an agreement stipulating compensation of an agreed amount (or some alternative course of action) upon breach of a contract. The penalty clause will not necessarily reflect the true cost of the breach, which may be difficult to estimate in advance of the event.

Penetration Extent to which a product or an advertisement has been accepted by, or has registered with the total of possible users, usually expressed as a percentage.

Penetration pricing Adoption of a lower price strategy in order to secure rapid wide penetration of a market.

People message sources *See* Message sources.

People orientated Inclined to be interested in people individually or collectively particularly before material goods. Used to indicate an attitude of mind appropriate to marketing activities.

Per capita income Total income of a nation averaged over its population, thus giving an arbitrary, but comparative measure of income per head of the population.

Per pro By proxy: through an agent. In relation to a signature on a letter, a representative signing on behalf of someone else. Abbreviation 'pp'.

Perceived benefit *See* Attributes.

Perceived image The impression held by people of an organization or a product.

Perceived value pricing The pricing strategy which is based upon the value put upon a product by the prospective customers and in relation to competitors' prices, as opposed to Cost plus pricing, which *see*. *See also* Market price.

Percentage-of-sales method   Means of arriving at a marketing or advertising budget by applying a pre-determined percentage to the total sales turnover of the previous year or to the current or future sales target. *See* Task method.

Perception   Personal interpretation of what one sees, hears, smells, i.e. the reception of sensory stimuli and conscious or unconscious application of them to form an acceptable interpretation of their meaning.

Perception by exception   Registering by consumers of particular distinction featured in a brand promotion. Is the basis of brand differentiation and the prerequisite is a unique selling proposition.

Perceptual mapping   Multi-dimensional maps of consumers' product positioning, often revealing indirect competition between different product choices.

Perfect binding   Method of binding used on books. The printed sections are folded and then sewn together on the spine. Glue is then applied and the cover is drawn on.

Perfect competition   Term used by economists to describe an open market situation, where free trade prevails without restriction, where all goods of a particular nature are homogeneous and where all relevant information is known to both buyers and sellers. Such conditions rarely, if ever, apply in fact but the hypothesis has been found useful in analysing the forces governing the operation of supply and demand factors in real life conditions.

Performance appraisal   Audit of actual achievement against forecast.

Performance-based compensation   A little used basis of paying an agency or consultancy based upon actual results obtained, e.g. sales, enquiries, column inches, etc.

Perk   Abbreviation from the word 'perquisite', defined by Webster as 'an incidental gain or profit in addition to regular salary or wages'.

221

Perimeter advertising Posters and other such displays in sports grounds 'around the perimeters'.

Periodical Publication which appears at regular intervals, e.g. daily, weekly, monthly.

Peripheral Any hardware item separate from the central processing unit. Common examples are terminals, modems and printers.

Perishables Goods with a limited sales life, such as fruit and vegetables.

Perquisites *See* Perks.

Persistent demand Continuing demand for brand, often in spite of increasing prices.

Personal computer *See* PC.

Personal interview Meeting between two or more people, with a view to discussing a project or proposition or eliciting answers to questions as in market research. *See also* Face-to-face selling.

Personal marketing Any marketing initiative which directly impacts upon individuals as opposed to groups of people.

Personal selling The process of making oral commerical representations during a buyer/seller interview situation. Colloquially referred to as face-to-face selling. Sometimes known as buyer/seller interface.

Personality (1) Term which attempts to aggregate that combination of traits which may indicate what a person will do, or how an individual will behave when placed in given or differing situations. (2) Well-known person such as may be used to feature in an advertisement or a campaign.

Personality promotions (1) Use of well-known persons to endorse a product or service. *See* Testimonial advertisement. (2) Use of readily identifiable, often gaily dressed, persons from whom a prize can be claimed if approached with the use of a promotional phrase or saying.

Personalized letter A standard letter to which is added, usually by computer programme, a personal touch such as the salutation.

Perspective Method for two-dimensional drawing in such a way that an impression of three-dimensions is given, e.g. by drawing converging lines away from the basic outline.

Persuasion Personal process with aim of changing a person's attitude or behaviour with respect to some object. In marketing, the development in a person of a desire to purchase a product or service or, more properly, to acquire the perceived benefit.

Persuasive communication Any form of communication which is primarily intended to exercise persuasion, e.g. advertising, editorial publicity, sales presentations, speeches, films and filmstrips, etc.

PERT (Project Evaluation and Review Techniques) A discipline applied to the methodical planning of complex systems, e.g. major events or large building projects. Can be applied to major marketing plans.

Peter principle To come to an end. In business the practice whereby people tend to be promoted until they occupy positions for which they are incompetent.

Phased or zonal distribution Distributing goods to one area or one group of customers at a time, until a national network has been established. *See* Zone.

Photocall A staged photographic event with the intention of gaining editorial publicity.

Photocomposition Typesetting by photographic means, in which light is transmitted through a grid bearing the outlines of lettering on to photosensitive material which can then be used for artwork.

Photogenic Attractive in photographs. *See* Telegenic.

Photogravure Printing process in which the subject matter is photochemically etched into a polished copper cylinder. Used widely for large-circulation colour magazines.

Physical distribution Movement of goods, and all that such movement implies, from the manufacturer to the user, via various channels of distribution.

Physical distribution management The management of the distribution function.

Pica A printer's unit of measure, a 12 point em, i.e. approximately ⅙ inch.

Pick and point A user-friendly method of selecting programs, software applications, or sub-routines within them, from a pre-defined form rather than by typing in the commands and filenames from the keyboard.

Pictogram Diagram representing figures in a more easily interpreted way, e.g. a pie chart.

Pictorial presentation Expression of data or information in picture form in order to ease, or further, comprehension.

Picture caption Heading or description of photograph for publication.

Pie chart Pictorial presentation, showing the parts of a total activity or performance as sectors of a circle. May also be used to contrast the behaviour of two sets of variables by comparing the angular dimensions and/or area of each piece and changes occurring over time.

Piece News item or feature.

Pied type Used by printers to describe words or lines of type rendered meaningless by displaced or wrong letters.

Piggy-back export schemes Government-supported export service in which would-be exporters are put in touch with existing exporters who assist them.

Piggy-back promotion Where a product is accompanied by another product or a voucher for one, e.g. a free sample.

Piggy-back selling In which an established organization accesses its services for use by a smaller business for a consideration. Has particular reference to overseas activities.

Piggy-backing To enclose an additional mailing piece with a mailing which is already programmed to take place.

Pilot Test survey to check mechanical or operating details before embarking upon a major study.

Pilot launch A pre-launch test in a small area to check the strategy before rolling out to the whole market. *See* Test market.

Pioneer selling *See* Commando selling.

Piracy Illegal use of a software program. Usually when someone avoids paying for 'license to use' by copying someone else's legal version.

Pirated products Use of another's trade mark, tradename, or copyright to gain the benefit of that established name or reputation. *See* Commercial counterfeiting.

Pitch   Colloquial term describing an agency presentation before a prospective client. Also refers to a sales pitch – a presentation by a salesperson to a buyer. *See* Presentation.

Placard   Small poster.

Place   One of the elements of the four Ps. It relates to the outlets and channels of distribution in marketing and also to delivery time in the business-to-business sector. *See* Marketing mix.

Place cues   *See* Cues.

Placebo effect   Power of suggestion, inherent in many advertising promises; usually a feature of Transference or Positioning.

Placement test   In such a test, products or packs are delivered to selected usage points for trial to be followed up by interviews collecting information on performance and attitudes towards them. *See* Extended use tests.

Placing   Process of selecting, organizing and implementing a choice between marketing alternatives.

Planned obsolescence   The somewhat controversial practice of designing products with a short lifetime, either because they go out of date or they cease to function as they should.

Planned selling   Operating selling activity along predetermined lines with calculated aims and goals, specified strategies and tactics, and monitored against these standards; it means guiding and controlling each sales interview against a plan setting its objectives, yet allowing some degree of variations to occur in achieving them, reflecting the human situations involved but keeping salesperson operation within a systematic schedule. Part of the overall marketing plan implemented by the sales force comprising all other sub-functions of marketing.

Plans board   Group of senior executives, usually in an advertising agency, who meet to assess a particular campaign or proposed strategy.

Plant utilization   *See* Down-time.

Plastic-comb binding   *See* Mechanical binding.

Plastics   Synthetic materials available in a variety of forms, sheeting, mouldings, extrusions and laminates. Have a wide range of properties, optical and mechanical, and are particularly resistent to water and to solvents and other chemicals. Available in rigid, semi-rigid, or pliable form. Basically of two types: thermoplastics (which soften or melt with heat), e.g. polyethylene, polyvinyl chloride (PVC), polystyrene; or thermosetting, which hardens (polymerizes) on the first application of heat, and thereafter maintain their form, e.g. phenol formaldehyde (Bakelite), urea formaldehyde. Some plastics can be 'blown' into expanded form with a variety of uses in packaging, e.g. foam plastic. *See* Blister pack.

Plate   Printing block or litho plate.

Platform   (1) Main copy theme of an advertisment. (2) The hardware and operating system base on which software applications and programs may be run.

Playback   (1) Reproduction on closed circuit of recorded material. (2) Reproduction of material, either live or recorded, through a loudspeaker to enable actors to synchronize with it.

Plinth   Wooden platform used as the floor of an exhibition stand.

Plotter   A type of printer which has a specialized application in the production of complex drawings such as technical illustrations.

Plug   Promotion of product or company by medium without charge. Often used as a testimonial in conversation.

PMT   Photo-mechanical transfer. Method of reproducing artwork or typesetting in which an image from the original is exposed onto photo-sensitive paper to form a negative. This in turn is converted into a positive paper which is a facsimile of the original.

Pocket envelope   An envelope with the flap on the short edge.

Point   (1) Unit of type – 0.0138 inches, 12 points to the pica, approximately 72 points to the inch. (2) Full-stop.

Point-of-purchase   Arguable alternative term to point-of-sale, but may differ in some respects, e.g. in mail order where the point-of-purchase differs from the point-of-sale in terms of time span, or where vending machines are in use.

Point-of-sale (POS)   Usually referring to retail sales outlet. Place at which a sale is made; also refers to publicity material used there, e.g. posters, showcards, display units, dispensers and leaflets.

Poll   (1) Public opinion survey. (2) To seek information.

Polybag   A means of distributing promotional literature, magazines, samples or products by enclosing them in a flimsy polythene container or envelope.

POP   *See* Point-of-purchase.

Pop-up   Promotional piece often used in direct mail whereby a flat enclosure 'pops up' when removed from the envelope. Equally, the same device can be inserted into a magazine to gain high attention.

Popular price   Pricing technique intended to appeal to a majority of buyers.

Population   Total number in a group, whether geographical area or specialized group.

Portfolio   Presentation kit used by salespeople when interviewing prospective customers.

Portfolio analysis   (1) Analysing elements of the marketing mix. (2) Analysing product performance within the product range.

Portrait   Describes an illustration or piece of print in which the vertical dimension is greater than the horizontal one. Opposite to landscape.

POS   *See* Point-of-sale.

Position   The choice of a special location for an advertisement in a magazine, e.g. front cover or facing matter. Also refers to a particular slot in a television advertising break, or on the radio.

Position media   Advertising media with fixed site or position, such as posters. Usually used as a blanket term to cover poster and transport advertising.

Positioning theory   Advertising style devoted to owning a part of the consumer's mind, so occupying a position of trust and loyalty for the brand concerned.

Positive option   In direct mail, the recipient is invited to respond and to ask for specific information or, indeed, to place an order. *See* Negative option.

Positive recall rating   The extent to which an advertisement can be remembered after appearance or broadcast, using either a prompted or an unprompted question.

Post peak   Time following peak viewing or listening times in broadcast media.

Post purchase   Referring to arrangements made after a purchase has been completed.

Post-purchase advertising   Reassuring customers that they have made the right decision; intended to stimulate word-of-mouth recommendation through brand personality. May also encourage buyers to make repeat purchases.

Post-purchase dissonance   *See* Cognitive dissonance.

Post-sales service Promotional activities designed to maintain customers' goodwill and support with a view to repeat sales. *See* After-sales service.

Post-test Evaluation of a campaign or an advertisement after it has run and has had time to have an effect. Could also apply to a new product launch.

Postal research Use of the post for research purposes as against personal or telephone interviews.

Postcall analysis Reviewing achievements following sales interview. *See* Kerbside conferences.

Poster Placard displayed in public place.

Poster panel Fixed position for poster advertising, usually found in underground/railway trains and stations or other transportation media.

Poster site classifications Based on type of location, category of road, and degree of visibility, for each poster site.

Poster sizes These are in multiples of one standard size called Double crown, which *see*.

Postscript In a direct mail letter, the use of a 'PS' is thought by some to add attention value to the advertising message.

Potential user Likely future user.

pp *See Per pro.*

PR Used alternatively and confusingly as the abbreviation for both Public relations and Press relations, both of which *see*.

Pre-approach Preparation of all relevant material in relation to objectives prior to a selling interview.

Pre-campaign exposure Assessing impressions or attitudes about a brand or a concept prior to a campaign. Used to develop refinement in campaign strategy.

Pre-coded Questions to be put and the possible answers which may be received in a survey are keyed to enable easy tabulation of results using a numerical coding system. This facilitates computer analysis making possible the rapid handling of a high volume of data.

Pre-empt spot In television, an advertisement spot bought in advance in a particular time segment at a discount but which will not be screened if another advertiser offers to take up that time at the full rate.

Pre-paid cards *See* Reply card.

Pre-peak Time prior to peak viewing or listening times in broadcast media.

Pre-sales service Activities by sales force or their supporting organization to provide prospective customers with advice or help in their movement towards a purchasing decision.

Pre-selected campaign (PSC) National poster campaign, sold as a package, either aimed geographically or for a specialist category. *See also* Impactaplan.

Pre-sorting To group together mailing pieces in order to gain a preferential rate from the postal authorities in consideration of geographical bundling.

Pre-test Test of product or advertisement prior to full scale testing programme.

Pre-testing *See* Product evaluation. *See also* Product testing; Concept testing.

Pre-testing copy Exploratory research to check the efficacy of a particular piece of advertising copy prior to its being used in an actual advertisement. *See* Advertising research.

Preferred position   A particular part of a newspaper or magazine in which an advertiser wishes to appear. An additional charge is usually made. *See* Facing matter.

Premium   Additional price charged in return for some commercial benefit over and above the product itself.

Premium offer   Special offer of merchandise at a reduced price in consideration of purchasing a particular product, as evidenced by the sending in of a qualifying number of labels or coupons. Usually conducted as a self-liquidating operation.

Presence   Refers to a form of measurement which endeavours to indicate whether members of a target audience are actually present during the transmission of commercials as well as the programmes within which they are slotted. Crude viewing figures require modification for translation in terms of attention value.

Presentation   Meeting in which proposals are put to an audience in a planned and usually formal manner. Much used by advertising and research agencies but also used by companies communicating with distributors or, for example, publishers desiring to influence main opinion formers.

Press   All periodicals, whether national, local, trade, or technical.

Press advertising   Advertising in the press. *See* Advertising.

Press conference   *See* Press reception.

Press cuttings   Excerpts on a particular subject cut from any kind of periodical. Used as a monitoring device to indicate the extent to which a subject is receiving publicity. *See* Cuttings.

Press date   Date on which a publication or a section of a publication is due to be passed for press. *See* Copy date.

Press mentions   Brand or company references in the media.

Press packs Kit of documents, samples and other related items for issue to journalists, providing them with comprehensive coverage of an event or news item.

Press puffs Complimentary brand or company references in the media.

Press reception Meeting to which press representatives (editors, journalists, reporters) are invited in order to be informed of an event, and to have the opportunity of questioning or commenting.

Press relations That part of public relations and/or marketing communications activity aimed at establishing and maintaining a favourable relationship both with and through the press. Not to be confused with public relations.

Press release Written statement describing an event or item which is considered to be of sufficient interest to readers for an editor to publish some reference to it. Sometimes referred to as a news release – a more appropriate term as it includes the use of broadcating media.

Press visit Visit by members of the press to a place of interest, usually coupled with a special event, such as the official opening of a new establishment or launching of a new activity.

Pressure selling Forceful selling effort. Referred to as high pressure selling when the effort is perceived to be aggressive. *See* Low pressure selling.

Prestige advertising *See* Corporate advertising.

Preview Showing of a film, commercial or advertising campaign to a select audience, in advance of general public viewing.

Price Agreed exchange value forming the essential basis for a trading agreement.

Price awareness Extent to which consumers react to, or are aware of, price differences between competing brands.

Price cues *See* Cues.

Price cutting Selling at prices below the commonly accepted level for the product or commodity concerned.

Price-demand elasticity Relationship between the selling price of a product and the volume of demand which will be generated as a result. High elasticity is indicative of a product for which demand will be very sensitive to changes in price. This is often to be found in highly competitive markets and is more closely associated with non-essential commodities. Low elasticity will apply to essentials and particularly in a monopolistic situation. Price-demand elasticity should never be taken to imply that reducing prices will inevitably lead to increasing demand or that increasing prices will result in a reduction in demand; the reverse may actually occur in both cases. *See* Giffen goods.

Price determinant One or more of factors affecting the final price of a product or service. Often used to describe merely the major determining factor in establishing a price.

Price discrimination Charging different prices to different markets or classes of buyers. Occurs most commonly as between cash and credit or instalment purchases but will also reflect the value of particular outlets.

Price/earnings ratio Quoted price of an ordinary share divided by the most recent year's earnings per share.

Price haven Securing a favourable position in brand loyalty where changes in price will not affect company sales volume.

Price index Sequence of price changes expressed against a base year, usually starting at 100. *See* Indexing.

Price leadership   Attributed to that company which initiates new price levels.

Price list   Sheet of paper on which is printed a schedule of prices for a product or service.

Price mechanism   System of allocation of scarce resources according to effective demand, expressed through price and price movements.

Price range   Prices from the lowest to the highest available for a particular type of product. Frequently used to describe the whole spectrum of prices within a company's product range.

Price sensitive   In which the demand for a product or service decreases quickly following a rise in price, and vice versa. *See* Law of supply and demand.

Price skimming   High initial selling price in markets where price is not likely to be elastic. May be set to secure a quick return, to recover high research and development costs, or to take advantage of a patent.

Price structure   Detailed prices and discounts, the amount of detail depending on whether prepared for trade or the final user or consumer.

Price tag   Price declared on an item or in an advertisement describing an item.

Price war   In which two or more organizations progressively decrease their prices in order to gain increased market share.

Pricing mix   Policy adopted in setting prices of particular products to meet competition.

Pricing plateau   Round figure for selling price, above and below which sharply increasing elasticity tends to occur, hence fixing of price at £4.99 rather than £5.

Pricing strategy   Deliberate planning of the pricing structure in relation to factors such as consumer wants, product attributes and competition in such a way as to ensure overall profitability. Such a strategy must have regard to price-demand elasticity as well as encompassing such variables and incentives as volume discounts, commission and premium offers.

Pricing tactics   Short-term pricing manipulation used in an effort to stimulate brand switching or an increase in the share of total market.

Primary advertising   In which demand for a product group in general is generated by advertising, say, for a trade association. Can be referred to as generic advertising. *See also* Co-operative advertising.

Primary colours   The colours which, when combined with black, go to make up a full colour illustration. They are yellow, magenta (red), and cyan (blue).

Primary data   Information which is specially collected by means of a research programme carried out for a specific purpose. *See* Secondary data.

Primary media   The main channels of communication in a marketing communications programme, as opposed to all the minor media which may be used in a support role.

Primary readership   Readership figures based upon initial purchasers of a publication, e.g. paid for by any member of a household. *See* Secondary readership. *See also* Tertiary readership.

Primary research   *See* Primary data.

Prime time   Those transmission hours in television and radio which attract the largest audiences.

Principal   Person or organization who appoints and directs an agent (e.g., export agent) who is acting on his/her behalf for instance in another country.

236

Print media Blanket term covering printed media and distinguishing it from broadcast or position media.

Print run Quantity involved in any print order or publication.

Printed matter *See* Matter.

Private brand Retailers' or wholesalers' own brand. *See* Distributors' brand and Own label.

Private carrier Carries goods according to specific contracts and is under no obligation to provide scheduled services.

Private label *See* Own label.

PRO *See* Public relations officer.

Processor *See* CPU.

Pro forma invoice Document stating the value of a transaction, used to notify the proposed despatch of a consignment of goods. It is frequently used as a means of obtaining prepayment or of permitting the buyer to obtain exchange control sanction for the necessary remittance from another country.

Pro rata freight Proportion of freight charges due as a result of cargo being delivered to a port short of the port of destination.

Probability Basis of sampling theory; providing sufficient history of an event is known, then the probability that it will occur again is calculable.

Probe Used to obtain further information when the initial inquiry does not produce a satisfactory response, or to make sure at interview that the respondent has answered the question fully.

Procurement All those activities within an organization which contribute towards the placement of an order. Synonym for Buying, or Purchasing.

Product acceptance Measurement deciding degree of success of product launch.

Product attributes The positive features of a product from which the 'benefits' are selected for promotion. These, in turn, must be chosen to match customer requirements.

Product benefits Factors which go towards satisfying the requirements of a customer. Fundamentally, the purchasing decision is based upon the perceived product benefits rather than the product itself or its specification or performance. *See* Consumer want.

Product champion Person having responsibility for a particular product or service in respect of promotion and other aspects of marketing. *See* Brand manager.

Product clutter Wide range of products, many past their useful life, usually clogging the attempt to streamline effective marketing management.

Product cues *See* Cues.

Product development Activity leading to a product having new or different characteristics or consumer benefits. Such developments range from an entirely new concept to meet a newly defined consumer 'want' to the modification of an existing product or indeed its presentation and packaging. It forms part of a process which has to be continuous to arrest the decline era within the intrinsic life cycle of any existing product.

Product development cycle Chain of events leading up to the birth of a new product, i.e. concept, mock-up, prototype, preproduction batch, full production.

Product differentiation Policy which emphasizes those features which distinguish one product from other similar products.

238

Product diversification   The adoption of a completely different range of products, may be aimed at existing markets or to utilize spare capacity. Objective is often as a hedge against a decline in demand for present product range, or to provide a more stable business base.

Product evaluation   Of particular relevance to new products, product evaluation is the means by which the value of a product to a customer is determined in advance. This is of special importance in developing a pricing strategy but, in practice, should go much deeper in order to categorize each of the product benefits in relation to each of the market segments. From such essential background knowledge develops not only the marketing strategy and the media mix, but also the basic selling platform and the advertising appropriation.

Product image   Concept which describes what consumers believe the product to be or do, regardless of its literal accuracy or otherwise. Often their conclusions are made on value judgments without recourse to trial of alternative products. *See* Brand image.

Product life cycle   *See* Life cycle.

Product line   Group of products having related characteristics or a common market. A number of product lines might make up a product portfolio. *See* Product portfolio.

Product manager   *See* Brand manager.

Product-market scope   Markets served by specific products; suppliers are established in this market and are able to use existing reputation to introduce related product types.

Product mix   Range of products which, when viewed as a whole, provides a more than proportionate return than the sum of the individual items if marketed in isolation. Such a return can be achieved by adding complementary products to an existing range and sold to the same market without significant additional expense. Alternatively, existing products with minor modifications involving little further expense can find a demand in different market segments. A product mix can be such that seasonal demands for one are offset by those of another, thereby maintaining continuity of production and distribution resources. Yet again, the mix can be so structured as to embrace products in each of the stages of the product life cycle. *See* Synergy.

Product parity   In which two or more products have equality in terms of performance, price and availability and are thus 'undifferentiated'.

Product performance   Relates to the intrinsic attributes of a product. These may not necessarily be in line with its specification, nor, for that matter, the requirements of all potential customers; cf. the Anglo-French Concorde.

Product placement   Securing one's own product as part of the set or scenery in a television, film-making, or theatrical production.

Product-plus   Element in the product, or its presentation, which gives it an advantage over its competitors and is perceived as such by purchasers of it. *See also* Competitive advantage, Competitive edge, and Differential advantage.

Product portfolio   Based upon the Boston Consulting Group's concept which categorizes all products into one of four classifications. These are commonly shown in the diagrammatic form of a box (hence the Boston Box) with the horizontal axis representing market share, and the vertical market growth. Products having high market share in a market with high growth are referred to as stars; those with high market share and low market growth are cash cows; low market share and high market growth are problem children (or wildcats or question marks); finally with both low market share and growth the products are classified dogs.

Product positioning   Examining the perception of a product in relation to its competitors in terms of a series of predetermined criteria, i.e., consumer benefits. And then to take such communications actions as are necessary to move it to a stronger or more desirable perception, viz, to change its position in relation to its competitors.

Product/price parity   Near homogeneous products at identical prices.

Product quality differentiation   Distinguishing a brand from competition by highlighting a quality feature that may or may not be unique to the brand concerned.

Product range   Full list of available products made by any one firm.

Product testing   *See* Anonymous product testing.

Product, weighted distribution   Distribution weighted to allow for the known disproportionate influences in different outlets. Weights will usually be determined by relative significance of factors, e.g. level of purchasing power or areas of light or heavy usage, e.g. of 'hard' or 'soft' water.

Production   The process of converting artwork into plates for reproduction.

Production department   People in an advertising agency dealing with planning, progress (traffic), production, proofing and vouchers, which *see*. *See also* Traffic.

Production orientation   Condition in which a company is preoccupied with the problems associated with producing goods with scant consideration for what the individuals comprising the market want or are prepared to pay.

Production schedule   Programme of work necessary to produce promotional or other material.

Professional services marketing   The application of the marketing concept and function to professional practices, such as lawyers, architects, consultants and accountants.

Profile   Detailed description of subject, often a person, or groups of subjects. Sometimes expressed as percentages against predetermined criteria, intended to make identification of the subject, perhaps the target user or consumer, readily possible.

Profit Often used to describe the surplus resulting after a defined trading period but must be regarded as the first essential charge upon a business, being a reward for engaging resources in conditions of speculative risk for the satisfaction of consumer demand. It furnishes resources to invest in future operations and consequently its absence must result in a decline in effective capital resources and ultimately competitive extinction of the business.

Profit accountability Practice requiring an executive to take responsibility for the profit performance of his/her own functional unit.

Profit centre Application of responsibility accounting to a unit or centre of activity through which profits are accrued.

Profit earnings ratio Often styled the P/E ratio, this refers to the number of year's earnings by which a company is valued according to its quoted share prices.

Profit potential Estimation of likelihood or otherwise of a particular product or venture achieving a profit.

Pro-forma invoice Document sent in advance of the despatch of goods for prior payment. Used often where the customer's credit rating is unknown or is suspect.

Program A set of instructions which can be applied to most data processing or computerized functions.

Programme A schedule in a marketing plan indicating the various actions which should take place in order to achieve the objectives.

Progress chasing Function of department responsible for the satisfactory progress of work through an organization.

Progress payments Interim payments made while work is in progress. Often applies to building work.

Progressive obsolescence Gradual periodic restyling of goods in order to outdate established models.

Progressives Set of proofs taken from the individual blocks or plates constituting a four-colour set for the purpose of checking clarity and correct alignment. *See* Four-colour set.

Projection (1) Forecasting process (extrapolation) using trends in a time series to estimate future values. (2) Psychological research technique to identify true attitudes, for example, towards a product, rather than the socially acceptable reasons which may be put forward by respondents.

Projective tests Research technique, usually qualitative, requiring respondent to complete an open-ended question.

Promotion *See* Sales promotion.

Promotional clothing Hats, shirts, sweaters, blouses, and other such garments upon which are emblazoned company or corporate logos, brand names, or slogans. Strongly associated with sponsorship.

Promotional mix Range of promotional activities selected for use by a company at any one time.

Promotional platform Central theme for a publicity campaign.

Prompt (1) Providing a number of alternative answers in a questionnaire to enable a respondent to select the one most appropriate to his/her beliefs. (2) Mastheads or magazine covers used in readership research to help respondents remember the titles they have read, or the product they have seen advertised.

Proof Preliminary printing, usually by a manual process, to facilitate checking and approval prior to final mechanical printing. *See* Block pull.

Proof of purchase Evidence that a product has actually been purchased, such as the package, or part of it, a label, bottle cap, receipt, etc.

Proof-read The checking of typesetting in proofs for an advertisement or publication.

Propaganda Putting across a biased and misleading point of view: to convert others to a cause. Not to be confused with public relations.

Propaganda selling *See* Missionary salesperson.

Propensity to buy An attitude of mind which directs and supports an inclination to buy one product as against another. Can be as a result of having a positive perception of the company which, in turn, by definition, is the outcome of a public relations campaign.

Proposition In short form, the selling or advertising platform upon which an advertising campaign will be based. *See* Unique selling proposition.

Proprietary goods The goods which are manufactured and sold under standards laid down by a ruling authority, such as that for drugs and pharmaceutical preparations.

Prospect Arising from an initial enquiry, which is subsequently filtered out into a qualified sales lead, i.e. prospective customer.

Prospecting Using direct mail, advertising or other medium to generate sales leads. *See* Hit list.

Protective tariff A charge or duty applied to imports in order to afford some protection to home-produced competitive products.

Protocol A set of formal rules against which, for example, computers may communicate with each other.

Prototype First working model or initially constructed version of a product. To all intents and purposes, the prototype is the product in appearance, characteristics and performance. Its existence facilitates numerous judgments, tests and management decisions regarding future developments.

Provincial press   Newspapers, circulating daily or weekly in a restricted geographic region, e.g. a city or county. Otherwise referred to as local press or regional press.

Proxemics   Use of space or minimization of space in personal communications.

Pseudo product testing   In which the same basic product is presented in a variety of ways, e.g. different packs, to a test group who are asked to give a preference rating. This determines customers' capability of discerning differences, or lack of them, and gives an indication of the virtues of each form of presentation. *See also* Anonymous product testing.

Psychogalvanometer   Measuring device used in advertising research to determine the emotional effect of advertising messages by reaction to the rate of perspiration flow exhibited by the viewer.

Psychographic segmentation   The breaking down of markets into smaller groups of people chosen for a common lifestyle, e.g. interests, activities and opinions. Also can apply to personality or consumption patterns. *See* Psychographics.

Psychographics   A technique devoted to the segmentation of markets using psychological criteria to distinguish between the different segments.

Psychological hook   Emotionally disposed towards a favoured brand; brand loyalty achieved by appeals to subconscious desires.

Psychology of selling   Explanation of the sales process which lays emphasis upon the workings of psychological factors and particularly their manipulation by salespeople to secure a favourable response to their propositions.

Public affairs   Term used usually to describe PR activities in relation to Government, pressure groups and sometimes financial affairs at a corporate level, i.e. excluding customers and prospects and probably employees. Alternative term Corporate affairs.

245

Public lending right   Right of authors to receive payments from a central fund for their books lent out to the public by local public libraries in the UK.

Public relations   Conscious effort to improve and maintain an organization's relationships with such publics as employees, customers, shareholders, local communities, trade unions with a view to strengthening reputation, i.e. building corporate image. Not to be confused with Press relations.

Public relations consultant/consultancy   Individual or firm employed by an organization to advise and/or act on its behalf in the field of public relations.

Public relations manager   An executive responsible for planning and implementing a public relations programme, sometimes in conjunction with a PR consultancy. Such managers sometimes report to the marketing director or another functional board member, such as the company secretary, but increasingly public relations is directly responsible to the CEO.

Public relations officer   Executive responsible for planning and implementing the public relations policy of an organization.

Public service advertising   Non-commercial advertising, sometimes provided by media at reduced rates or free of charge, and concerned with the welfare of the community in general.

Publication date   Officially stated date when a publication becomes available for purchase or distribution.

Publicity   Process of securing public attention for messages to be imparted. *See* Advertising; Public relations; and Sales promotion – all of which fall to some extent within the category indicated by this term. In USA refers to editorial publicity.

246

Publicity manager   Person responsible for managing a company's publicity. *See* Marketing communications manager, Advertising manager and Marketing services manager.

Publics   Discrete and identifiable groups of people to whom a corporate image is to be projected and whose goodwill is important to an organization in the achievement of its overall objectives. Such audiences will include shareholders, employees, customers, government, local community, and opinion formers, all of which go to form the audience for a public relations programme. Sometimes referred to as stakeholders.

Publisher's statement   Statement by a publishing company of the circulation and other information relating to a particular publication. Not necessarily independently audited. *See* ABC.

Publishing   Business of producing books, magazines, newspapers, and other periodicals, and distributing them to the public via bookshops, newsagents, mail or other outlets.

Puff   Reference by individual or organization, usually in the media, to a product or company with the intention of providing favourable publicity.

Pull   *See* Block pull.

Pull-down menu   A list of options that can be 'pulled down' on the screen from a menu bar. *See* Graphical user interface.

Pull-out   Separate section or supplement to a publication which is loose and may be pulled out.

Pulsation method   Short-term periods of intensive advertising followed by a pause and then another 'pulse' of advertising, as opposed to Drip, which *see*.

Punnet   Specialized paperboard carton, or wooden container, open to inspection of contents and used principally for dispensing soft fruit by weight.

Purchasing agent/officer Representative of buying firm group. *See* Buyer (1) and (2).

Purchasing motives *See* Buying motives.

Purchasing patterns Refers to individual, or collective, purchasing behaviour within a market.

Purchasing power Extent to which an organization, group of people or a geographical area with funds available, whether committed or otherwise, has the ability to make purchases during specified time periods.

Push/pull strategy Two options open to a manufacturer to move his products through a distribution channel. One is to advertise heavily and thus create a consumer demand which forces retailers to stock a product. The other is to promote actively the product to retailers and wholesalers and encourage them to take stocks in anticipation of a developing consumer demand.

Pyramid selling Form of franchising where personnel are recruited against financial standards of entry and help to establish a distribution network of commission agents.

Q

Quad crown Poster size equal to two double crowns. *See* Double crown.

Qualified circulation *See* Controlled circulation.

Qualified sales lead An initial contact (e.g. an enquiry) which has been followed up and proved to be a potential customer.

Qualifying   The process of checking whether or not a particular prospect is genuine in terms of wanting a product in the foreseeable future, and has some means of paying for it.

Qualitative research   Deals with data frequently difficult to quantify; often expressed as value judgments by individuals from which any collective general conclusions are difficult to draw. Such research usually involves group discussions or interviews.

Quality control   Important procedure usually involving the random inspection of goods with a view to maintaining specified standards.

Quantitative research   Research findings which may be expressed numerically. They may then be subjected to mathematical or statistical manipulation to produce forecasts of future events under differing environmental conditions.

Quantity discount   Reduction from list price in consideration of the purchase of a particular (larger) quantity of a product.

Quarterly   Publication issued four times a year.

Quartile   Any of four parts into which, in statistics, a population is divided. In a cumulative frequency distribution, the lower values occur in the lower quartile, the higher values in the upper quartile and the remainder in mid positions around the median value.

Quasi contracts   While no actual contract exists, the courts would hold on such a basis that one party nevertheless has an obligation towards another.

Quasi retailing   Outlets selling services rather than goods, including estate agents, banks, hotels, and undertakers.

Queen's Award to Industry   Annual awards made on 21 April in recognition of outstanding achievement by firms in exporting or in technological innovation.

Query A facility to access data held in a database. Provides rapid access to predefined information as specified by file or record type.

Questionnaire Base document for research studies which provides the questions and the structure for an interview and has provision for respondents' answers. Requires considerable skill in design, involving understanding of human nature and communication processes.

Quid pro quo A concession given to a person or organization in response to an equally valuable concession on their part.

Quota (1) Structure of a sample specifying number and type of persons required for interviews. (2) Sales target figure for salespeople that may be expressed as required minimum performance or act as threshold for commission payment.

Quota sample Preselected groups for interviewing, constructed so as to represent the known characteristics of the whole population.

Quotation Specific offer, verbal or written, of goods or services, the acceptance of which will form a contract.

Quotation closes Submitting a selling proposal with the formal quotation.

Quotes Quotation marks or inverted commas used at the beginning and end of a quoted passage or word.

R

Radio rating points The equivalent of TVRs on radio.

Ragged In which no attempt is made to line up or 'justify' lines of type setting, i.e. one edge or both edges are left 'ragged'.

RAID (Redundant array of inexpensive disks) A technique which spreads data over several smaller interconnected disk drives instead of a single large one. RAID provides faster data retrieval and better protection against data loss, so if one disk crashes then data can be quickly reconstructed from redundant data on the other disks.

RAM (Random access memory) 'Volatile' or 'dynamic' memory comprising one or more electronic microchips which can be read from or written to by a computer (contrasted with 'static' memory such as hard disks).

Ranking Established alternative choices in order of preference.

Rate card Document issued by publishers or advertising contractors showing the charges made for various types and sizes of advertisement and including the relevant mechanical data to govern advertisement production.

Rating Applied especially to broadcasting media and meaning the relative audience or viewership achieved by a programme or advertisement, as compared with others, e.g. a popularity rating. Used also in research studies. *See* TVR.

Rationalization In reference to products, the elimination of items in the range which bring in the minimum return and call for a disproportionate effort to sustain demand. Rationalization leads to a concentration of resources into those products from which a maximum return can be expected.

Reach Synonym for cumulative audience.

Read most Term used in assessing the effectiveness of an advertisement in the press. Respondents are asked to indicate whether, if they noted an advertisement, they then 'read most' of its copy. This data can then be expressed as a percentage of total readership.

Reader Someone who has 'read' a publication or periodical as opposed merely to having 'received' it. Hence the difference between circulation and readership. A person receiving a publication, whether free or at a price, may never read it. Thus there could be fewer readers than the circulation or print order might imply. Equally, the opposite might apply. *See* Pass-on readership.

Reader involvement Copywriting with the aim of gaining the participation of the reader; a particular facet of local newspapers and radio.

Reader service A facility provided by a periodical whereby readers are helped to obtain further information about a product by completing and mailing a postage paid reply card. *See* Bingo card.

Reader service card *See* Bingo card.

Readership Number of people who read a publication as opposed to the number of people included in its circulation. *See* Circulation.

Readership profile Classifications of readership of publications expressed in percentage form relative to total readership.

Readership replication Extension of the claim period for readership research where a second reading event occurs during or after original claim period, so introducing error into estimated readership figures, leading to overestimation of readership. *See* Parallel readership.

Readership survey Measuring the number of people reading a periodical including the initial person to receive or purchase it: also their demographics and perceptions. As opposed to circulation. *See* National readership survey (NRS).

Reading and noting Readership research index of actual audience for advertisements appearing on particular pages or average pages in specific publications. *See* Page traffic.

Real income   Income as expressed in terms of the goods and services it can purchase.

Real time   The concept of a computer responding instantly to information it receives and producing its results immediately (contrasted with Batch Processing).

Rears   Spaces available on the backs of buses for advertisement posters. Especially suitable for certain products, e.g. garages, motor tyres and spares, travel, and driving school services.

Reassurance   Post-sales back-up in order to maintain a customer's support and to overcome any doubts or second thoughts about a purchase. *See* Cognitive dissonance.

Rebate   Scheme by Post Office whereby second-class letters that are posted in bulk can qualify for a rebate.

Rebating of commission   A procedure whereby an advertising agency is remunerated by a fee rather than the media commission. In which case, the commission is subtracted from the gross charge, thus giving the client a net rate.

Recall   (1) Spontaneous: where an informant's memory is allowed to suggest information without guidance or assistance. (2) Prompted (aided recall) or assisted memory: where informant is shown possible alternatives, or part of the actual subject matter, as a memory stimulus.

Reciprocal trading   Arrangement between organizations whereby their roles as seller and buyer are interchangeable, i.e. they buy from and sell to each other. Commonly found between member companies of a group but also exists between independent firms where mutual interests may thus be economically served. *See* Transfer prices. *See also* Contra-deal.

Recloseable pack   A package or container which, after opening, can be re-sealed and re-used, e.g. a screw top jar.

Recognition (1) Method of testing effect of advertising. *See* Recall. (2) Advertising agencies apply to controlling media organizations (NPA, PPA, ARIC and ITVA) for recognition and are then entitled to receive commission from media owners. It is difficult for an agency to operate if denied this form of recognition, which is most frequently a credit-rating device but may also be used as a means of applying pressure to conform. *See* Above-the-line advertising.

Recognition tests Study of consumer's recall of brand message with or without an aided recall.

Recommended retail price *See* List price.

Record Like a medical record, it is a mixture of information common to one entity, such as a person.

Recruitment advertising Advertising designed to recruit staff of any kind. Consists mostly of classified and semi-display advertisements. *See* Display advertising.

Redemption Process of trading in or redeeming coupons, vouchers, special offers, trading stamps and the like in exchange for a stated product or benefit.

Reduced instruction set computer *See* RISC.

Re-engineering A radical change in a process or system in order to achieve a breakthrough in business performance.

Reel fed Printing by reel in web offset and gravure printing rather than with flat sheets of paper.

Reference group Market segment under consideration for a promotional campaign.

References Getting people outside the organization, particularly customers and users, to give endorsement to a product. This might take the form of a case history which can be produced as a leaflet and/or published by a suitable periodical. *See* Referral *and* Third party endorsement.

Referral   The use of a person's or company's name as an endorsement of product or service. Of all of the message sources which may persuade a prospect to become a customer, probably the most powerful is 'third party endorsement'.

Reformat   *See* Format.

Regional press   *See* Provincial press.

Register   Alignment of colours in a printing process so that a sharp, well-defined image is reproduced rather than a blurred one.

Registered design   Design which is legally registered thus providing protection against its unauthorized use by any other person or organization.

Registered trade mark   *See* Trade mark.

Regression analysis   Mathematical technique for establishing the relationship between observed and quantifiable variables, both past and present.

Regular model   Standard basic model in the product range, usually the one achieving density sales volume.

Relationship marketing   The deliberate building of extra strong relations with existing and past customers, based upon the rationale that new and further business from that source is easier, faster, and much less expensive than gaining new customers. The development of effective relationships should involve a wide range of one's own staff with as many relevant customer staff.

Relative market share   Share of market segment relative to largest competitor.

Relaunch   Repeating the launch of a product usually with some new feature. Frequently associated with a product which has failed or which is in need of revitalizing.

Release *See* Press release.

Release date The date upon which a news item is to be announced officially, before which no mention should be made either in the press or elsewhere. *See* Embargo.

Release form A document to be signed by a person appearing in an advertisement giving permission to use such photographs or illustrations of that person. This may well involve a fee.

Remainder A term which applies to goods for which the demand has not met supply and which are, therefore, being offered at a much reduced price. A typical example is where a publisher sells off a stock of books at bargain prices as an alternative to pulping them.

Reminder advertising Expenditure devoted to overcoming memory lapse. Accounts for a significant proportion of advertising.

Reminiscence Improvement in retention of factual data over time without further relevant communications. *See* Sleeper effect.

Repeat purchasing Products subject to frequent usage, usually of low unit value and bought regularly for habitual consumption. Convenience plays a large part in such purchasing and substitution will often occur if the preferred brand is not readily available, e.g. newspapers, tobacco, office supplies. *See* Convenience goods *and* Buy classes.

Reply card Used, for instance, in a direct mail campaign, in which a card is enclosed usually prepaid, to encourage a reply. *See* Bingo card.

Repositioning Putting a competitor's claims, concept, or image in perspective and then stating your own claim in form of compensation.

Representative *See* Sales representative.

Reprint   Copies of an advertisement printed after appearance in a publication.

Repro pulls   Good quality proofs of typesetting, usually for use in making up artwork, or in enlarging for display purposes.

Reputation   *See* Corporate image.

Reputation monopoly   Virtual monopoly gained by establishing a unique brand image for which consumers believe there is no genuine alternative.

Requested circulation   In which people receive copies of a periodical free of charge but only 'on request' and probably upon their meeting certain criteria as, for instance, their being involved in purchasing decision making. *See* Controlled circulation.

Resale price maintenance   Agreement between trading concerns regarding prices at which goods may be sold. Prohibited in UK under the 1964 Resale Prices Act so that suppliers may now only publish a recommended retail price (RRP).

Research   *See* Marketing research.

Reserve price   Minimum selling price. Most often used at auctions but may occasionally apply when stock is being cleared at reduced prices.

Resources   In regard to a marketing or marketing communications plan, this refers to the availability of suitable staff and outside services to implement the programme. Financial resources are included under the heading 'Budget'.

Respondent   Research informant. *See* Informant.

Response   Reaction evoked by a stimulus.

Response elasticity   Degree to which consumers react to a stimulus, normally an advertising campaign or a promotion.

Response function Set of numbers, often in percentage form, defining the relative value of given numbers of advertising impressions per person or section of the target population.

Response handling Service provided by some media to handle enquiries arising out of advertising. *See also* Fulfilment house.

Response mechanism Part of any advertisement or promotional item which sets out deliberately to generate some action, e.g. an enquiry, a sales lead or an order.

Response rate Measure of advertising effectiveness, e.g. in direct mail, the number of replies per thousand; in other forms of advertising, the number of replies per insertion. Taken in conjunction with readership/viewership figures for example, this measure enables a comparative cost per inquiry structure to be compiled for use in media selection.

Retail audit Study of preselected sample of retail outlets, providing information on the sales volume, sales trends, stock levels, display and promotional effectiveness of brands, the suppliers of which pay a subscription in return for the regular supply of such information.

Retail outlet Physical point or premises at which goods are retailed. Usually associated with a specialized service or category of business, e.g. co-operative, supermarket, chemist, general store, diary, etc.

Retail price index *See* Cost of living index.

Retailer Person or organization which sells goods to the general public, usually through the operation of a shop or store, i.e. a retail outlet.

Retailers' cooperatives Retail buying groups owning and operating a wholesale facility for members and often selling under a common brand name. A common feature in agricultural marketing for sale of specific commodities to farmers and market gardeners.

Retainer A fee paid to a person or organization which holds itself ready to provide a service as an when it should be required.

Retention strategy The basis of relationship marketing which exploits to the full the existing customer base to encourage further purchases, or larger and/or more frequent purchases. Existing customers take more interest in, and read more frequently, the suppliers' advertisements and direct mail shots. Also, the cost per purchase is many times lower than that of a new customer. *See also* Conquest strategy

Retention time Length of time normally in which there is an 'opportunity to see', e.g. a month or more with a monthly publication as against a few seconds for a television or radio commercial. Can also refer to the length of time an advertising message is retained in the memory which, in turn, is a measure of Impact, which *see*.

Retiring a bill Refers to a bill of exchange which is paid on its due date.

Retouch To modify a photograph or negative by hand, using paints, dyes or chemicals, in order to improve or change it in some way, or to introduce additional features or eliminate existing ones.

Retrospective analysis Study of a situation after the event; colloquially referred to as 'post mortem'.

Return Applied often to a direct mail campaign where the number of replies is expressed as a percentage of the total number of mailers sent out. A common, but misleading figure, as a norm is 3%. The term is also used in relation to the number of orders received in a direct marketing operation. *See* Response.

Return address The address to which a mailing should be sent if it cannot be delivered.

Return on investment Expresses the ultimate measure of business performance. Often expressed in percentage terms, it may refer to a measure of profitability against total assets, employed net worth, or working capital. In many cases, it is used specifically to measure the relative success or otherwise of any particular business venture. Known also as Return on Capital Employed (ROCE).

Returns (1) Measure of income arising from an investment. (2) Applies to goods returned, damaged, unsatisfactory or surplus, to a supplier for credit.

Reusable container A selling feature of a product in that the packaging can have a secondary, or after-use, when the primary product has been used.

Revenue-cost projections Valuing future costs necessary to achieve given levels of revenue.

Reverse out *See* Negative setting.

Reverse plate Printing block in which the contents – illustrations and lettering – are in white upon a black or coloured background.

Review board *See* Plans board.

Revise The repeat printing of a proof but with all the corrections made.

Revolving credit Fixed periodic payment to credit company allowing purchases up to a fixed amount determined by a multiple of 12, 24, or 36 months, but where the credit facility does not cease unless cancelled.

Reward Important benefit offered or implied in an advertising promise. *See also* Romance.

Rifle approach Part of niche marketing in which following a precise definition of the target audience, a very specific and relevant message is sent in order to gain maximum effectiveness. The opposite of a Blunderbuss approach, which *see*.

Right of resale   Legal term to cover circumstances under which a seller of goods still in possession may resell goods, even though he may not hold title to them. Any surplus on the transaction accrues to the original supplier, after the expenses of the seller have been met.

RISC (Reduced instruction set computer)   A computer based upon a processor which is designed to execute sequences of fewer and simpler processing instructions rather than a large variety of complex ones, resulting in faster response times.

Rival brands   Competing brand choices, often of nearly homogeneous goods.

Robot salespeople   (1) Purely mechanical sales effort by salespeople. (2) Dispensing machines, vending machines.

ROI   *See* Return on investment.

Role playing   Acting a part in a simulated face-to-face interview, usually at a sales meeting or training session.

Rollout   A full scale campaign following a test or trial in order to assess the effectiveness on a much smaller sample audience, e.g. a test market. Can be used in direct marketing or merchandising, and sometimes refers to a step-by-step campaign phased over a period of time.

Roman   The upright alphabet as distinguished from the slanting letters of italic; the normal text type. This line is roman ⸤⸥ is marked on the proof margin to order a change to roman letters.

Romance   Important benefit offered or implied in an advertising promise. *See also* Reward.

ROP   Run of paper, which *see*.

Rorshach test   Series of ink-blots shown to subject who is asked to suggest what they represent. The ink-blots have no set meanings but the subject reveals own feelings and attitudes in his/her answers.

Rotogravure   *See* Photogravure.

Rough   Illustration or design of a layout for an advertisement or other printwork in rough form. *See* Scamp.

Rough out   First edited assembly of film shots in correct order and sequence according to script instructions.

Round-up   Detailed study of single subject by several reporters.

Rounding off   Mathematical procedure for eliminating small insignificant numbers or decimals of numbers, by taking the nearest significant value.

Routing salespeople   Designing a calling pattern for salespeople to ensure systematic rather than haphazard coverage.

Royalty   A payment in consideration of the right to use a piece of original material, e.g. authors receive a royalty of, say, 10% of cover price on all books sold by a publisher.

RPI   Retail price index.

RPM   Resale price maintenance.

Rub-offs   A technique in which a specially prepared surface is rubbed off to reveal a prize draw number or gift.

Rule   Solid line in printing.

Run   (1) Period of printing an edition. (2) Quantity to be printed.

Run of paper   Instruction to a publisher indicating that no special position is sought for an advertisement, i.e. it can be placed in any convenient part of the advertising space of the publication. A lower charge is usually payable in such circumstances than where a specific position is demanded.

Run-of-week spot An arrangement whereby a TV contractor undertakes to transmit a commerical during a particular week but, since a discount is allowable, will not specify the exact time of transmission.

Run-on Additional quantities of printed material over and above the original print order. Thus, an advertisement in a periodical can be 'run-on' whilst the machine is still set, thereby providing additional copies at a relatively low price, due to there being no additional setting up charges.

Running costs Costs incurred in operating a business or service.

Rush *See* Film rush.

S

Sachets Unit packages, usually made of flexible plastic to contain liquid or powder in sufficient quantity for one person at one time, e.g. shampoo, sugar, coffee.

Sack Originally open-ended hessian container, but now more commonly made from multiwall paper or from plastic, used largely for bulk packaging of powders or granulated materials.

Saddle stitch To fasten with wire staples through the back fold of a leaflet or brochure.

Sale of goods The law relating to contracts for the sale of goods from the Sale of Goods Act 1979.

Sale or return Colloquial term for practice whereby only goods resold are charged to a dealer, any unsold goods being returnable for full credit. *See* Consignment selling, to which this is related.

Sales agency Organization or person having the right to negotiate business with a third party on behalf of a principal, selling his/her goods or services according to a laid down agreement. The essence of an agency is that the agent drops out of the contract once it has been signed by the principal parties.

Sales aid Any tangible element of sales promotion, leaflet, film projector or sample, which acts as a back-up to a salesperson in presenting his/her proposition to a buyer.

Sales analysis (1) Investigating company sales performances, especially in statistical form. (2) Published version of actual sales performance shown in tabulated form.

Sales approach Positive proposition or theme adopted by salespeople to win a favourable reaction from prospects.

Sales barometer Means of comparing the level of sales performance against preset standards.

Sales budget Tabulation of anticipated accounting figures covering sales revenue and direct selling costs, shown in predetermined divisions of time, products, territory or market segment. Used as a means of control by comparing actual with budgeted performance and taking remedial action, where possible, to restore any shortfalls.

Sales campaign Implementation of the selling strategy. Sometimes mounting a specific selling operation for a product, a market segment, or a geographical area, in isolation from the normal sales activity.

Sales calls Visits to customers or prospective customers by a salesperson.

Sales conference Gathering, often annual, of all the personnel involved in selling, and often marketing, activities in a company to review past performance and examine targets, incentives, and techniques for the future.

264

Sales contest   Competition for salespeople who are rewarded for achieving a specified sales target.

Sales control   Use of system or procedures to enable supervisory personnel to monitor the performance of the selling operation, particularly in relation to the field force, using predetermined aims or goals.

Sales costs   Costs of field selling effort.

Sales coverage   Distribution of selling agents or sales outlets reaching potential markets.

Sales drive   Particularly active selling campaign.

Sales effort   Extent of selling activity.

Sales engineer   Salesperson having a knowledge of engineering or of the technical aspect of a product so as to be able to discuss intelligently the application of the product with all the technical implications.

Sales feature   Aspect of a product which can be shown as a customer benefit.

Sales folder   Portfolio of selling aids.

Sales force   Group of salespeople, directed by a national or regional sales manager.

Sales forecasts   Projections of likely sales, given certain defined criteria and making defined assumptions. Often based upon historical data. Not identical to sales targets which relate purely to the salespeople they concern.

Sales goods   Items reduced in price for quick clearance.

Sales impact   Measure of response to sales activity and performance.

Sales incentives (1) a) Financial incentives to salespeople by provision of commissions, prizes, bonuses, etc. b) Non-financial incentives such as award of status symbols. (2) Promotional devices and gifts offered to trade buyers, potential customers, or to distribution channels, in order to promote sales or extra selling effort.

Sales inquiry Request from sales prospect for sales literature or quotation. (Enquiry is a general term used for requests for non-sales information.)

Sales interview Meeting between a salesman and a potential customer in which an attempt is made to close a sale having previously provided all the information necessary to satisfy the prospect's requirements.

Sales kit Sales presentation, communicational selling aids and administrative stationery and equipment carried by the salesperson for the transaction of business.

Sales letter Any promotional letter sent out to customers or prospects. Increasingly personally addressed as part of a direct mail campaign, where it might summarize or highlight the main features of the accompanying enclosures.

Sales lead Piece of information or a contact which may ultimately lead to a sale being transacted. *See* Sales inquiry.

Sales literature Pamphlets, leaflets, point-of-sale showcards, etc. which give product information to potential customers.

Sales manager Executive responsible for sales force management, directly through field sales managers or through branch or area organization. Often also controls some internal sales service, which may or may not include transport, credit, repair, maintenance or other services.

Sales management Organization, direction, control, recruitment, training and motivation of the field selling effort within the planned marketing strategy.

Sales manual   Guide to operating instructions, terms of employment and policy document issued to salespeople as a supplement to sales training and supervision.

Sales meeting   Gathering of all salespeople usually led by a field supervisor, for a training session or for dissemination of information.

Sales mix   Breakdown of sales revenue by product groups and normally expressed in percentage terms.

Sales mobility   Indicates extent of ability and positive or negative attitude shown in responding to customers' requests for out-of-schedule visits.

Sales office manager   Executive responsible for managing the sales office and, in particular, ensuring that the necessary back-up is provided to the sales force in using company resources efficiently, thus exerting maximum persuasional effect upon customers.

Sales organization   Structure and distribution of the sales personnel, head and branch offices or warehouses and possibly shops, where company-operated. Can also be applied in same way to organization of sales staff in a mail order operation.

Sales orientation   Where the selling of a product is regarded as the primary task as against the satisfying of the customers requirements. *See* Marketing orientation.

Sales penetration   Extent to which total market potential has been realized, i.e. the proportion of people in that market who have become users or consumers of a product or service.

Sales pitch   Content and style of salesperson's presentation to prospective customers.

Sales planning   Determining sales objectives and selling activity quotas in an effort to achieve pre-set sales targets.

Sales platform   Main selling proposition upon which a particular campaign is to be based.

Sales policies   Company policies enjoined upon the sales force in order to promote uniform achievement of marketing objectives.

Sales potential   Share of a market that a company believes is achievable when its plans and strategies have been fully implemented.

Sales power   Measure of company strenth in selling effort and achievement compared with that of competitors' equivalents.

Sales promotion   Any non-face-to-face activity concerned with the promotion of sales, but often taken also to exclude advertising. In consumer marketing, frequently used to denote any below-the-line advertising expenditure and having close connections with in-store merchandising.

Sales prospects   Likely customers for a particular company or industry.

Sales push   (1) Marketing activity where merchandising has the dominant role. (2) Synonym for Sales campaign.

Sales quota   Goal set for person, product, territory, or market segment in selling activity or sales performance terms. *See* Quota.

Sales records   Collections of data relating to sales achieved by product category, geographical location, customer type, etc.

Sales report   Analysis of selling activity and performance.

Sales representative   Salesperson usually associated with technical or professional selling, although often acknowledged as a facade created by salespeople and their managers in an effort to embellish their function.

Sales research   Study of field and office activities in an effort to discover means of improving sales force productivity.

Sales resistance Rational or irrational opposition to a buying proposition. Will either be dispelled by salesperson effort or persist irrespective of how, or the extent to which, the proposition is presented.

Sales revenue Income from sales. Turnover.

Sales service All the productive, clerical and administrative facilities which are provided as a support to the activities of the sales force in order to service customer requirements.

Sales spiel *See* Sales pitch.

Sales strategy Plan of the sales activities undertaken to achieve set objectives including territory targets, methods of selling, rates of calling and budgets; a subsection of established marketing strategy.

Sales targets Quantitative sales objectives set as a positive statement of company requirements as compared with sales forecasts which are related more to an objective assessment of anticipated events based upon external factors not within the company's control. *See* Sales quota.

Sales territory Geographical area, market segment, or product group within which individual salespeople are responsible for developing sales.

Sales tools Synonym for sales aids.

Sales volume Sales achievement expressed in quantitative, physical or volume terms.

Salesman/Saleslady (1) Retail sales staff in a store. (2) Employee of wholesale or manufacturing distributor calling upon retailers or other potential customers soliciting orders. *See* Sales representative.

Salesmanship Practice of informing and persuading persons or organizations of the value of a purchase and expressing that value in actual benefits unique to each prospect.

Salient attributes Those features of a product which a customer finds most attractive. *See* Attributes.

Salting The insertion of fictitious names into a commercially offered mailing list for one-time use only in order to check mis-use by having such names routed back to the list broker. Sometimes called a Sleeper or a Seed.

Same size Instruction to a printer or production house to reproduce an original in the same size. Commonly abbreviated 'SS'.

Sample (1) Representative item or portion used by salespeople to assist in convincing buyers of product's quality. (2) Representative microcosm of the entire population or universe taken to represent the characteristics of the whole. Accuracy of resultant information may be calculated according to sample size and sampling technique used.

Sample case Mobile container used, for instance, by salespeople for carriage, protection and demonstration of samples of their company's products.

Sampling error (1) Bias in one or more aspects of a sampling frame. (2) Standard error. *See* Deviation. *See also* Normal distribution.

Sampling frame Control data for research study; specifies parameters and structure for each sample.

Sampling offers Invitations by manufacturers to potential customers to 'try' the product by taking a free sample or lower-priced trial pack.

Sampling point Geographical location convenient for contacting a predetermined cluster of informants.

Sandwich board Advertising poster carried by a person in public, usually in the form of two displays, one at the front and one at the back, suspended over the shoulder and thus 'sandwiching' the carrier.

Sans serif Plain and simple style of lettering without serifs, e.g. This sentence is set in sans serif. Arguably not so legible as lettering with serifs. *See* Serif.

Satellite broadcasting Use of satellites for live transmission of television and radio signals.

Satisfiers Core of promotional campaigns offering recognition, self-respect, achievements, or self-realization as secondary needs.

Saturation campaign Intensive use of mass media in a single campaign.

Saturation coverage Heavy weight of advertising in short period. Often effective but expensive.

Saturation point Level at which any futher expansion of distribution in a market is unlikely to be achieved and where further sales are restricted to the potential arising from replacement needs or population growth.

SC paper Super calendered paper. Highly compressed paper with smooth finish.

Scaling Ranking order of items in a market research to show the strength of respondents' feelings towards a subject.

Scamp Rough design or layout of advertisement or other promotional material.

Scanner A hardware device with associated software which takes in an optical image and digitizes it into an electronic data image. Scanners are used to create computerized versions of photos, illustrations or other graphics which cannot be input into a computer by conventional means (e.g. by using a keyboard).

Scattergraph   Graph with a scale for each two variables; values of variables are plotted in pairs, one for the X axis and one for the Y axis. When a line is drawn to pass through the centre of the points, it indicates the line of best fit. Once drawn, it can then be used to estimate the most likely level of expenditure necessary to achieve the return shown against the matching point on the other axis.

SCC   Single column centimetre, which *see*.

Schedule   *See* Advertising schedule.

Scheduling   Normally refers specifically to detailed arrangements for commercials or advertisements appearing in the media. *See* Media schedule.

Scheme advertising   Advertising normally of a below-the-line character. *See* Theme advertising.

Schwerin test   Research method for study of respondents; involves observation of changes in ranking of products after exposure to advertising.

SCI   Single column inch, which *see*.

Screening   Procedure by which new or modified product ideas are assessed in a methodical way against key factors for success. Products not meeting the essential criteria are thus eliminated at an early stage in their development. This is a discipline which should be imposed early on in the concept development stage in order to eliminate unnecessary wastage of resources on ideas which are unlikely to be successful.

Script   (1) Manuscript or typescript for publication. (2) Synonym for broadsheet. (3) Text of a commercial film or broadcast.

Sealed-bid pricing A matter sometimes arising out of government tendering in which applications will be held until a given time when all bids will be opened and a contract awarded to the lowest quotation. Thus, such pricing has to be based upon what prices it is anticipated will be offered by all the competitors. In other words, a blind bid usually not subject to negotiation. *See also* Tender.

Seasonal concentration Limiting sales or promotional campaigns to appropriate segments of the year.

Seasonal discount Discount offered by media owners to encourage business during what are considered to be slack periods in the year.

Seasonal rate Rates in advertising which vary according to the time of year.

Second generation product Product which evolves from one already on the market and eventually supersedes it. Term commonly used in areas of rapid technological development, e.g. electronics.

Secondary coverage Area in which reception of radio or television channel is subject to variation; usually the area concerned is catered for by another channel but is within the outer area of another. *See* Overlap.

Secondary data Information which already exists, e.g. internal company records, government and other official statistics. *See* Primary data.

Secondary meanings Adopted popular terms or expressions effectively re-naming branded goods, (e.g. Coke for Coca-Cola). May be deliberate by supplier or coincidental by consumers.

Secondary needs Human characteristics that often prevail after all basic human needs have been reasonably met – mostly relevant to affluent societies but may be copied by others even if basic needs are still unsatisfied.

Secondary readership   Indicates extra readership of a publication, e.g. by the members of a household whose head buys the publication or by people in an organization which subscribes to it, sometimes referred to as 'pass-on readership'.

Seed   Inclusion in a mailing list of check names and addresses to monitor usage, speed of delivery, or improper use by third party sometimes referred to as 'sleepers'.

Segmentation   Breakdown of a market into discrete and identifiable elements, each of which may have its own special requirements of a product and each of which is likely to exhibit different habits affecting its exposure to advertising media. Other marketing factors such as optimum price, quality, packaging and distribution are likely to differ as between one segment and another. Typical breakdowns are based upon age, social standing, income, sex, geographical location, leisure pursuits. *See* Market segmentation.

Selective attention   Noticing the unusual, gaining attention because it is different. *See* Selective perception.

Selective distribution   The use of only a selected number of outlets rather than using all the possible ones which are available.

Selective perception   Seeing in an advertisement something beyond its basic meaning that reflects one's own basic concept; so perceiving a hidden meaning whether that be contrived or unintended.

Selective positioning   (1) Choice and continuity of a special position within a type of advertising medium, aimed at a specific target audience. (2) Decision process for deciding what market segment and what appeal to offer to achieve a given position in the consumer's mind.

Selective selling   Selling which is confined to those customers and prospects which satisfy a minimum standard of performance or some other limiting factor. Formerly a common practice for the distribution of speciality products but breaking down as mass marketing techniques are more widely exploited. *See* Exclusive agency agreement.

Self-image One's perception of oneself. Normally, how one perceives that others see oneself not how one is.

Self-liquidating offer Special offer (or gift) made available to purchasers of a product, and designed to yield sufficient revenue to defray the cost of the offer and also perhaps reduce the promotional costs involved.

Self-mailer Direct mail piece that can be posted without envelope or wrapper; a form of postcard.

Self-selection Merchandise arranged in a retail store in such a way that customers may make their own choice without further assistance. The sale is then completed by a sales assistant. Distinguished from self-service where the sale is completed at a checkout point.

Self-service store Retail outlet where customers help themselves to prepriced goods from shelves or other displays, and pay for their purchases at suitably located cash tills or in total upon departure. *See* Checkout.

Sell-by-date Date marked on goods to indicate the time by which they should be purchased in order that they be in perfect condition.

Sell-in Achieving effective distribution among retail outlets to prepare for a promotional campaign.

Sellers' market Excess of demand over supply creating market imbalance and making sales effort less obligatory on the part of suppliers. *See* Buyers' market.

Selling Process of persuasion leading to a continuing trading arrangement, initiated and perpetuated at either a personal or impersonal level but commonly confined to oral representation supported by visual aids.

Selling agent Salesperson representing an organization but not necessarily on the organization's payroll. *See* Commission.

Selling proposition The particular benefit which is to be used in a campaign, it having been selected as having the strongest appeal for a particular potential market. *See also* Appeal and Product benefit.

Semantic differential Choice from an arrangement of pre-selected phrases to enable informant to register one with the closest affinity to his/her own opinion. Often expressed in a complete spectrum, e.g. excellent to poor, from which respondent chooses the description most nearly corresponding with his/her own views.

Semi-display advertising Paper-set classified advertisement in which some additional devices are incorporated such as bold face or heavy rules.

Semi-solus Advertisement which appears on a page containing another advertisement but which is not positioned adjacent to it.

Semi-structured Research conducted by interviewer with guidelines but in which certain key questions may need to be answered.

Seminar Meeting set up for the dissemination of knowledge in which a 'leader' discusses a subject with his/her audience rather than expounding it. Frequently a small and informal grouping, but can be organized on a large scale of conference proportions.

Sentence completion Establishing attitudes or opinions by providing incomplete questions that the respondent may answer in any fashion he/she chooses. Often portrays the irrational areas of motivation that are difficult to elicit and summarize from a conventional interviewing situation.

Sequential Taking events one at a time in an orderly fashion, usually according to some agreed procedure.

Sequential sampling Continuous analysis of research findings as they are received such that when no further changes occur no further data is thought to be necessary.

Serial Broadcasting, publishing, or filming of continuing story in sections, usually without a predictable end. *See also* Series.

Series (1) Broadcasting, publishing, or filming of similar or related stories usually for a limited season. *See also* Serial. (2) Term in statistics for orderly arrangement of numerical data, usually in a sequence.

Series discount Discount given by advertising media owner in consideration of an undertaking by an advertiser to book a series of insertions within a given minimum number of issues.

Serif Tail or cross stroke in a type face, at one or both ends of a main stroke, intended to improve readability. This book is set in a serif face. *See* Sans serif.

Server A type of computer which provides services for other computers connected to it, usually via a network. A common example is a file server which provides archive or database services to remote and usually less powerful client computers.

Service contract An arrangement whereby an organization contracts to keep a piece of equipment in good working order for an agreed period of time.

Service department Part of an organization concerned with providing after-sales service to customers; frequently involved with the handling of complaints which require tactful replacement or rectification to avoid temporary or permanent loss of goodwill.

Service fee Charge made, usually on a predetermined annual basis, by an advertising or public relations agency for the service it provides. Increasingly used instead of, or in addition to, the earlier convention of commission income. *See* Commission (3).

Service industries Suppliers of services not directly involved with manufacturing, e.g. travel, entertainment, health, insurance, professional and personal treatment.

Services Work carried out for others by an individual or organization where no transfer of goods is involved, e.g. banking, insurance, travel.

Set (1) Collection or group of people, items, numbers, or ideas. Each object in the set is a member or element of the set. Set theory is the branch of mathematics concerned with sets, their operations, and the properties concerned with their operations. (2) Where filming takes place.

Set-off A term in printing referring to the unwanted transfer of ink from one sheet to another or to the printing roll itself.

Set solid Lines of type which are set close up to one another, without any spacing.

Share of mind The extent to which a particular brand will be thought of in relation to a specific product category.

Share of voice Within a particular product category the promotion of a brand compared with that of its competitors will represent its share of voice leading on to an equivalent share of mind.

Shed Large shell type building, usually out of town, for retailing such products as DIY, furniture and electrical goods.

Sheet (prefixed 4, 8, 16, 32, etc.) Means of describing the dimensions of a poster based on multiples of a double crown, i.e. a double sheet poster measuring 30 in × 20 in. Therefore, a four sheet poster would measure 60 in × 40 in.

Shelf life Limit of time during which a product may be stored on a retailer's shelves before natural deterioration will render it unfit for sale. *See* Date coding.

Shelf talker Printed material on shelves in self-selection or self-service stores promoting particular brands and obviating the necessity for sales talk by shop assistants.

Shell scheme   Standard design of individual booth provided by the organizer of an exhibition.

Shift in demand   Change in the pattern or extent of consumer demand.

Shipping note   Delivery note used by exporters to notify the docks of an intended consignment specifying the vessel and sailing date.

Shooting   Synonym for filming; in colloquial usage.

Shooting script   Schedule of activities in film making which relates each part of a script to the accompanying visual and sound effect.

Shop audit   *See* Retail audit.

Shop traffic   Number of potential customers passing through a retail outlet at any one time. Frequently used as a cumulative figure for set time periods.

Shoplifting   Stealing from retail stores with intention to evade payment for them leading to stock 'shrinkages'.

Shopper   Retailer's customer.

Shopping centres   Urban marketing developments planned and operated under local government regulation and providing for a full representation of shopping facilities in the interests of the local community.

Shopping goods   Generally applies to the more expensive specialities or consumer durables which are not bought on impulse. Consumer behaviour towards purchasing such goods is characterized by exploration of information, with comparison of performance and prices, before coming to a decision which may be joint and several rather than individual. The time taken in 'shopping around' may be considerable: hence, the term 'shopping goods' *See* Convenience goods.

279

Short rate   Difference between the rate paid by an advertiser at the end of a period between the actual number of lines taken up by advertising in a publication and the estimated lines upon which an original quotation was based.

Shotgun approach   Sales messages sent to a very general range of prospects without any degree of targeting, either the media or the message. Sometimes referred to as a Blunderbuss approach.

Shoulder time   Time immediately preceding or following peak-time.

Showcard   A piece of cardboard with printing on it to promote a product.

Showcase   Cabinet made of glass or clear plastic to display products protected against deterioration and pilferage. Though extensively used at point-of-sale, showcases are widely used at public and private exhibitions, e.g. hotel foyers, where an indication will be given of where displayed articles may be purchased.

Showthrough   Print on reverse side of a sheet showing through.

Shrink wrapping   Enclosure of goods in a transparent film of plastic which is 'shrunk' onto the goods by the application of heat. Often used as an alternative to an outer container where protection is not a key factor but display is. Used especially for dispensing fresh foodstuffs in self-service stores and supermarkets. *See* Blister pack.

Shrinkage   Difference between physical stock-take and book stocktake. May be a result of recording or counting errors by supplier or customer but is often a consequence of pilferage.

SIC   Standard Industrial Classification.

Sidehead   Subheading appearing to the left or right of a column.

Sight draft   Bill of exchange payable on sight.

Signals, buying Indication of a prospect's willingness to make a purchase perceived by a salesperson as the preliminary to the use of closing techniques.

Significance (1) Generally used to suggest relevance. (2) Statistical term with similar meaning but with more precise implication. Statistical tests are used to establish the significance level, e.g. T-tests (taking differences between average values) and Chi-tests (testing differences between distributions).

Silent salesperson Point-of-sale material embodying display and especially attention-getting contents used as a merchandising technique. Is also often used to describe packaging.

Silk screening Method of printing by which ink is forced through a fine mesh on which have been superimposed opaque areas, representing the reverse of the design, through which ink will not pass. Much used in the production of high quality point-of-sale material.

Simulation Representation of one system by means of another. In particular, the representation of physical performance by computers, either equipment or models, to facilitate the study of such systems or phenomena to train operators etc. (BS 3527).

Single column centimetre (scc) Standard unit of measurement for print advertisements; one centimetre in a column. *See* Single column inch.

Single column inch (sci) Obsolescent measurement in newspapers and magazines in UK, based upon the depth of type matter contained in a single column. *See* Single column centimetre.

Single selling proposition Out of all the customers benefits, one is selected as being the best selling argument at a particular time, rather than diluting the proposition by sending out too many messages to have any impact. This is an alternative to the Unique selling proposition (USP) as more and more products become undifferentiated without there being any unique features to put forward.

Single source Information or data received or compiled from one origin alone, most often in connection with a research study.

Situation assessment Review of current position, particularly to consider exploiting an opportunity or remedying a problem.

Situation report Report on the current situation or circumstances; often shortened to ... sitrep.

Sixteen sheet Most popular size of poster consisting of eight double crown sizes. *See* Double crown.

Skewness Distribution of data which differs from a normal distribution in that the mean and the mode are located at different points.

Skimming price Price aimed at appealing to higher income groups. *See* Penetration pricing.

Slant Central theme adopted by writer on a particular issue.

Sleeper *See* Seed.

Sleeper effect Studies which have shown that, even after the purely factual information within it has been forgotten, attitudes may still have shifted in favour of an advertisement, indicating that an attitude change has been effected. This is known as the sleeper effect.

Sleeper products Products remaining in the range that have no major importance but continue to achieve low volume sales.

Slogan Catchwords, phrase or sentence associated with a product or company, encapsulating a particularly pertinent selling point in a succinct and sometimes entertaining fashion.

Small ads *See* Classified advertising.

282

Small order problem   Arises from receipt of orders of insufficient unit value to justify handling; such a problem can be overcome by using dropshipment via intermediary stockists, by making such orders subject to deposit of cash price in advance of delivery or by fixing a minimum order size/value.

Smart card   Plastic card similar to a credit card but incorporating a chip embodied in it, giving the card both intelligence and memory.

Snip   Bargain.

Social marketing   Application of the marketing concept to non-commercial activities such as those connected with community, welfare and social services. Thus, it can be argued that marketing has a relevance to government, both national and local.

Socio-economic groups   Breakdown of population into sections to represent main subsections of a community according to selected economic and social criteria. The groups are designated by a letter series, namely, A, B, C1, C2, D, E, in which A and B represent the minority of higher income receivers in the scale, D and E the lower skilled, lower earners and C1 and C2 occupying a position midway between these extremes. Introduced by the IPA in 1962, as an aid to media distribution analysis, the scale has been the subject of wide contention, since it is felt to be inadequate to reflect the facts of market segmentation in an era of rapid social changes. On the other hand, complex problems of social measurement are involved in any attempt to set up any superior alternative.

Sod's law   Obtuse incongruity of inanimate objects, e.g. the door to a telephone booth will always seem to be on the opposite side to one's approach. *See* Murphy's law.

Soft goods   Textiles or merchandise manufactured from textiles.

Soft marketing   *See* Soft selling.

Soft news Articles in newspapers and magazines with an element of news but mainly expressing the opinions of publications or a contributor. *See also* Hard news.

Soft selling Couching the selling message in a subtle or oblique way, as against a blatant or hard selling approach. Sometimes known as 'low pressure selling'.

Software All computer programs (operating systems, applications, etc.) as opposed to hardware.

SoHo (Small-office/Home-office) A term describing the market for computer goods suitable for a small business or work environment.

Sole agent Someone who represents another on an exclusive basis in relation to a specific product or service, or for a particular region.

Sole trader One-person trading concern, representing the simplest and earliest form of business organization.

Solid In which type or body copy is set without any space between the lines, e.g. there is no Leading, which *see*.

Solus position Position of isolation (i.e. separated from any immediate, especially competitive, announcements) of a poster or press advertisement, for instance.

Sound track Narrow area running alongside the film which carries the sound recording. Is often used to refer to the actual sound recording itself.

Source credibility The extent to which a message source is respected by the recipient.

Space Term used to describe pages available for advertising purposes in a publication; constitutes the product available for sale after text matter has been accommodated.

Space buyer *See* Media buyer.

Span of control Breadth of control, measured in numbers of personnel and the rigour of their duties, which a manager or executive may supervise effectively.

Spatial gaps Distances between manufacturing or supply point and distribution outlets.

Special feature Part of a publication, or a separate publication, devoted to particular event or interest, ostensibly for readers' benefit but often to attract associated advertising expenditure.

Special position Insertion of an advertisement in what is regarded as a distinctive position in a publication, e.g. outside or inside covers, or facing matter. Such a selection frequently involves a higher charge being made to the advertiser and advance action on his/her part to secure it.

Speciality goods Goods not always available in conventional outlets and sold direct to the home from leads obtained by advertising, such as double glazing, encyclopedias, insurance. Requires speciality salespeople.

Speciality salesperson Sales personnel who are usually confined to one product or at most a limited range of products and frequently where there is a once-only selling opportunity or at least little likelihood of a repeat sale in the immediate future.

Specific offer Precise proposition by the seller with a view to securing a contract to use or purchase a product or service.

Specification In marketing, this relates to the specified characteristics and performance required of a product, expressed in quantitative as well as qualitative terms. In production terms, specification is a schedule of parts or a list of ingredients from which a product is manufactured.

Spectacular (1) Large, outdoor, electrically illuminated sign. (2) Unusual direct mail piece. (3) Elaborate special TV programme, irregularly scheduled. (4) Advertising theme providing entertainment to promote a brand where there is nothing new or unique to offer.

Speech synthesis   Also known as voice recognition. Inherent to multi-media systems as the audio related component. Where the computer can understand what you say and it can say things to you.

Spend   Short for expenditure. *See* Budget and Appropriation.

Spike   To disregard a news item. *See* Kill.

Spinarama   Triangular poster with three faces spinning from central pivot; usually located in shopping centre or precinct.

Spine   The back of a book.

Spinner   Revolving stand on which products are displayed.

Spiral binding   *See* Mechanical binding.

Splash   Main news story, associated with front page of newspapers but not exclusively.

Split credit sales   Division of credit between salespeople for business obtained, where orders are secured from one sales territory but delivery is required on another. The arrangement may also apply to orders booked via a head or branch office which are then delivered in one or more sales territories; such apportionment assists in the compilation of sales statistics and comparisons as well as the payment of appropriate commissions to the salespeople concerned.

Split run   When the identical publication is printed and distributed in two or more separate production runs and deliveries to facilitate the insertion of different advertisements in each part run. The arrangement is often used to compare the measured effects of alternative pieces of advertising copy.

Sponsor   Organization financing sporting or other activities in order to gain coverage and prestige from its association with them.

Sponsored book   Book specially produced for an organization which undertakes to meet all or most of the production cost to the publisher, such publications being produced for public relations purposes.

Sponsored events   In marketing, part of a public relations programme to emphasize the name of an organization or product in a favourable light by paying all or some of the costs of a public sport or spectacle, e.g. cricket or motor-racing. The technique can be used in relation to any event which is likely to be patronized or otherwise come to the attention of the particular public the organization desires to influence.

Spontaneous recall   A respondent's ability to remember things seen or heard without any visual aids or other memory prompts. *See* Aided recall.

Spot   Single television advertisement appearance.

Spot colour   Small areas of colour on an otherwise black and white printing.

Spot lengths   Standard times for television commercials, e.g. 7, 15, 30, 45, and 60 seconds; 30 seconds being the base time. *See* Timelength.

Spread   Two facing pages in a publication over which one advertisement may be printed. *See* Centrespread.

Spread traffic   *See* Page traffic.

Spreadsheet   A software application used to manipulate quantitive information like cash flow charts.

Stable market   Describes a market where the volume of sales show little change when prices vary. Associated, but not to be confused with those products known as 'staples'. *See* Staple product.

Staff manager   *See* Line manager.

Stakeholders   *See* Publics.

Stamp trading   Incentive vouchers, usually in the form of stamps, issued by retailers in relation to value of purchases to encourage trading loyalty; stamps may later be redeemed for cash (a legal requirement), or goods chosen by the consumer from a catalogue and collected from a stocking and display point. The practice has been outlawed in N. America where it was found to be subject to abuse.

Stand out test   In consumer goods marketing, a package on shelf store test to determine how well the designed package shows up when compared with competitive offerings in close proximity and display.

Standard deviation   *See* Deviation (standard).

Standard error   Measurement of accuracy of statistical measurements of sample. Expressed in two dimensions; the parameters of accuracy and the confidence level at which the study was undertaken.

Standard industrial classification (SIC)   Comprehensive listing and coding of industries and services by the UK Government's Central Statistical Office (Central Office of Information), and published by Her Majesty's Stationery Office (HMSO).

Standard letter   Letter which is typed or printed many times over in the same format for sending to customers, suppliers, or any large group of people to whom the same message is to be delivered. *See* Direct mail.

Standard of living   Quality of life in a community normally related to its income and wealth and, for the individuals, the availability of goods within their incomes.

Standardized sales presentation   Prepared sales sequence following a definite course of action developed by experienced sales personnel for the benefit of new or inexperienced recruits.

Staple product Refers to products which are essentials, in constant demand, such as bread, milk, cigarettes, etc. *See* Convenience goods.

Star Expression used to describe highly successful, profitable products which have established competitive track records. *See* Cash cow.

Starch ratings Method of measuring advertisement effectiveness in the USA. *See* Reading and noting.

Statement Financial document showing net total of outstanding accounts owing to the seller by the buyer after taking into consideration all due allowances and payments received. Usually but not always a monthly issue.

Static market Market which has a pattern over time substantially free from fluctuations, particularly of volume.

Statistical significance tests Extent to which there are real differences between different sets of data or research findings.

Status inquiry Form of checking upon the credit worthiness of a prospective customer, sometimes known as 'credit rating'.

Status symbol (1)Non-financial incentives offered to salespeople. (2) Prestigious products bought more for purposes of ostentation than for their utility; buyers may or may not make extensive use of such purchases.

Statute of Limitations UK legislation, fixing period within which outstanding debts may be legally collected: outside such period the indebtedness lapses.

Step-and-repeat Printing process in which a small image will be repeated a number of times over, e.g., labels.

Stereotype Printing plate cast in one piece from a matrix or mould.

Sterling area Group of countries using the British pound as a reserve currency, agreeing to permit free transfer of funds amongst members and to operate joint control over exchanges of sterling area currencies for other external currencies.

Sticker Label, poster or other printed sheet intended for sticking on window, letter, envelope or other medium for display purposes.

Still Single frame printed from photograph used in a continuous film. Generally refers to a photograph rather than the movie-film as such.

Stimulus Initiating step or incentive intended to provoke a predictable response.

Stochastic model A contrived, simulated situation where chance or random variables are used. Involves the use of conditions of uncertainty, and is an advanced form of linear programming. *See* Shift in demand.

Stock The type and quality of paper or film.

Stock control A methodical checking procedure in which the quantities of products or components are monitored in order that quantities can be kept within prescribed maximum and minimum levels.

Stock financing Element in the marketing mix; involves the marketing advantages of carrying stock sufficient to meet agreed levels of demand.

Stock footage Film or video held in a library for hire in making a commercial.

Stockist Stockholder of a specific range of goods for sale on behalf of a particular supplier.

Stocktaking Physical or manual counting of trading stock. May sometimes be used to describe an inventory, which includes the counting of all assets within the firm and not just stock.

Stockturn Rate at which trading stock is sold and replaced.

Stop motion Photographic technique for animating inanimate objects.

Store audit *See* Retail audit.

Store demonstration Public demonstration of machines, product, or equipment held in a store.

Store traffic Number or extent of people coming into or passing through a retail outlet.

Storyboard Sequence of sketches designed to show the main elements of television or cinema commerical.

Strategic alliance Two or more companies working together, for instance, in attacking a particular market place where their respective assets complement one another. *See* Joint venturing *and* Business partner.

Strategic business unit A specific profit centre within an organization.

Strategic cascade The rationale here is that a company in its whole planning operation starts with the 'business objective' (profit), leading to a number of business strategies, one for each function, e.g. by means of R&D (a new scientific process) or marketing (increase market share). The business strategy of marketing now for the department concerned becomes the marketing objective. The marketing strategy is then the way in which this objective will be achieved, for example by means of an aggressive marketing communications campaign. This strategy, in turn, becomes the objective (say, sales leads) for the marketing communications department, and so on. Thus there is a 'cascade' of strategies.

Strategic innovation New product development, market development, or diversification policies in the search for profitable markets.

Strategic planning   *See* Corporate planning.

Strategic pricing   Practice for establishing the optimum price at which a product is to be offered to the market. *See also* Tactical pricing.

Strategic window   A period of time during which a market opportunity will exist, with the likelihood that it will cease after the window is closed.

Strategy   Plan, sometimes in outline only, for reaching certain objectives, usually quantified and more often on a relatively long time base.

Stratification   Structuring requirements or procedure laid down within a research survey questionnaire for the uniform control of interviews in such a way as to permit reliable summaries and comparisons of results to be drawn up.

Stratifying the market   *See* Market segmentation.

Strawboard   Paperboard manufactured from straw rather than woodpulp. Used mainly in box making and book covers due to high rigidity.

Strengths and weaknesses   Used to categorize elements and characteristics of products or organizations to assess positive and negative features, particularly for competitive comparisons. *See* SWOT.

Stringer   Assistant to correspondent in media.

Structured   A firm set of questions in a research interview so that all answers follow a predetermined pattern.

Stuffer   Piece of publicity matter intended for general distribution with other material such as outgoing mail or goods, e.g. 'envelope stuffer'.

Style   Rules concerning spelling, grammar, punctuation, and layout in publishing or broadcasting material.

Style obsolescence Deliberate restyling of goods in an attempt to outdate models already on the market.

Sub (1)Preparing copy for publication. (2) Abbreviation for sub-editor.

Sub-head Bold type in or preceding a line of printing but inferior or secondary to a main heading.

Subjective perceptions Conclusions existing in the mind, not subject to rational thought or reason. Basis for many modern advertising techniques.

Subliminal projection Delivery of an advertising message below receiver's level of awareness, but which registers in the subconscious. May be visual or audio or both. The use of subliminal advertising is illegal in the UK and a number of other countries where it is not regarded as a fair means of exercising persuasive influence.

Subsample Subsection of a sample.

Subscribed circulation The part of a publisher's circulation which is paid for, as opposed to being distributed free of charge. *See* Controlled circulation.

Substitute goods Two alternative basic products where one can, and often is, used as a substitute for another. A price increase for one will lead to an increased use of the other.

Suggestion selling Presenting selling arguments by suggestion, whereby the prospect may feel he/she has arrived at a conclusion (favourable to the selling agent) as a result of his/her own persuasions.

Superior In typography, a small number set above a word indicating a reference to be found at the foot of the page or at the end of the chapter, or even the book or publication.

Supermarket (1) Self-service store of over 2000 square feet and having three or more check-out points, mostly having a wide range of fast-moving merchandise, including a high proportion of foodstuffs, usually at premium prices. (2) Site where many traders operate their business on their own account under the same roof.

Supersite Large tailor-made posters or displays, often hand-printed or cut out so as to give a three-dimensional effect.

Superstore *See* Hypermarket.

Supplement Special feature section of a publication.

Supply and demand *See* Law of supply and demand.

Supporter A customer or client who, when asked, will give a positive reference to a product. This is a reactive, as opposed to a proactive, situation. *See* Ladder of customer loyalty.

Survey Study based on sampling techniques.

Suspect In the 'Ladder of customer loyalty', this represents the initial target audience or market segment. Little is known about such a person and what, if any, is the Propensity to buy, which *see*. *See also* Prospect.

Swatch Sample of ink, paint, plastic, fabric or other material for purposes of colour matching.

Sweepstake Prizes are awarded on a completely chance basis upon the submission of a winning leaflet or ticket.

Switch selling In which an inferior, non-existent or non-available product is put on offer in very favourable circumstances in order to draw the attention of potential customers to whom an alternative but less commercially attractive proposition will then be made. Rendered illegal by an order under the Fair Trading Act, 1973 and also outlawed by the British Code of Advertising Practice.

SWOT analysis A mnemonic for Strengths, Weaknesses, Opportunities, Threats. Situation assessment used in marketing planning.

Symbol Distinctive sign or graphic design denoting a company or product. Often a pictorial presentation of a company or product name. *See* Logotype.

Symbol retailer Member of an independent group of retailers who join together for joint bulk purchasing and sometimes for co-operative marketing.

Symbolic association Association of ideas, relating ideas or symbols to other functional or abstract things.

Symptom (1) Deviation from normal, suggesting a problem. (2) Characteristic of a situation.

Syncro marketing Technique for using up spare production capacity during regular slack periods, particularly seasonal trades.

Syndicated Multiclient project with no one client exercising exclusive rights.

Synectics Group discussions to generate creative thinking. Group members are normally chosen to represent difference rather than similarity.

Synergy Term used to identify the condition where the combined effect of two or more courses of action is greater than the sum of the individual parts. In marketing, frequently applied to the measure of overall effectiveness through the co-ordinated operation of the many elements comprising the marketing mix.

Systems parameters Limits to which variables in a system may be taken. May involve the lower and upper limit of expenditure or of likely response or achievement.

SX A slower and less powerful microprocessor than a 'DX' of the same type.

T

T-Test   Statistical test to measure differences between two average values.

Table   Data laid out in rows and columns. Inherent in spreadsheets.

Table of random numbers   Tabulation of numbers where the numbers have no repetitive order or pattern, usually listed in rows and columns of five digits. Used for selecting people or items at random for sampling purposes.

Tabloid   Newspaper with a small page area.

Tabulation   Putting data into tables, usually of a numerical order.

Tachistoscope   In advertising research, a projection device used to measure the thresholds at which the features of an advertisement are registered. Is also used for measuring visual impact of an advertisement when exposed for only a short time.

Tactical pricing   Short term variations, usually reductions in price, to stimulate sales.

Tactics   The detailed components of a strategy. In marketing, the marketing strategy is a short statement of how the objectives are to be achieved. The media plan gives a comprehensive run down on the actions to be taken, i.e. the tactics to be employed.

Tag line   *See* Base line.

Tallyman   Collection agent for loan/insurance companies.

TAP   *See* Total audience package.

Target audience   Group of people, or segment of a market to whom an advertising appeal is specifically addressed.

Target group index   Continuous survey of adults in which their purchasing habits in detail are related to their media exposure, thus facilitating accurate media planning.

Target market Group of people or companies to which an organization aims to sell its products.

Target marketing *See* Niche marketing.

Target weights Used for weighting advertising expenditure; a means of varying expenditure according to the influence of demographic factors. *See* Weighting.

Targeting Choosing a medium which will direct an advertising message at a narrowly defined market segment. *See* Segmentation.

Tariff Customs duty charged on selected imported goods.

Task method Means of calculating the budget for an advertising campaign by relating it to the objective(s) to be achieved, rather than by using any given amount of money arrived at in a more arbitrary fashion.

Tax incidence Point where ultimate tax burden is located.

Tax, turnover Tax levied as the proportion of the price of a commodity at each level of distribution. Commonly known as VAT (value added tax).

TC *See* Till countermanded.

Tear sheet Press advertisement torn from a newspaper or periodical and sent to an advertiser as evidence of its publication. *See* Voucher.

Tear strip Strong membrane in a heat-sealed package which, when pulled, is intended to cause the package to open easily.

Teaser Advertisement which by withholding information about the product and/or sponsor, is designed to arouse widespread attention through the operation of curiosity. Often takes the form of a poster or series of posters.

Technical press Periodicals dealing with technical subjects. Usually grouped together as 'trade & technical', referring in effect to all publications directed to a non-consumer public.

Teleconference A telecommunications connection of vision and sound in which people in different areas around the world can meet together, each remaining in their own location.

Telegenic Characteristic of a person whose features will appear attractive on television. *See also* Photogenic.

Telemarketing Alternative term for Telephone selling, which *see*. Also includes use of telephone for research purposes.

Telephone answering service Automatic or manual servicing of calls or inquiries through the telephone network.

Telephone interviewing Use of the telephone for market research purposes.

Telephone selling Selling operation in which the telephone is used to contact potential customers, and to solicit orders without any personal call upon customers' premises.

Teleshopping Placing an order by phone on a supplier.

Television consumer audit Organization of a sample of viewers who report findings and thus enable television impact on population to be measured.

Television rating (TVR) One TVR represents 1 per cent of the total TV audience expressed in terms of homes or individuals, so establishing a comparative unit of measure.

Televisual audience data Result of research into television viewing behaviour and patterns.

Temporal gaps Differences between volume of manufacturing output and volume of consumer purchases being met through stock-holding.

Temporary exports Samples or exhibits required to be re-imported within an agreed period of time.

Tender Offer to supply goods or services at a price: usually a detailed document outlining all the conditions which would relate to any ensuing contract. Commonly associated with Government contracts for building, construction, service or period supplies.

Terminal A device which can be used to input or receive information to and from a computer system, usually comprising a VDU or screen with keyboard, but may also be a cash register, telephone handset, bank cash dispenser, etc.

Terminal emulation Using a screen from one computer to utilize software which allows you access to a different type of computer.

Terminal markets Markets dealing in futures where dealers and importers have the opportunity to buy supplies at currently ruling prices. Especially common in the sale of agricultural products, e.g. wool, but also used for many other basic commodities, e.g. metals.

Terms of trade Ratio of index of export prices to index of import prices, showing a relationship for comparison purposes between levels of prices at home and overseas.

Territory Geographical region in which a representative is called upon to sell his/her products.

Tertiary readership Indicates readership of a publication seen casually during or while waiting for some other activity, normally outside the home, e.g. at hairdressers or surgery.

Test area or town Relatively small geographical location selected as representative of a larger market to be used to try out a proposed campaign. *See* Test marketing.

Test close Requesting the buyer to place an order for the purpose of establishing the extent to which he/she is ready to buy and thus enabling the interview to be conducted economically.

Test marketing Method of testing a marketing plan on a limited scale, simulating as nearly as possible all the factors involved in a national campaign; usually carried out in a restricted but representative location, often a particular TV region. This procedure enables a marketing company to obtain an indication of likely market acceptance without the full commitment and expense of a national launch. It also exposes the product and the plan to competitors, and consequently the results of the test can seldom be regarded as absolutely conclusive.

Testimonial advertisement Piece of promotion which uses the implied or explicit patronage of a product by a well-known person, or organization. *See* Personality promotions.

Tetra pack Four-sided container, usually constructed from waxed paper and designed for dispensing liquids, e.g. milk, frequently in portions for individual serving.

Text Solid typematter as distinct from headlines.

TGI *See* Target group index.

Thematic apperception test Series of pictures shown to subject who is asked to complete or provide a story about these pictures. Indicates attitudes and reactions to particular themes such as branded products, or advertising promises.

Theme advertising Advertising, normally of an above-the-line character. *See* Scheme advertising.

Theory of demand Branch of economic theory concerned with the determinants of choice, involving selections of sets of purchases from among the many available. Involves the study of conflict between incomes, prices, and marketing interactions in order to make predictions on likely future behaviour patterns. *See also* Elasticity of demand.

Thermography A process whereby lettering can be printed on paper such that it is raised, thus simulating embossing.

Third age   *See* Grey market.

Third party endorsement   *See* Message source.

Threshold goals   Minimum level of achievement acceptable.

Through-the-door advertising   Direct mail, door dropped leaflets, samples and coupons.

Through-the-line agency   An outside agency offering both above-the-line and below-the-line services. A 'one stop shop'. Also called a total communications agency.

Throw-away   *See* Give-away.

Thumbnail   Miniature sketch.

Tie-breaker   An open-ended question in a competition designed to reduce the number of qualifying winners by asking for an opinion or statement, for instance on the reasons for preferring a particular product.

Tied house   While referring mostly to public houses, could apply to other retail outlets where they are owned by, or receive all their supplies from one source.

Tied loan   Loan from one country to another but conditional on the borrower buying specified goods or services to the value concerned from the lender country.

Till countermanded   Stipulation in contract that it will run until stopped by the advertiser.

Time series analysis   Using historical data and statistical techniques to secure projections of future events.

Time segment Periods of time in television broadcasting during which commercials are booked. Often, each time segment has a different charging rate as audiences are constantly changing during broadcasting periods. *See* Break.

Timetable Part of a marketing or marketing communications plan which deals with the timing of each proposed activity and the relation, one to another, of each.

Timelength Time of a commercial spot in television or radio. *See* Spot lengths.

Tip-in Insert, smaller than page and not bound in. Pasted to adjoining page.

Title or Credit title List of executives and performers in a television or film programme.

Token An alternative to money, used mostly in vending machines where they comprise small circular discs made of either metal or plastic.

Top-down planning/budgeting In which the formula for the plan and the allocation of the budget are set by top management, sometimes without any detailed consideration of what needs to be achieved. As opposed to Bottom-up planning.

Top-of-mind Within a broad product category, the brand which comes out top in a customer survey into 'share of mind'. This may or may not be the brand leader, i.e. holds the largest market share, since top-of-mind is a perceptual measure of a brand's position rather than the actual position in the market place.

Torture testing Putting products under extreme stress to breaking point.

Total audience package Commercial spots spread across time segments, usually at discretion of media owner, throughout broadcasting hours.

Total communications agency *See* Through-the-line agency.

Total paid circulation *See* Paid circulation.

Total quality management (TQM) An important management procedure in which high quality standards are set for all operations, including marketing, and subsequently measured and monitored. Many business practices are expected to conform to laid down national and international standards from which they may gain an important competitive advantage.

Total quality marketing In which all aspects of 'quality assurance' (BS 5750) are exploited in marketing terms, e.g. manufacturing, quality control, pre-sales, sales and post-sales service.

Tote system Service offered by British Rail involving a tote bin specially designed for the transport of goods in bulk. Particularly applies to movement of materials in granular, powder or liquid form.

Touch screen video An IT system in which information is accessed simply by touching a particular part of a VDU screen which contains a display of all the sources of information available.

Town hall test *See* Hall test.

TQM *See* Total quality management.

Trackball A 'mouse' which is integral to a portable PC.

Tracking A system of monitoring a campaign as it progresses in order to be reassured that it is 'on track' towards attaining its ultimate objective.

Tracking study A continuous monitoring procedure, for instance of the effect of an advertising campaign upon the awareness or perception of a product.

Trade *See* Distributive trades.

Trade advertising *See* Trade promotion.

Trade counter   Sales point in a retail or wholesale outlet where provision is made to supply 'the trade'. Has particular application to the building trade.

Trade cycle   Periodic oscillations (of about 8–10 years) in the level of business activity ranging from booms or peaks to depressions or troughs. Due to government action after World War II, the extremes of the trade cycle have been considerably reduced, permitting more steady growth, but the phenomenon has re-appeared in recent times under the pressure of inflationary increases in the costs of energy and materials induced not only by the action of producers but as a response to fears of resource exhaustion. No government has found it easy to control the resulting barriers to continued growth and the diminution of employment prospects. (*See* Business cycle.) An upturn in trade would appear to await discovery and exploitation of alternative sources of supply.

Trade discount   Special discount offered to trade customers who in turn sell to the general public.

Trade fairs   Fairs held in a selected national market to show and promote goods made in another country or made under licence or other arrangements in the country concerned.

Trade-in   An old good is used in part exchange for a new good of the same kind to offset paying the full price.

Trade mark   Mark used in relation to goods so as to indicate a connection in the course of trade between the goods and the proprietor or registered supplier. Registration under the appropriate Act provides exclusive right of usage.

Trade press   Strictly referring to periodicals dealing with particular trades. *See* Technical press.

Trade price   Discounted price for the benefit of another in a trading position and not usually open to a consumer.

Trade promotion   Mounting a marketing campaign to the retail trade in an effort to persuade retailers to stock and display the company's products. *See also* Sell-in.

Trade setting   Typesetting by a trade house on direct instructions from a client or agency, usually working to tight specifications and resulting in higher quality output. Compare Paper setting.

Trade show   Synonym for exhibition, but often used to describe an exhibition for non-consumer markets.

Trading down   Selling at low prices to achieve high volume; most usually involves lower grade or deteriorated products, where the price structure will permit such a strategy. *See* Trading up.

Trading stamps   *See* Stamp trading.

Trading up   Selling at high prices supported by a high level of service in order to secure exclusive custom and high profit ratios. *See* Trading down.

Traffic   (1) Progressing and scheduling of activities in an advertising agency to ensure events take place on time and are completed according to requirement. (2) Pattern of movement of customers in a store, observed or induced.

Traffic count   Count of persons (or vehicles) passing a particular point during a specified period of time.

Traffic department   Used in advertising agencies for function similar to progress chasing in industry.

Tramp steamer   Independent vessel available for the carriage of any type of goods.

Trannie   Colour transparency.

Transfer lettering   *See* Dry transfer lettering.

Transfer prices   Special prices charged to an associated company carrying no profit and usually making no allowance for marketing costs, e.g. delivery. *See* Reciprocal trading.

Transfer pricing   Pricing policy adopted by organizations under common ownership where each organization is expected to achieve profit targets even when supplying to associate companies.

Transference   Style of advertising suggesting by abstract means an association between a brand and some unrelated but significant factor; often the appeal is to the subconscious.

Transient medium   *See* Intransient.

Transnational   New term applying to companies transacting or managing business across national boundaries on a large scale. Often used as an alternative to Multinational, which also *see*.

Transparency   Transparent colour film used for making plates, prints, or for projection.

Transport advertising   Special form of poster advertising sited on or inside buses, main line and Tube railway trains, or other forms of transportation, e.g. taxi-cabs and trucks. Also refers to posters exhibited at railway stations, bus stops, airline terminals, seaports and the like.

Transpose   Switching one digit, letter, or word with another.

Trans-shipment   Goods transferred to another vessel to complete the journey to their ultimate destination. A means of diversion from main transport lines to more isolated places.

Traveller   *See* Salesman/Saleslady.

Travellers' cheques   Personalized credit forms issued by banks, usually for overseas travel and redeemed by signature. Replaceable in the event of loss, they reduce the necessity for holding large amounts of currency which involves greater risk of loss.

Travelling exhibition   Exhibition designed to be fully mobile. May be generally mobile on a planned circuit, e.g. by road, or confined to a rail or sea network, e.g. exhibition train or ship.

Treasury bill   Bill of exchange issued by the British Government and payable within three months. Holding is mainly confined to the large joint stock banks in connection with fiscal controls within the economy, but other finance houses especially the building societies, for example, may purchase them as a good form of liquid reserve.

Treatment   Sequential descriptive document in film making, giving a detailed outline of the form a film is likely to take. Used generally with same meaning in relation to any form of planned communication.

Tree   A graph or diagram of information structure containing no 'cycles' and allowing for only one route between any pair of nodes. A tree is typically used as a model for a system's software file structure where one 'stem' of the tree, representing say a 'folder', can subdivide into two or many 'branches', or 'files', and so on.

Trend analysis   Extrapolation of historical figures for the purpose of studying their significance.

Triad   Test of selection, usually from three products offered to informant – one varied in some way from the other two – with an invitation to choose the one preferred.

Trial close   Attempt by salesperson to close an interview or assess the direction in which it is progressing by asking specifically or even indirectly for the order before the proposition or demonstration has been completed. *See* Test close.

Trial order   Small order, placed specifically to judge the value or quality of a proposition, prior to placing a substantial order or sequence of orders.

Trial purchase   Initial order, sometimes small, occasionally at special price to test suitability of goods.

Trickle-down   Collective move by consumers to buy lower-priced brands.

Trimmed size   Final size of a leaflet, brochure or other print job.

Trolley   Mobile wire basket to carry goods in a supermarket.

Try and buy   *See* Sale or return.

Tube   Cylindrical pack made from soft metal, e.g. for toothpaste, rigid metal, e.g. for cigars, plastics, e.g. for cosmetics, or fibreboard, e.g. for maps.

Tube cards   Advertisements inside railway compartments, particularly associated with Greater London Tube train network.

Turn   Continuation of a news item in another column or page.

Turnkey   Commercial or industrial contract involving several suppliers of specialist skills to be subcontracted by the main supplier.

Turnover   (1) Total period sales figure of a business or organization, expressed by value or volume but usually the former. (2) In recruitment, the measure of the mobility of staff in an organization.

Turnover, rate of   Number of times the average value of stock is sold during a period. Formula for calculation:
$$\frac{\text{value of sales at cost}}{\text{average stock at cost}} \times 100$$

Turnover of salesperson   Number of salespeople leaving employment of a company during a specific period of time, usually expressed as a percentage of the sales force.

Tutorial   An introductory lesson to a software program which allows you to learn at your own pace.

TVR   Television rating; indicates coverage of target audiences by individual programmes or advertisements on commercial television. *See* Rating and Television rating.

Two-colour   Number of colours used in printing an advertisement or publication. Usually black plus one other.

Type   Characters made of metal or plastics and used in printing.

Type area   Space which is available on a page in a publication for printing.

Type family   *See* Family.

Type mark-up (TMU)   A typographical visual giving the specification of the type to be used, and showing the approximate layout of all of the visual components of, say, an advertisement.

Typeface   *See* Face.

Typographer   Person, frequently but not always an employee of an advertising agency, who produces type layouts or type markups, i.e. accurate specifications from which a printer can carry out typesetting.

Typological analysis   Combination of households into 'generic' classifications. The aim is to establish distinct profiles for given families or households.

U

Ultimate consumer   Person or persons who actually consume or use a product or service, as distinct from the shopper or buyer who may be no more than a purchasing agent, such as housewife.

Ultra vires   Transactions outside normal established procedures.

Unaided recall   In market research, the asking of a question from a respondent without giving any guidance as to what the answer might be. *See* Aided recall, Spontaneous recall *and* Recall.

Uncoated paper   Paper that has had no coating applied to its surface.

Undercut   To offer a product or service at a price set deliberately lower than that of the competition.

Undifferentiated marketing   Products or services aimed at the entire population without any attempt to offer or suggest a unique benefit.

Undifferentiated products   Products which are intrinsically identical and for which it is necessary in competitive terms to develop some perceived difference, e.g. gasoline.

Unilateral   One-sided proposition, decision, or agreement.

Unique selling proposition (USP)   Product benefit which can be regarded as unique as a primary selling argument. Often replaced by single selling proposition.

Unit pack   Pack which contains only one product or unit.

Unit pricing   Pricing each item so that the price by volume or weight is clearly indicated. Makes price comparison easier for the shopper and has been the subject of regulation by the Office of Fair Trading and the European Community.

Universe   Population (or subsection of the population) from which a research sample is drawn.

UNIX   A multi-user multi-tasking operating system, of which many commercial variants exist such as AIX, ULTRIX, HP-UX and SVR4.

Unjustified type   A piece of body copy in which the line ends, right, left, or both, are uneven, i.e. not lined up. Sometimes referred to as 'ragged'. *See* Justify.

310

Unloading Disposing of goods in a market at a low or concessionary price. *See* Dumping.

Unprompted response In response to a market research question a respondent gives an answer which is not in anyway guided or prompted.

Unsolicited goods and services Unsolicited goods sent or delivered for sale or hire become the property of the recipient if notice is given within thirty days to the sender and they are not retrieved. And if not collected within six months, without notice, the goods become a gift to the recipient.

Unstructured interview A method of gaining research information but without the use of a rigid questionnaire. The interviewer will know which general topics to cover but they will be raised and answered informally so as not to inhibit the breadth of the respondent's answers.

Unweighted sample A research sample before any weightings have been applied. *See* Weighting.

Up-market Market segment where higher prices dominate the buying behaviour.

Upgrade What you need to do to the chip in your computer when it runs out of sufficient power to run the software.

Upper case Capital letters in printing or typescript. *See* Lower case.

Uppie Unpretentious, Privately Individually Egoist.

Upset price Lowest price at which negotiations can begin. Often used in auctioneering as the price from which bidding is invited.

Upwardly mobile People who aspire vigorously to move upwardly towards a higher socio-economic position.

Usage pull   Technique ascribed to Rosser Reeves in USA, to discern the proportionate change in usage of a product as between those who are familiar with its advertising and those who are not.

User friendly   Goods easy to use or operate, service or maintain.

User group   An independent group of users who organize meetings and lobby manufacturers for product changes.

USP   Unique selling proposition, which *see*.

Usury   Generic term for the lending of money in return for payment of interest, usually at a fixed rate of interest regardless of the rate of repayment.

Utility   (1) Psychological satisfaction derived from a purchase – the converse of the modern use of the term as defined in (2) below. (2) Sufficient to perform a prescribed function without elaboration. Utility goods prevail during emergency conditions, e.g. war.

V

Vaccine   A program which is an absolute must to use if you value the integrity of your data.

Vacillating customer   Customer unwilling, or unable, to determine own needs when presented with positive proposition.

Validation   A term used in market research whereby a sample of interviewees or respondents are followed up to confirm that contact has been made, and in the right manner. This confirms the accuracy of the research programme, and also gives an indication of the extent to which the interviewers are acting properly.

Value-added   In its simplest form, the change in value from, say, raw material to the finished product. An important element in arriving at the actual cost of a product as opposed to its price, to which it may bear little or no resemblance.

Value-added tax (VAT)   Tax levied on a product at each stage of manufacture or distribution related directly to the estimated or actual increase in sales value. Successor to purchase tax in UK. *See* Tax turnover.

Value analysis   Examination of every constituent of a product to ensure that its cost is no greater than is necessary to carry out its function. Sometimes referred to as value engineering.

Valued impressions per pound   (1) Number of readers divided by the advertising rate. The VIP index shows how many readers are bought for a given sum of money. (2) Weighted media target multiplied by media weight and divided by cost of advertisement.

Value judgement   Subjective expression of opinion unsupported by fact or available data.

Variable costs   Accounting term for costs that vary directly with output, as opposed to fixed costs.

Variance   (1) Management accounting term indicating the difference between a budgeted item and its actual cost or performance. (2) Statistical term for the arithmetic mean of the square deviations of the values from the mean. (3) In a dispute, disagreement between executives on questions of policy or strategy.

VCR   Video cassette recording.

VDU (Visual display unit)   Strictly speaking the TV screen of a terminal, but can be used to include the keyboard as well.

Vehicle   Particular publication or channel used to carry advertising message.

Vending machine   Purely automatic dispensing of solid or liquid products on insertion of specified coinage. Also used for services, e.g. laundering. *See* Robot salespeople.

Vendor   Person or organization with products or services to sell.

Verified free distribution   Audited figures indicating the number of copies distributed of a free newspaper.

Vertical circulation   Business publication for persons at all levels in a specific industry or profession, e.g. *British Printer. See* Horizontal publication.

Vertical integration   (1) Refers to the merging of companies producing different things but contributing to the same ultimate product, e.g. between a car seats producer and a windscreens manufacturer. (2) Company operating at more than one level in channels of distribution, typically as both manufacturer and distributor, e.g. Boots the Chemists.

Vertical market   Selling of a product or range of products restricted to one type of classification of market. Compare with Horizontal market.

Vested interest   Material involvement of a person or organization in the outcome of a venture or the maintenance of the status quo.

Vet   Study for inaccuracies.

Video cassette recording   In which electronic signals representing sound and vision are superimposed upon a magnetic tape contained in a cassette for easy handling. The signals so stored are subsequently available for playback via a television monitor or screen as and when required.

Video conferencing   A discussion or meeting involving two or more people in different physical locations who can see and hear each other using electronic communications.

Video news release (VNR)   A specialized form of news release in which an actual programme is made and recorded in a form suitable for public transmission. Such video recordings are then distributed to television stations in the same way as a printed news release.

Video tape recording   Pictures and sound recorded magnetically on tape which can then be reproduced upon a cathode ray tube. Often used for television commercials and programmes but also suitable for many forms of instructional training and evaluation of personnel.

Vignette   A gradual shaded-off edge of an illustration or background colour from dark to light produced by the gradual reduction in size of the halftone dot.

Vinylite   Plastic matrix.

VIP   Valued impressions per pound.

Virtual reality   Software and hardware which attempts to simulate real life scenarios without the risk (physically or financially) of making mistakes, e.g. nuclear power plant modelling.

Virus   A destructive software program that searches out and 'infects' other programs usually rendering them inoperable. Viruses can be unwittingly transmitted from one computer to another by modem connection or by introducing an infected floppy disk.

Visiting cards   Business cards identifying caller usually confined to name and organization but may also include nature of business and occasionally a sales promotion message.

Visual   Drawing or illustration of an advertisement or other piece of promotional material, finished to an adequate standard for presentation to a client. *See* Layout.

Visual display unit   *See* VDU.

Visualizer   Designer responsible for producing visual ideas for the interpretation and execution of an advertising brief. Usually, but not necessarily, an employee of an advertising agency.

VNR   *See* Video news release.

Voice mail   A telephone system which enables one to send a message without actually speaking to the person concerned.

Voice over   Narration with narrator not on screen, possibly with still photograph, used for commercials.

Volume discount   *See* Quantity discount.

Volumetrics   Data giving product consumption figures according to viewing or readership of particular media channels or publication measured by percentage in media costs per thousand viewers and readers.

Voluntary chain or group   Association of independent traders using collective power for purchasing, promotional and development purposes. A chain usually confines its membership to retail buying while a voluntary group is based upon a wholesaler in association with a group of retailers.

Voluntary controls (advertising)   System of self-control adopted by UK advertising practitioners to ensure that advertisements conform to a defined code of practice. *See* ASA and Codes of Practice.

Voucher   Free copy of a periodical sent to an advertiser or agent as evidence of an advertisement having been published. *See* Tear sheet.

VTR   Video tape recording

W

WAN (Wide area network)   Interconnected computer systems (or LANs) covering an extended national or international geographical area.

Want   Desire by a person to possess a product or a service. Usually prerequisite to a purchase, but not always so, since a customer may buy a product which he/she needs even though he/she may not want it. *See* Need.

Warehouse   Storage site for finished goods. Provides local availability prior to sale.

Warranty   Commitment by supplier that his/her products will perform as specified and that, should they not, some form of compensation or corrective action will be provided.

Waste circulation   Parts of a circulation which are of no value to the advertiser but which he/she nevertheless has to pay for in his/her campaign.

Watermark   Image which appears on paper when held up to the light. Often used for branding papers.

Wealthy empty-nesters   Couples whose children have left home and who are also well-off.

Wear-out   In research where respondents become weary of answering questions. Also, in advertising where an advertisement stops having an effect, i.e. it is 'wearing out'.

Web-offset   Method of offset-litho printing in which paper is fed into the press from a reel as compared with a sheet feed.

Weekly   A periodical which is published once a week.

Weighted average   Individual group averages multiplied by values assigned to each group. Weighting is a statistical technique for adjusting averages according to their significance in the total.

Weighting Adding to the importance of one series of data compared with another by multiplying by an appropriate factor.

Wet-on-wet Multicolour printing process in which one colour is printed onto another while the ink is still wet.

Whannies We have a nanny.

White goods Consumer durables, such as refrigerators, washing machines and dishwashers.

Whole plate *See* Full plate.

Wholesaler Intermediary between the retailer and manufacturer. Usually buys goods in quantity at a discount and sells them in small batches at higher unit prices. An important facility for distribution of goods of smaller manufacturers, especially in non-urban areas, but also has a high utility in cities for urgently required immediate supplies.

Wide area network *See* WAN.

Widow Very short line in typography: usually just one word or part of a word. Sentence is often re-written so as to shorten it and thereby eliminate the 'widow'.

Window dressing (1) Displaying goods in a shop window to best advantage to attract custom. *See* Display. (2) Arranging goods or presentation in such a way as to impress another party; sometimes used to describe an artificial situation with the intention to mislead.

Window of opportunity A finite time ahead, having both a beginning and an end, and during which period actions can be effectively taken.

Window shopping Visiting shops without an immediate intention or inclination to buy.

Windows Microsoft Corporation's GUI software which runs on top of the MS-DOS operating system.

Windows NT   A Windows-based GUI and combined operating system from Microsoft which features many advanced features such as multi-threading.

Wire binding   Continuous double series of wire loops run through punched holes on the spine of a booklet or calendar.

Woopies   Well-Off Older People.

Word artists   Descriptive term for originators of brand names.

Word association test   A market research technique in which a respondent is asked for feelings, or other words, associated with a given word.

Word engineers   Descriptive term for advertising copywriters.

Work study   Systematic recording and critical examination of existing, and proposed, ways of doing work, as a means of developing and applying easier and more effective methods and reducing costs. Is increasingly applied to marketing organization, especially, for example, sales force operation. (Definition quoted from the BSI Glossary of Terms in Work Study.)

Workgroup   A deliberately formulated group of people who are electronically interconnected via the computer network for the purpose of interworking, e.g. a major project staffed by people from different sites.

Workload schedule   Forward plan of work for executive and sales personnel.

Workstation   A desktop computer terminal with its own computing power (as distinct from a dumb terminal) connected to a network (LAN or WAN).

World class   Term used in benchmarking to indicate best practice worldwide.

Write-off Reducing the value of an asset to zero either for tax benefit, trading advantage, or to reflect its true market value. Often leads to its disposal.

WYSIWYG 'What you see is what you get.' Only effective if the screen fonts and printer fonts are the same. Otherwise you only get something close to what you see being printed out.

X

X (X bar) Statistical symbol for average.

X.400 An E-mail protocol.

X-height Standard height of a lower case letter in typography, usually measured by referring to the letter 'x'.

Y

Year books *See* Annuals.

Yellow Pages A business telephone directory classified under trade or commercial sub-headings.

Yield Profit or revenue attributable to a product or company's shares. May be expressed in absolute or relative terms.

Yuppie Young, upwardly mobile professional.

Z

Z chart   A diagram charting values over a period (frequently one year) and showing simultaneously monthly figures (or weekly or daily), cumulative totals and the moving averages. It normally takes a Z shape, hence its title, and is of use in clarifying the trends present in the data displayed. A main feature of Interfirm comparisons, for example.

Zapping   With reference to a commercial channel in which a viewer switches to another channel whilst the advertising slot is in progress. More importantly with recorded programmes, the commercial break is fast-forwarded thus eliminating any advertising value.

Zipper tone   Adhesive plastic sheets with varying tones of grey. For application to artwork to give halftone or shading effect.

Zone   Any territorial area in which for the time being marketing operations are confined.

Zone pricing   The market for a product is divided into zones in which different price levels are fixed.

Zoom   Fast action of continuous change in focal length in a special lens giving the impression that the television or film camera has moved rapidly towards the object being focused, or vice versa when used in reverse.